P9-CRO-271

A GREATER LOVE

A Greater Love

PRINCE CHARLES'S

TWENTY-YEAR AFFAIR

with

CAMILLA PARKER BOWLES

CHRISTOPHER WILSON

WILLIAM MORROW AND COMPANY, INC.
New York

LIBRARY OF CONGRESS CATALOGING-IN-PUBLICATION DATA

Wilson, Christopher, 1946–
A greater love : Prince Charles's twenty-year affair with Camilla Parker Bowles / Christopher Wilson.
p. cm.
ISBN 0-688-13808-X
1. Charles, Prince of Wales, 1948– —Relations with women. 2. Great Britain—Princes and princesses—Biography. 3. Bowles, Camilla Parker. I. Title.
DA591.A33W57 1994
941.085′092—dc20
[B] 94-9529
CIP

Printed in the United States of America

First U.S. Edition

1 2 3 4 5 6 7 8 9 10

BOOK DESIGN BY PATRICE FODERO

To
MARTA CHAIKOVSKA
and
FRANK PETERS
—no greater friends

$\mathscr{C}$ONTENTS

INTRODUCTION

IT WAS, AND IS, A GREATER LOVE: GREATER THAN THE PRINCE OF WALES COULD ever summon for his wife, or for any other woman.

For nearly a quarter of a century Prince Charles has found, in Camilla Parker Bowles, a spiritual haven. It is one of history's wry jests that, just as with his predecessor David, Prince of Wales, the woman to whom he finally gave his heart should be married to someone else.

The discovery that Charles had loved, throughout his marriage, someone other than his wife came as a *coup de foudre* to the outside world. In an instant, the remedial work done by King George VI and his daughter Queen Elizabeth II to bring back a precious luster to the House of Windsor was gone. The illusion was shattered.

Courtiers at Buckingham Palace, fearful for the future, became convinced that Charles's unswerving devotion to Mrs. Parker Bowles was the one factor that could bring down the monarchy. They call it "The Problem."

But not one of *them* was informed, at a very early age, that one day he would be king. The prince has almost a sixth sense about his destiny which may yet confound his critics, both within and without the palace walls. At present he is undergoing a very public period of rehabilitation; it may well be that the humbling process he has been forced to endure will make for a stronger, yet more amenable, monarch when his time comes. Certainly there was a danger, before the fall, that a certain arrogance and myopia were beginning to infect his princeship.

In January 1993 a six-minute fragment of a conversation he had shared with Camilla Parker Bowles three years earlier surfaced, in an eerie and sinister way. Whatever its genesis, the effect on Charles of the publication of the so-called Camillagate tapes was to effectively blow away forty-four years' work—a lifetime of making himself acceptable to the people whom one day he would rule.

For this act of duplicity—apparently loving one woman while secretly devoted to another—the Prince of Wales took an unprecedented hammering, and it is fair to say at the time of writing that equilibrium has not yet been restored. Opinion polls showed, again and again, how the British nation could not stomach the thought of Charles's cheating on their number-one cover girl, the one with the caring heart and perpetual smile. His popularity rating slumped from second (behind Diana) to last (behind Fergie).

With his public acceptance that the royal marriage was over, and the very real evidence that it had been a complete sham, the historians began sharpening their quills in readiness for their epitaphs on the House of Windsor. It does not take much to puncture the pundits' faith in an outdated institution whose power base has been eroded and whose function is now almost entirely ceremonial; and, indeed, suddenly there were some very good reasons to believe the monarchy might not survive the death of Queen Elizabeth II.

But history has a way of soothing fears and healing wounds; and it is not unreasonable to suppose that soon the nation's anger at having been so willfully cheated will give way to a better tolerance of Charles's unusual circumstances and apparently discreditable behavior. But forgiveness can come only with understanding, and a clear understanding is possible only if those who care about royalty are furnished with the full facts of Charles's affair with Camilla Parker Bowles.

This I have attempted to do, as it is my conviction that the incomplete versions which have appeared to date have all distorted the facts by concentrating on Diana, her life and problems. Inside the royal circle, now that the dust is settling, it is possible to see what an irrelevance she has become to the dynastic future of the House of Windsor. She is Queen Caroline to history's King George IV—a forlorn figure on the outside, knocking to be let in.

No, what is most important to the future of the world's leading royal house is that Charles should acquit himself impeccably as Prince of Wales and superbly as king. He can do that, to borrow a phrase from his great-uncle, only with the help and support of the woman he loves. There is room, in these enlightened times, to accept Charles's irregular love life for what it is—an accident of history—and to tolerate its continued existence.

In a sense, of course, the House of Windsor are hoist by their own petard: It was they, under King George VI, who created the notion of a royal family. One generation on, that notion is in tatters, simply proving that it is better to invest one's higher beliefs in the monarch as an institution, rather than one half of a marriage duo, for royal marriages have traditionally had a habit of coming unglued.

Charles and Camilla exist; they will continue to do so. Those who have a certain sympathy for thwarted love will be encouraged, I hope, by the following chapters, but the story is no cozy romance. People, both children and adults, have been hurt by this Cupid's accident; many others, millions maybe, feel cheated for one reason or another by what has happened.

More than any other, Diana feels cheated. But as the following pages amply demonstrate, she knew about Camilla all along—she was warned of the married woman's existence even at the moment when she first met Charles on a Sussex hayrick. Camilla was too omnipresent, and Charles's courting of Diana too chaste, for the penny not to drop—even for a girl who was far from being a woman of the world.

When, during his courtship of Diana, Charles was discovered to have entertained a blonde overnight on the Royal Train, the world's press believed it must have been Diana—but she knew differently. The irony was not lost on her that while the world predicted that he would ask her to marry him, and secretly supposed that despite her virginal appearance they were behaving as young lovers do the world over, he sought the delights of the marital bed elsewhere.

With the benefit of hindsight it is possible to see that there is *another* version of events than the one which has been put forward so forcefully over the past two years. It is generally supposed that if Diana considered Camilla at all, it was only as the vague threat which all former girlfriends pose to a future wife. Innocently, she walked up the aisle of St. Paul's Cathedral knowing that, from now on, Charles was all hers. That certainly is the picture painted in Andrew Morton's apologia, *Diana: Her True Story.*

The reality is somewhat different. It was clear from the outset that this was a dynastic match, one which was wanted by Charles in order to perpetuate the line and silence the critics—including his own father—who claimed he neglected his duty by remaining unmarried. Equally it was wanted by Diana for reasons of ambition. She was determined to turn it into a love match if possible, but it never happened. It was that cynical a piece of social engineering.

Charles's obsession with Camilla barely wavered under the onslaught of his young wife's charms. Once, in all their married life, Diana nearly won him round: She detested his country house, Highgrove, since it had been chosen by Camilla, and almost managed to persuade him to move away from Gloucestershire. She reasoned that, away from the immediate influence of Camilla, Charles might respond more warmly to her; but it was not to be, and soon after that, the marriage started to slip away.

But this story is not merely a *ménage-à-trois,* for into its pages from time to time strides the handsome, purposeful figure of Brigadier Andrew Parker Bowles, Camilla's husband of twenty-one years. It is his part in this extraordinary love story which perplexes people most of all, for he has never once shown the slightest flicker of emotion over the stories about his wife and the prince, and has acted with commendable decorum even under the most extreme provocation.

This almost saintly behavior cannot altogether be explained and, in their frustration, jealous souls have branded him a latter-day Ernest Simpson. It is true both men were married to a woman a Prince of Wales loved; it is true both were officers in the Household Brigade—but there the similarity ends, for he continues to enjoy a harmonious marital relationship with his wife, and those who predicted divorce for the couple have been proved completely wrong. It is, in conventional society, an alien concept that a man may happily share his wife with another—but then, Charles and Camilla and the brigadier do not inhabit conventional society, but a high-octane version of it, which has its own arcane rules.

In religious terms, of course, Charles is in grave moral danger, and since he will be the custodian of the Church of England once he ascends the throne, this is something he should be addressing. So say some of the bishops in one of the chapters of this book: It is their belief that he cannot become supreme head of their Church unless he is purified in some way. Some Church figures speak of a celibate existence for the rest of his life, which may look perfectly acceptable from where they sit in the General Synod, but not to a red-blooded male who is still relatively young, healthy, and fit.

The Church-versus-Crown arguments that are detailed in this book are crucial because they demonstrate that, sooner or later, there will be a showdown which neither side can win, and yet another part of the monarchy's traditional role is likely to be eroded through a willful lack of desire to adapt to the times.

Camilla, it is said, always looked to her great-great-grandmother Alice Keppel as a role model. Alice's tenure as King Edward VII's favorite mistress—La Favorita—was long and uncontroversial. But though it is hard to look ahead, it is likely that Camilla's place in the history of Britain's monarchy will be even greater than her illustrious forebear's, for with all her love and affection for Charles, she is still in danger of dealing a mortal blow to monarchy in Britain, should she choose to divorce.

Yet strangely, this is not the view of the most seasoned royal of all, the queen mother. It is clear that from the outset she approved of her grandson's relationship with this married woman, actively encouraging it, seeing it as a piece of history. Quite what she thought this encouragement would do to the furtherance of his marriage is harder to ascertain, but then, she and Diana never saw eye to eye. Her view of the love affair was adopted, possibly with slightly less relish, by her daughter the queen.

What is left, now that the cat is out of the bag, is for the royal machinery to make the Charles-Camilla-Andrew imbroglio an acceptable fact of life, yet in this they have signally failed.

Successive royal biographers have pointed to the sorry lack of talent in the present "management team" of the House of Windsor plc, as they like to call themselves. In these pages are detailed instances where misleading information has been disseminated, apparently in order to buttress the Prince of Wales's position with regard to his relationship with Camilla. A franker, bolder approach is what is required in order to assuage an affronted public who feel that the Royal Wedding of 1981 was an expensive sham, and that they have been made to look fools by waving their Union Jacks while Charles stood at the altar thinking about Camilla.

This is an imperfect story, which has its origins in a child who knew very little love and found it increasingly hard, as he went through life, to gather any more to him.

As the boy became a man, he found in the shape of Camilla Parker Bowles someone in whom he could put his trust, with whom he could share his fears, and under whose watchful gaze he could go about acquitting the loneliest job in Britain. It is an imperfect love story, but then, we live in an imperfect world.

A GREATER LOVE

Chapter 1

NTO THE NIGHT

ERKELEY SQUARE IN LATE OCTOBER. WITH THE FIRST FROST STILL A WEEK OR two away, Mayfair clings on to the last vestiges of summer warmth. The huge plane trees have been stripped bare, the thick carpet of leaves at their feet swept away.

In the country, among the higher reaches of British society, the season has moved on. Pheasants have replaced grouse as a prime target; fishing rods have been put away. Huntsmen have hauled their scarlet out of the cupboard and burnished their boots.

In London, though by now the debutantes have scattered to the four winds, the party season has begun. Though fashions alter, the immutable London season goes on; it has barely changed in half a century.

October 1972: Britain's political leaders, Edward Heath and Harold Wilson, had come to an uneasy truce about Britain's membership of the European Community. The bloody war in Vietnam was on the verge of a cease-fire; Dr Henry Kissinger was holding secret meetings with the North Vietnamese in Paris, flying on to talks with President Thieu of the South in Saigon.

Britain was involved in an unedifying scrap with Iceland. The Cod

War erupted with fishing boats and Royal Navy frigates firing on one another. A flight to New York cost £58 and a bottle of Pol Roger champagne £2 17s 6d.

The queen, together with Prince Philip and Princess Anne, toured Croatia as part of their visit to the Communist-ruled state of Yugoslavia, while at home a memorial service was held for her libidinous cousin Prince William of Gloucester, who had died two months earlier in an airplane crash.

The most eligible bachelor in the world was a twenty-four-year-old sublieutenant in the Royal Navy—if not quite a man of the world, then someone who had already seen more of it than most of his contemporaries.

Charles Philip Arthur George, prince of the United Kingdom and possessor of an elegant array of subsidiary titles, had been known by the title Prince of Wales for three years, and while both he and the nation still relished the novelty of this new appellation, to many he was still simply Prince Charles.

Though much had been written about the boy, little was known of the man. From a remote Scottish public school he had disappeared into the anonymity of Cambridge University and from thence, a year before, into the Royal Navy in the tradition of his father, grandfather, and great-grandfather.

To satisfy the diktat of the Duke of Edinburgh, Charles also learned to fly, spending some of the summer months of 1972 familiarizing himself with Royal Naval Wessex helicopters and aircraft of the Queen's Flight. Soon he was to return to the navy to endure the low point of his service there—as a lowly officer on the coastal minesweeper HMS *Glasserton*. But that autumn, the sobersided prince allowed himself a little light relief. He was young, fit, not unhandsome—and ready to fall in love.

In the pursuit of women, he pictured himself as a younger version of the man he most admired—his cousin Prince William of Gloucester. William was everything a prince should be—tall, dark, staggeringly good-looking, and formidably attractive to women. He broke all the rules in a straitlaced family which had survived the Swinging Sixties completely untouched by the decade's loucheness: While in Tokyo he lived with an older woman who was a double-divorcée and mother. She was an artist who painted him in the nude—then displayed the picture in an exhibition. Soon she was supplanted by another older woman, also a divorcée and mother. William could take his pick of beautiful women, and did.

Charles, in awe of his thirty-year-old cousin, wanted to follow suit. William's heroic death in an air race near Wolverhampton that summer only served to strengthen Charles's resolve in that regard—he would take up where William had left off; he would find beautiful women, woo them, conquer them, leave them.

This was easier said than done—the reality was that his conquests so far were neither exciting nor numerous. While an undergraduate at Trinity College, Cambridge, he discovered the pleasures of the bedroom with Lucia Santa Cruz, the glamorous daughter of the Chilean ambassador to London. Three years older than the prince, Miss Santa Cruz was employed by the master of Charles's college, Lord Butler, as a research assistant on his memoirs, *The Art of the Possible*. Butler later recalled: "The Prince asked if she might stay in our lodge for privacy, which request we were very glad to accede to," and so to bed. But the relationship came to an end at about the time Charles graduated.

The prince then entered a brief but ultimately unsatisfactory liaison with Lucinda Buxton, who later became an exceptional filmmaker but, in preference to marriage, chose instead a single life in the company of women. Charles also enjoyed a friendship, though hardly a passion, with Sibella Dorman, the daughter of the governor-general of Malta, Sir Maurice Dorman. An invitation to the George Cross island, where the couple were spied rubbing suntan oil onto each other, was reciprocated with an invitation to Sibella to join Charles on the Royal Yacht *Britannia* after he was crowned Prince of Wales. But the relationship soon fizzled out.

And that was about it. Charles's biographer Penny Junor observed: "He had a number of girlfriends . . . but the relationships were mostly platonic. Not a natural womaniser, he was far more likely to present a girl with some hideous practical joke—like the envelope he gave to one which exploded with rubber bands when she opened it—than a single red rose.

"Like most public schoolboys who have been cloistered in an all-male preserve for five years of their adolescence he was awkward with the opposite sex, unsure of himself, and had never had much opportunity to overcome his diffidence. His peers could practise and make fools of themselves in anonymity. He could never be anonymous."

He also lacked opportunity. In the months leading up to October 1972 he toured Canada and the United States, sailed to Fiji, Bermuda, and Barbados—then went on, in different forays, to France, Kenya, Germany, and Gibraltar. This was in addition to his military duties in first the RAF, then the Royal Navy. Meeting girls was a problem.

But not in Berkeley Square. Not in Annabel's.

Considered by many to be the best nightclub in the world, it was then, as now, an unflashy place which boasted neither hostesses nor floor shows nor gaming tables. Instead, it comprised a dark set of basement rooms decorated in discreet English country-house style, with paneled walls hung with pictures by Augustus John, Sir Edward Landseer, Sir Alfred Munnings, and the royal court painter Sir Oswald Birley, father of the club's founder, Mark Birley. There were separate bars decorated in dark green, a dining room and dance area, a vaulted ceiling held up by brass columns which were polished daily; the ethos was one of sophisticated seclusion.

Its critics would argue that there is a smugness about its denizens, a self-congratulatory ease in the knowledge that they are part of an English inner circle that excludes the socially ambitious, the untrustworthy, and those of lesser birth. In addition, the only journalists ever allowed through the doors were those who accepted the Trappist vow of silence over events that took place inside. It took a long time, for example, for the story to leak that the model Sandra Paul, now married to Home Secretary Michael Howard, had been propositioned—to her disgust—by Ted Kennedy in there. The mustachioed Lord Lucan was a regular, but that was another story altogether.

Into these surroundings royalty may venture, sure in the knowledge that they may safely let down their hair; and in the 1970s Annabel's was a safe launch pad for those early steps into adulthood where the young can flirt and enjoy the heady scent of cheap music far away from the curiosity of the common herd.

There, in the dark, in the basement of the house where King George III's lady of the bedchamber Lady Isabella Finch made her home, history was about to be made. Under the awning and down the steps came a party which included the twenty-two-year-old Princess Anne, newly back from her tour of Yugoslavia, followed by Prince Charles, snatching a rare night's carousal after a dreary shore posting at HMS *Dryad* in Portsmouth.

It was a unique sighting of the prince and his younger sister out on the town together, but it was those who accompanied the royal siblings who would give those gifted with foresight a special frisson. These escorts included the suave Gerald Ward, a Berkshire landowner whose father commanded the Household Cavalry and was appointed Silver Stick in Waiting to the Queen—dual posts which one day would become familiar under the custody of another officer. Ward, who was ten years Charles's senior, was to remain a close friend of the prince through the troubled years ahead.

And then there was the twenty-five-year-old Camilla Shand, a relatively unknown girl-about-town with an interest in horses, clear blue eyes, and a nicely rounded figure.

Miss Shand, when she had a job, was a secretary, but she was not to be confused with someone who needed to work in order to live. Her lineage was aristocratic—some said royal. She had been a debutante in 1965 and had enjoyed the fruits of the London social round for the past six years. Most of her friends were married, but for several reasons this sexy but unremarkable-looking woman remained single.

Camilla lived in a rather unusual place for one of her wealth and social standing—the Cundy Street flats at the back end of Belgravia. Though one of her forebears had made his name and family fortune from building the estate for the Dukes of Westminster, she herself occupied the only part he did not build—an ugly postwar seven-story block which, with its three neighbors, had taken the place of elegant stuccoed terraces bombed flat in the war. Mozart wrote a symphony yards from where she lived; yet the sight of the tall and drably constructed towers set against the pillared, white-painted mansions of Belgravia was about as inharmonious as it was possible to get. Victoria Coach Station, with its rumbling buses belching black fumes, was the nearest landmark.

Miss Shand had no obvious royal connections, but her landlady in the two-bedroomed ground-floor flat was Lady Moyra Campbell, the daughter of the fourth Duke of Abercorn, who had been a Maid of Honor to the queen at her coronation, and whose mother was a close friend of the queen mother and was Mistress of the Robes in that royal household. Lady Moyra moved out when she married an Irish landowner, and Camilla's flatmate became Virginia Carington, beautiful daughter of the Conservative politician and former Guards officer Lord Carrington.

Camilla was no stranger to Annabel's, though it had only lately become attractive to the young. Across Berkeley Square, ten minutes' walk away in Swallow Street off Piccadilly, lay the deserted remnants of the only challenger for the blue bloods' nocturnal attentions, Sybilla's.

Opening in 1966, the nightclub was named after Camilla's cousin Sybilla Edmonstone. She was all Camilla was not—beautiful, celebrated, incredibly trendy. The contrast between the two girls' lives was best demonstrated in that year when two events took place almost simultaneously. On the one hand, there was Camilla's rather staid coming-out dance at the Dorking home of her uncle Lord Ashcombe, where the most exciting event was a car crash involving two silly debutantes, one of whom broke her nose. On the other hand, there was the opening of Sybilla's.

Co-owned by George Harrison, then a godlike being by virtue of the Beatles' worldwide acclaim, and baronet Sir William Pigott-Brown, its first night was a sensation, the greatest manifestation yet of the Swinging Sixties. All four Beatles were present; the Rolling Stones had held back their tour of America to be there. It was a blessed moment of synchronicity, when for a brief time class barriers were breached and pop stars of lowly birth mixed with the earls of Lichfield and Shelburne, Lord Eliot, the children of Lord Harlech, and such figures of the moment as Vanessa Redgrave, Julie Christie, and Rudolf Nureyev.

And there, center stage with all eyes on her, was Camilla's cousin Sybilla. At twenty-two she had the face and figure of a model, the adulation of the *beau monde,* and an impressive fortune stemming from her great-grandfather Marshall Field's Chicago stores empire. Her name and face had become synonymous with the freewheeling spirit of the age; her very presence was enough to make grown men go weak at the knees.

So very different from the fledgling Camilla Shand, whose charm for the opposite sex was a rumbustious earthiness, rather than a goddess's awe. But then her upbringing lacked the cosmopolitan élan of her older cousin's.

Though, as we shall learn, there were hidden depths to her family, Camilla seemed on the face of it an unlikely date for the Prince of Wales that night in 1972. Her father, who described himself as an "educational films representative" when she was born, lived in London but preferred the country where he pursued the fox with vigor and his business interests with rather less success.

She was not related to the dukes of England, nor to any foreign royal houses—the two areas where Charles might expect to find a future bride. She was not then the possessor of a personal fortune, and of the girls in her debutante year she was possibly one of the least photogenic. In addition, she was known to have enjoyed a lively love affair with an army officer called Andrew Parker Bowles, at thirty-two eight years her senior, which those who knew the couple predicted would end in marriage.

But Parker Bowles, a serving major in the Blues and Royals cavalry regiment, had been posted to Germany. And in the preceding summer months Camilla had spent much time at the Guards' Polo Club at Windsor together with her friend Carolyn Gerard Leigh and Andrew Parker Bowles's sister, Mary Ann Paravicini, whose husband, Nick, was a Life Guards officer and polo-playing friend of Prince Charles's.

The connection had been established. It was at a party soon after Charles and Camilla met that, with typical joie-de-vivre, she made her historic proposal: "My great-grandmother and your great-great-grandfather were lovers. So how about it?"

Factually, she was accurate. Between 1898 and his death in 1910, King Edward VII enjoyed a close physical and intellectual relationship with the Honorable Mrs. George Keppel, a woman twenty-eight years his junior. Of all his extramarital relationships, this was the most profound, and Charles, well versed in his family's history, knew of the special role Alice Keppel played in the life of his ancestor as confidante and hostess.

Had he studied more closely the photographs of Alice Keppel, he would have seen an eerie resemblance between the two women. But there were more similarities—many more—between Alice and Camilla. And in the end, Camilla would achieve a greater footnote in history than her celebrated great-grandmother.

Ahead of him the prince faced the prospect of the chilly wastes of Lincolnshire, where he would undertake a week's refresher course flying RAF Jet Provosts, and beyond that the even less congenial surround-ings of the RAF's Advanced Flying Training School in Anglesey. But that night in the warmth and dark of Annabel's, Camilla Shand's proposal echoed again in his ears. Champagne corks popped and romance was in the air.

Princess Anne and Gerald Ward danced to the hits of the day, Eric Clapton's "Layla," the Bee Gees' "Run to Me," Michael Jackson's "Ain't No Sunshine," Roxy Music's "Virginia Plain," and when things slowed down, Charles and Camilla took to the floor for Python Lee Jackson's "In a Broken Dream" and Faron Young's "It's Four in the Morning."

At four in the morning they were no longer in Annabel's, but in the ground-floor flat of Stack House, Cundy Street, discovering a passion which was to last many long years; years of joy and sometimes of adver-sity, but years where never once the love would die.

TWO MISTRESSES

T WAS HISTORY REPEATING ITSELF. THOUGH THERE ARE UNCANNY SIMILARI-
ties between Charles and Camilla's love affair and that of the
Prince of Wales and Mrs. Simpson, it is the relationship between
Camilla's great-grandmother and Charles's great-great-grandfather that
casts the greatest light over present-day events.

Alice Keppel was born in 1869, the youngest daughter of Admiral
Sir William Edmonstone and Mary Elizabeth Parsons. Edmonstone, the
fourth baronet, descended from the Stuarts by a fifteenth-century marriage: King Robert III's daughter Mary married Sir William Edmonstone
of Culloden, and in 1445 they were given the family seat of Duntreath
Castle on the Stirlingshire side of Loch Lomond.

Set in uncompromising Scottish moorland and with the backdrop
of two austere, bald hills, Duntreath appeared a forbidding edifice with
a courtyard and tower at each corner. Yet its stark grandeur belied the
comforts within, and its solidity and history were arguably a proper
setting from which a king's mistress might emerge. "It was romantic, of
a standard of luxury without equal in those days; gay with a touch of
Frenchness in its *salons en enfilade* and premeditated perspectives. The

25

atmosphere of the place was complex: half-medieval, half-exotic," wrote one member of the family.

As Alice passed from childhood into adolescence, her human qualities became more marked: *honest, energetic, practical* were the adjectives used, mirroring those of another woman almost a century later. She was noted for exceptional kindness—"her nature was without pettiness, prejudice or malice," wrote one biographer. "Even as a girl her tact was remarkable." In a different age, when the *beau monde* were privy to the king's raffish ways while preserving the news from the hoi polloi, her charm and good nature uniquely shielded Alice from attack once she became Edward's mistress.

Her upbringing was indeed aristocratic; but as a younger daughter she was unlikely to bring a great dowry to her future husband. Nonetheless she married for love, not money, accepting the proposal of the Honorable George Keppel, third son of the seventh Earl of Albemarle. He was twenty-six and an officer in the Gordon Highlanders; she was twenty-two when they married in 1891.

Despite the lack of money on both sides, contemporaries thought she had done well—for Alice, like her descendant, was not one of the celebrated beauties of the age. Dame Rebecca West noted: "Her charm was not in her looks; George indeed was the only real beauty of the two. Alice had no distinctive characteristics of face or figure. She was endowed with a bright pale skin, and those Scottish eyes that have the quality of a clear stream but with a noting, concerned quality, as if she were a theatre sister in a well-run hospital." Just as with Camilla, her charms lay elsewhere than in striking physical beauty, though each was the possessor of an imposing bosom. Hugh Walpole noted: "Mrs. Keppel is great fun. I do like her. She's like the sergeant in the guard with a sense of humour."

Her husband's family, despite their Dutch origins, were by the late nineteenth century an intensely grand English family. Arnold Joost von Keppel joined the Prince of Orange on his first trip to Britain in 1688, and remained one of his closest allies after he ascended the throne as King William III the following year. He was created Earl of Albemarle and made a Knight of the Garter—"for his *beaux veux,*" observed Sir Harold Acton drily.

This intimacy with the monarch extended, unusually, over three generations with the second and third earls also being made Knights of the Garter. The connection with the throne was maintained, albeit in a watered-down form, through succeeding generations—George Keppel's own father, the seventh earl, was treasurer to Queen Victoria's household as well as twice being under secretary of state for war. His mother, Sophia Macnab, was an unusual choice of wife for an established aristocrat and courtier in that she was the daughter of the prime minister of Canada, Sir Allan Napier Macnab. A soldier, lawyer, businessman, and politician, Macnab owed his massive fortune to speculation in real estate, and his knighthood to the zeal with which he suppressed the Canadian rebellion of 1837.

A contemporary described Alice's husband thus: "One of those tall and handsome Englishmen who, immaculately dressed, proclaim the perfect gentleman." He was also a womanizer and, though from a grand family, perpetually short of cash—a situation that remained unrelieved until King Edward got him a job in trade, working as an agent for his friend Sir Thomas Lipton, the grocer.

On the face of it, and in the light of subsequent events, the youthful match did not augur well. Yet it lasted more than fifty years, from 1891 to 1947, when the couple died within weeks of each other.

Three years after their marriage at St. George's, Hanover Square, their first child, Violet, was born. In adulthood she was to become notorious in her own right when, as Violet Trefusis, she embarked in 1918 on a turbulent love affair with the writer Vita Sackville-West. Lesbianism, a form of love which was not acknowledged to exist by Queen Victoria, was still deeply shocking, even in the sophisticated salons of Mayfair.

When Violet was not quite four, an incident occurred which was to change her mother's life. On February 27, 1898, the Prince of Wales came to dinner with the Keppels at their Wilton Crescent, Belgravia, home. In the words of his biographer Sir Philip Magnus, "an understanding arose overnight"—and an affair started that would continue until the king died. The historian Richard Hough put it more graphically; the relationship "warmed with the speed of a bonfire."

The couple had already met: While inspecting the Norfolk Yeomanry, of which he was colonel-in-chief and in which George Keppel served as an officer, the prince saw Alice and asked his friend Lord

Leicester to introduce them. They subsequently met at Sandown races when she was accompanied by Sir John Leslie. Then, wrote Leslie's granddaughter Anita: "HRH gave Leslie to understand that his presence was no longer required. Whimsically, my grandfather used to describe that certain look—blending shrewd appraisement and admiration—that crossed the Prince's face as his eyes travelled over Mrs. George Keppel's lovely face and fashionably curved figure."

"She was attractive enough to interest him sexually; entertaining when he was bored, patient when he was cantankerous, sympathetic when he was ill, unobtrusive when he appeared in public," noted the writer Theo Aronson. "Like all successful mistresses Alice was part-lover, part-wife, part-mother." No more accurate description could be found of Alice's descendant.

Less than two years after the royal love affair began, a second daughter was born to Mrs. Keppel. Successive historians have balked at addressing the question of the child's parentage—but certain factors point compellingly toward Edward's being the father. Alice's marriage, by this stage, was nine years old. From the beginning of the affair the king was virtually a daily visitor at the Keppel houses, first in Wilton Crescent, then in Portman Square. From the outset George Keppel was a quiescent player in this ménage-à-trois, and indeed had romantic interests of his own to pursue. It would not be unreasonable to assume that the physical side of their relationship was by now dormant, even though to the end the pair maintained a devoted affection for each other.

Furthermore, it is highly questionable whether Keppel had even fathered Alice's first child. Violet was generally assumed to be the daughter of an earlier paramour, the recently widowed Ernest William Beckett, the future Lord Grimthorpe, and in later life her lover, Vita Sackville-West, told the writer Philippe Jullian that Beckett was indeed Violet's father.

Additional evidence of the platonic nature of Alice's relationship with her husband may be found in the caustic aside of the Marchioness Curzon to her husband: "Mrs. Favourite Keppel is bringing forth another questionable offspring! Either Lord Stavordale's or H. Sturt's!" Since Alice gave birth to no further children, it may be supposed that she suffered a miscarriage soon after, but clearly the multiplicity of sexual dalliances she enjoyed does tend to point to a conjugal inactivity between husband and wife.

One further, and telling, piece of evidence came sixty years later, when the child born to Alice in the first months of sexual intrigue with the king decided, in old age, to write her memoirs. Sonia Keppel entitled the book *Edwardian Daughter,* the neatest of double entendres and the most illuminating pointer to her true parentage.

If Sonia Rosemary Keppel was Edward's daughter, that would make her King George V's half sister. It would make Sonia's daughter Rosalind a first cousin of King George VI, and her granddaughter Camilla a second cousin of the queen. It would also make Camilla a second cousin once removed of Prince Charles. The serendipity of this coincidence would not be lost on either.

Edward's affair with Alice Keppel was barely three years old when he ascended the throne as King Edward VII. He was sixty, she was now thirty-one. Their way was made easier by George Keppel's good-natured complaisance: "He was extremely handsome, a tall army officer with a bristling moustache, an aquiline nose and a hearty laugh. Very fond of women himself, he raised no objection to the Prince's friendship with his wife, to whom he was deeply attached; and when his income proved inadequate for the sort of life he was called upon to lead—and his wife's bank managers to whom she was, as her daughter said, 'irresistibly attractive' could help no more—he cheerfully went to work for Sir Thomas Lipton, who obligingly found him employment at the Prince's instigation," wrote the historian Christopher Hibbert.

Mrs. Keppel fulfilled more than a mere bodily need for the king and, such was the graceful and unassuming way in which she conducted herself, her presence by his side was accepted at all levels, including, grudgingly, by Queen Alexandra herself. By the time Edward and Mrs. Keppel met, the royal marriage was thirty-five years old, the queen was aged fifty-four and had become isolated in her deafness.

Anita Leslie, in her book *Edwardians in Love,* observed: "When Edward's niece Princess Alice came to stay at Sandringham, she found Mrs. Keppel delightful. She never flaunted herself or took advantage of her position as the king's favourite. Queen Alexandra was very fond of her and encouraged the liaison. There was a lot of gossip about their relationship and unnecessary sympathy for Aunt Alex—who didn't need it, as she welcomed the relationship."

Just as her great-granddaughter would do eighty years later, Alice hosted dinner parties for her royal paramour—on one occasion she was famously placed next to the kaiser "so she might have the opportunity of talking to him." The Keppels and the king would make annual trips at Easter to Biarritz, and the Keppels also made regular visits to Sandringham.

The king, benevolent in incipient old age, took great delight in Alice's two daughters, and it was said that they had grown up "rolling their hoop with a Sceptre." As the younger—Camilla's grandmother Sonia Cubitt—later recalled: "Sometimes Kingy would come to tea with Mama, and was there when I appeared at six o'clock. On such occasions he had devised a fascinating game. With a fine disregard for the condition of his trousers, he would lend me his leg, on which I used to start two bits of bread and butter (butter side down), side by side. Then, bets of a penny each were made, and the winning piece of bread depended, of course, on which was the more buttery."

This kindness was repaid by the dedication with which Alice Keppel served him, as mistress and helpmeet. Lord Hardinge of Penshurst, permanent head of the Foreign Office and viceroy of India, noted in a private memorandum: "Everybody knew of the relationship which existed between King Edward and Mrs. George Keppel. . . . I used to see a great deal of Mrs. Keppel at that time and I was aware that she had knowledge of what was going on in the political world. I would like here to pay tribute to her wonderful discretion, and to the excellent influence which she has always exercised over the King. She never utilised her knowledge to her own advantage, or to that of her friends; and I never heard her repeat an unkind word against anyone. It would have been difficult to find any other lady who would have filled the part of friend of King Edward with the same loyalty and discretion."

Friends of Camilla Parker Bowles would echo those sentiments at dinner parties and in private conversations almost a century later. As Sir Philip Magnus noted: "The truth is that in Alice Keppel the King had found not only a woman who . . . would excite him physically as well as relaxing him mentally (a rare combination in itself). On top of that he had found a mistress who could cherish him as fondly as a wife. No man, not even a monarch, could have asked for more."

There were other mistresses, of course—the Princesse de Sagan, the Countess of Warwick, and the actress Lillie Langtry among them—but it was with Alice that Edward was able to find the most profound relationship. She was universally known as La Favorita. What was remarkable was the forbearance of both Queen Alexandra and George Keppel—only once did the queen slip from saintly forbearance, as the historian Christopher Hibbert reported: "One day . . . glancing out of the window at Sandringham, she caught sight of Mrs. Keppel returning with the King in an open carriage. Mrs. Keppel had become rather stout by then and the sight of her imposing bosom alongside the rather portulent figure of the King, suddenly struck the Queen as ludicrous. She called her lady-in-waiting to come and share the view and burst into peals of laughter"—not something the Princess of Wales was able to do in a later generation.

Until Edward's death in 1910 Alice Keppel occupied an equal place in the king's innermost circle along with his financial guide, Sir Ernest Cassel; his adviser on military affairs, Sir William Esher; Lord Fisher, the first sea lord; Lord Hardinge; his private secretary, Sir Francis Knollys; and the Portuguese ambassador, the Marquis Luis de Soveral.

Remarkably, not only did the upper echelons of society open their doors to accept her, but so too did the queen. At a house party at Chatsworth, the Duke of Devonshire's seat, in January 1904, the king and Mrs. Keppel "with lovely clothes and diamonds" played bridge in one room while the queen was entertained with songs and music elsewhere. Nor, judging by the queen's unusual liveliness, was she in the slightest put out to be sharing a roof with her husband and his mistress.

Though Alice—like Camilla—hosted private dinners for her paramour, her public self-effacement was complete. Only when she ventured abroad with the king could she be treated as an equal. And in Biarritz, Edward's biographer Gordon Brook-Shepherd declared: "Alice Keppel *was* Queen."

For a month or so each year, from early March to early April, the couple would hold sway in the French seaside resort—he staying in a suite of rooms in the Hôtel du Palais while she was welcomed at the Villa Eugénie, the luxurious home of Sir Ernest Cassel.

They would meet each day at quarter past twelve and together they would stroll along the promenade, recognized by all and unhindered by all. Indeed, some illustrated French papers even went so far as to airbrush out the features of Mrs. Keppel whenever she was photographed with the king.

Then they would invariably lunch in his suite at the Hôtel du Paris, where, according to one historian, both drank copiously. But the soft Atlantic weather, French cuisine, and the absence of protocol allowed the king to unwind and pay full attention to his companion, paying her the compliment of treating her as an equal.

"Edward VII thought too highly of Alice to subject her to the indignity of a clandestine existence," wrote Theo Aronson, though perforce this courtesy could only be extended in a sympathetic environment. The king never took Alice on his annual visit to Marienbad, where in the course of his so-called "spa diplomacy" he would meet political and royal figures from all over Europe, and where a veil would have to be drawn over her presence. But he did take her on several occasions to Paris, where she forged an alliance with the ex-Empress Eugénie, widow of Napoleon III.

It was in Biarritz, however, where the king's life started toward its close. He arrived there in March 1910, after an unusual altercation with Queen Alexandra over the excursion, which, by now, was as annual a fixture as the Glorious Twelfth. He had caught a chill in Paris, and Alice nursed him until his health returned. Their sojourn in Biarritz was much longer than usual—seven weeks—and the longest continuous period the couple had ever spent in each other's company.

His arrival back in Britain in late April prompted another chill, which turned to bronchitis; within a week his life was all but over. Perhaps because of the exceptional intimacy they had shared on their recent holiday, perhaps because of the lengthening years of their relationship—they had been inseparable now for twelve years—Alice vehemently asserted her rights, as she saw them.

For six days, while the queen, alerted to the emergency, was hurrying home from a holiday in Corfu, Alice attended the king at Buckingham Palace. On Alexandra's arrival Alice sent her a letter which Edward had written her at the time of his appendix operation in 1902 which stated "if he were dying he felt sure that those about him would allow her to come to him."

Alexandra, faced with the unexpected demise of her husband, was violently resistant to the idea, but the clamorous Alice was eventually allowed in to see her lover once more. The king insisted that the two women kiss as an act of reconciliation, to which the queen frozenly assented. But as the monarch's condition deteriorated, a resistant and by now hysterical Alice was removed from the room.

Lord Esher wrote afterward: "Altogether it was a painful and rather theatrical exhibition, and ought never to have happened." The queen added, bitterly: "I would have not have kissed her if he had not bade me."

In bereavement Alice was inconsolable. Her daughter Sonia wrote: "A pall of darkness hung over the house, blinds were drawn, lights were dimmed, and black clothes appeared, even for me, with black ribbons threaded through my underclothes."

The king had made provision, through Cassel, for his mistress to buy a villa in Italy, but it was to be fifteen years before she did so. Instead, she took her entire family on a tour of Ceylon and the Orient, returning two years later to a new house in Grosvenor Square.

Life without her lover went on for another thirty-seven years—in 1925 she finally purchased a house in Florence, escaping to England when the Second World War broke out and returning when peace was declared. On September 11, 1947, she died, aged seventy-eight, of cirrhosis of the liver. She had never once been known to be indiscreet about her relationship with the king, and never kept a diary. Her dedication to him was utter and complete.

George Keppel followed his wife to the grave within weeks; it was said he could not see the point of living without her. They had been married for fifty-six years.

As one famous life came to its close, another had just begun. Alice Keppel's granddaughter Rosalind, married to a dashing army officer called Bruce Shand, gave birth on July 17, 1947, at King's College Hospital in London to a daughter, Camilla. History was about to repeat itself.

Seventeen years later, when the gossip columnists were looking around for a suitable label for the debutante Camilla Shand, they came up with the phrase "building boss Lord Ashcombe's niece." The Ashcombes, whose family name is Cubitt, were known as the people who built Belgravia and made the Dukes of Westminster rich.

As with all legends, this was only partially true but served as an identity tag for those who were unfamiliar with Camilla's rich ancestry.

Back in the eighteenth century, in the little town of Buxton in Norfolk, documents first recorded the existence of the Cubitt family. The name derives from the Anglo-Saxon, meaning "elbow." Thomas Cubitt, one of a widespread Norfolk yeoman family, was a tenant farmer living at Mayton Hall and working for Lord Yarmouth. It was debated whether his son William was "prodigal or incompetent," but either way by 1772 he was poverty-stricken and moved to Swannington, five miles away.

By the end of the eighteenth century, records were more comprehensive and there emerges Thomas Cubitt, described as a master builder and "the penniless son of a Coltishall farmer." Having trained as a carpenter, he married and fathered twelve children, as well as establishing a thriving builder's business, which was ultimately responsible for the construction of some of London's finest streets in Belgravia and beyond. Much of the Grosvenor estate, including the ultimate in grandeur, Eaton Square, together with Pimlico and a portion of the lesser suburb of Clapham were his responsibility, though much of the work was subcontracted as Cubitt aspired to become responsible for the standard of construction and the social quality of the work. Rather grander commissions followed, including the creation of Osborne, Queen Victoria's house on the Isle of Wight, and the remodeling of Buckingham Palace.

Cubitt's origins were humble, his ascent quite breathtaking. He became an adviser to Prince Albert and, unusually for one in trade, was recommended for a peerage. He died before it could be conferred and, unusually, the peerage was given instead to his son George. The family's arrival in the nobility took two generations and it settled in Surrey. It was Roland, the third Lord Ashcombe, who wedded Alice Keppel and King Edward's daughter, Sonia: they were married for twenty-seven years until the union was dissolved in 1947, the year that Alice and George Keppel died, and Camilla was born.

If Camilla's ancestry on her mother's side, with its roots in Scottish royalty and Dutch nobility, was gilded and wreathed in the aroma of love and intrigue, her father's ancestors had an equally fascinating tale to tell.

The Shands started life in Scotland, too—though as merchants, not kings. By the late eighteenth century John Shand was established in a minor way, to be followed in the business by his son Alexander Garden

Shand. As Camilla's Edmonstone ancestors were being raised to the baronetcy, Alexander was making his own way forward by marrying an heiress, Isabella Morton, on June 5, 1809. She brought to the marriage an estate in Banffshire, and after six years of marriage produced a son, Hugh Morton Shand.

But the wealth Alexander had so assiduously cultivated during his lifetime, and might reasonably have passed to his son and heir, disappeared overnight. Isabella having predeceased him, he made a deathbed marriage to his housekeeper and effectively dispossessed the son. So Hugh joined the army and sailed for India, as so many of similar backgrounds and financial circumstances did in the high days of Empire. Imbued as he was with his father's business acumen, it was not long before he established a trading company which brought the inevitable profits from the cornucopia of the Indian subcontinent. Returning to London, he bought a complete terrace of houses in Edwardes Place, Kensington, and the wealth he generated has effectively kept the family ever since.

For Hugh, marriage could wait—fortune came first; so it was not until he was forty that he took a wife. He chose Edrica, the daughter of the portrait painter Joshua William Faulkner, and the wedding took place in London in 1855.

By now the family was firmly based in London and three sons were born in a short space of time. The eldest, Alexander Faulkner Shand, was born on May 20, 1858, in Leinster Gardens, Bayswater. Educated at Eton and Peterhouse, Cambridge, where he read law, he went on to train as a barrister, picking up an honorary Ll.D. at St. Andrew's. But he was never called to the bar; instead, his life took a bohemian turn, with the increasingly hedonist and oenophile Alexander becoming part of the set that evolved around Beatrice and Sidney Webb. Economists and social reformers, the Webbs laid the foundations of the Fabian Society and set out to reform Britain's sociopolitical system, and while in this they may have failed, they did succeed in creating the *New Statesman* as a voice of the intelligent left.

Under this influence Alexander Shand became interested in the nascent study of psychology and wrote a book, *The Foundations of Character*. He became engaged to Constance Lloyd, the slim, graceful, and violet-eyed English beauty; but at the age of twenty-four she met and fell in love with the notorious homosexual Oscar Wilde. Constance and Wilde finally married when she was thirty-three, but Alexander had already found a substitute wife in the form of Augusta Mary Coates, whose paternal family had been doctors in Bath for five generations, but whose mother was a member of the Hope shipping family from Liverpool.

The marriage was not a happy one. Alexander's life-style was that of a dilettante, while his wife, who bore him a son, Philip Morton, was religious, straitlaced, and energetic. Constantly engaged in the pursuit of good works but personally "vague and hopeless," according to some who knew her, she expressed concern over the upbringing of her son but then largely left that responsibility to nannies.

Philip Morton followed his father to Eton and went on to King's College, Cambridge, before starting his lifelong love affair with France at the Sorbonne. He went to visit his grandfather in Florence, where Alice Keppel was soon to make her home, before embarking on a multi-faceted career which saw him become one of the most influential writers on modern architecture of the age, and one who was instrumental in introducing modern architecture to Great Britain. He counted among his friends many of Europe's leading architects including Walter Gropius, Le Corbusier, and Wells Coates.

Philip was a prolific writer and an acclaimed authority on food and, in particular, wine—an enthusiasm he shared with his father and grandfather, and which he was to pass on to his son. He also wrote copiously about apples and set up the Fruit Group at the Royal Horticultural Society. His character, like his career, was multifaceted—his friend Sir John Betjeman, later Poet Laureate, described him as "a man of compelling charm," but there was also a collection of enemies and broken marriages.

An extrovert, raconteur, and eccentric, he annoyed many of his associates with his outspokenness: His impatience and intolerance were legendary. His politics were described as "Red" by some—he voted for Labour in the 1945 election—but as "right wing" by others. Certainly he bore all the hallmarks of upper-middle-class intolerance—he was racist, sexist, and anti-Semitic—but in intellectual matters he was otherwise enlightened.

His rackety existence, numerous affairs, and general disregard for life's rules inevitably caused a falling-out with his father, and ultimately led to his being disinherited. In fact, a clause in his father's will specified that if any of the grandchildren gave money to their father they themselves would be disinherited.

He married four times, first to Edith Marguerite Harrington in April 1916. Exactly nine months later a son, Bruce Shand—Camilla's father—was born. Philip returned to the war—he served "a brief and undistinguished service" in the Royal Field Artillery—and that, effectively, was the end of the marriage. Edith remained close to Philip's parents, and Bruce was brought up by his grandparents with the assistance of a number of boarding schools.

But in 1920 Bruce's parents were divorced—whereupon Edith, the daughter of an accountant, became engaged to a golf-course designer and left for America. The child, still only three, was thus effectively deserted by both his parents. By the time he was six his father was living in France; father and son were not to meet again until 1935 when Bruce was eighteen—and then only by reason of Alexander Shand's death—and his mother remained in America.

At the time of the 1920 divorce Bruce's father met and married Alice Tunnere. Within a few short months a daughter, Doris, was born—but the marriage was soon over. By 1926 he was living in Lyons and obtained shares in a velvet-making mill. That year he married a Frenchwoman, Georgette Avril, whose family owned the mill, but that, too, ended in divorce with a great deal of publicity in the French evening papers and the judge directing Shand to "turn his attentions to another country."

He swallowed the rebuke and headed for England. There, in 1931, he married Sybil Sissons, the daughter of a Weybridge solicitor, and at last found contentment. With his wife he served during the Second World War at the Admiralty in Bath before returning to Lyons, where he died in 1960.

His stepdaughter from this marriage was Lady Stirling, wife of the architect Sir Jim Stirling; and with Sybil he had a daughter, Elspeth Rosamund Morton Shand. To her he dispensed a single piece of advice: "It does not matter whom you marry as long as he isn't a politician, a lawyer or a Welshman." Elspeth's husband, the future chancellor of the exchequer Sir Geoffrey (now Lord) Howe, was all three. As a privy councillor and uncle by marriage to Camilla Parker Bowles, Sir Geoffrey was able to offer firsthand advice in the crises which were to billow up in the years ahead.

By comparison to his father's wayward life-style, Bruce Shand devoted himself to a life constrained by convention. Though he may have expected to go to Eton, the decision was taken by his grandmother to send him elsewhere. "She was anxious that I should not go to Eton where both her husband and son (with neither of whom, sadly, had she enjoyed particularly harmonious relationships) were set on the road to modest intellectural prowess," Bruce Shand later recalled. "Rather illogically, and I think unfairly, she attributed the plethora of wives, four in all, that my father collected to the influence of that seat of learning."

His grandmother Augusta may have been right at that. Bruce went to Rugby ("a school I cordially disliked") and his life thereafter was a model of rectitude. After Rugby there was a brief spell in France before he went to a crammer in Pimlico. He was accepted by the army and joined the Royal Military Academy in 1935.

His heroic exploits with the 12th Lancers, a cavalry regiment, in the Second World War were racily told in his memoirs, *Previous Engagements*. He earned the Military Cross twice, was wounded, and taken prisoner by the Germans in 1942. On his release at the end of the war he met the twenty-four-year-old Rosalind Cubitt, whose father would shortly become the third Lord Ashcombe, and in the euphoria of a capital city released from the constraints of war, the couple married at St. Paul's, Knightsbridge, in the bitter chill of January 1946. Typically for this gallant soldier, based at Bovington Camp, no close members of his family turned up for the ceremony.

In the space of the next five years three children were born—first two girls, Camilla and Annabel, then a boy, Mark.

In adulthood Mark Shand was to lead an unstructured life more reminiscent of his Shand ancestors than the Cubitts or Keppels. Born when Camilla was four years old, he was educated at Milton Abbey, a substitute for the academically more demanding Eton, before plunging with enthusiasm into London life—his quite exceptional good looks and laconic style made him an essential adjunct to every fashionable party.

Eschewing university or the services, he took a fine-arts course at Sotheby's on leaving school before adopting a free-lance career as an art dealer, at one stage specializing in the Art Deco period. By the time he was twenty-two, according to the London gossip columnists, he was enjoying a liaison with Princess Lee Radziwill, the sister of Jacqueline Onassis, who was twenty years his senior. The relationship evolved from a house party in Barbados given in 1971 by Mark's uncle Lord Ashcombe for Jackie, Lee, and others; the month-long sojourn among close friends was otherwise most notable for the near death of John-John Kennedy, then ten, who all but drowned in Glitter Bay.

The house party was also attended by Camilla, who took along for company her flatmate from Ebury Street, Virginia Carington—a decision which resulted soon after in the peer, known as Mad Harry, proposing marriage to Virginia, despite a twenty-two-year age gap. Clearly the Barbadian air had special qualities for dissolving the generation gap.

While staying at Princess Lee's house in the West Indies, Mark met Caroline Kennedy, then a schoolgirl, and encouraged her to come to London to undertake the same fine-arts course he had studied. She arrived in Britain while the freewheeling Shand was enjoying a relationship with an American actress called Barbara Trentham, who was later to marry John Cleese. But for the time the eighteen-year-old daughter of the assassinated John Kennedy was in London—and just about the time his sister Camilla, then still single, was falling in love with the Prince of Wales—he embarked on a romance with her.

If alerted to their children's latest fancies, and not every parent is, Major Shand and his wife, Rosalind, must for a moment have marveled that, of three children, one should be dating the offspring of a queen and another the offspring of a U.S. president.

The relationship flourished despite Miss Kennedy's being involved in two bomb incidents—first when a car bomb exploded outside the house where she was staying, then again when she moved to the Onassis family flat in Mayfair. Mrs. Onassis was reported to have pleaded with her daughter, halfway through the Sotheby's course, to come home. When she refused, Jacqueline asked for special protection for her daughter through the American Embassy. She was said to have been beside herself with anger when Scotland Yard informed her that only top-risk targets enjoyed personal protection, and that Caroline must walk the streets unguarded like anyone else.

Caroline stayed the course, enjoying Shand's attention so much she sewed him a pair of boudoir slippers, but the relationship did not survive her return to the United States. Nevertheless, Mark remained friendly with the family while moving on to his next conquest, Bianca Jagger, whose marriage to Mick Jagger had ended in divorce.

By now he was the hottest ticket in town, and in February 1979 the *London Evening News* asked: Is This the Sexiest Man in London? It pointed out that Bianca Jagger, who had been his date for the past year, was fascinated by his expertise in aikido and the tattoo of a snake on his body; the newspaper ululated about "his shaggy locks, Nureyev hips and casual, bored manner." These attributes then earned the attention of American heiress Avril Payson Meyer, whose mother, Sandra, had been married to the British publisher Lord Weidenfeld, and the actress and model Marie Helvin, who had recently separated from the photographer David Bailey.

But as he matured, Mark Shand sought out new conquests of a different variety. His life had changed after a dangerous canoe trip into the headhunting backwaters of Indonesia, and before long he had become immersed in the plight of the elephant. Riding across India on one convinced him of their endangered nature and he wrote *Travels with My Elephant.* It was a best-seller, earned him the title Travel Writer of the Year, and moved him into a different class of writing from his previous attempt at authorship, a travel book called *Skullduggery,* with photographs by world-famous war photographer Don McCullin, described by one reviewer as: "a boys-together book—lots of drinking, hangovers, constipation, nights on the town."

He married the actress Clio Goldsmith, niece of the financier Sir James and daughter of the ecologist Teddy, in 1990. An article in a London newspaper suggested that, at forty-two, he had finally found a purpose in life. "Now it's time to put something back," he mused. "I've taken all my life."

That is not a phrase that could ever be used of his sister Camilla.

Chapter 3

HOUGH LATER SHE WAS TO ADOPT THE ADDITIONAL CHRISTIAN NAME OF
Rosemary, in deference to her Cubitt grandmother—Edward
VII's daughter—she was named at birth plain Camilla Shand.

Her recently demobilized father, Bruce, no doubt too busy during
the summer of 1947 with his new career as an educational films representative, left the task of registering the birth to his wife, Rosalind. Up
and about five days after the birth at King's College Hospital, it was she
who walked to the Lambeth Central office to fill out the necessary
paperwork to register her firstborn.

The newlyweds had yet to celebrate their second anniversary. Bruce
Shand, twice decorated with the Military Cross for his valor in France,
then El Alamein, had been wounded and captured by the Germans,
spending nearly three years in a prison camp at Spangenburg before
being released in the spring of 1945.

Handsome and urbane, Shand cut a raffish figure prior to his marriage, running with a much faster set than most of his Rugby contemporaries could hope to match. His friends were higher-born than he, but
such was his natural charm he was soon absorbed into the recherché life

of St. James's clubland, becoming a member of the two hundred-year-old Boodle's in his early twenties. A life of splash and dash at one stage brought him into sufficient financial difficulties from "frequent and expensive dinners at the Mirabelle, nights at the Four Hundred and considerable sociable drinking at the Ritz Bar" for Bruce to submit to the efforts of a committee of friends who were forced into sorting out his shaky finances as he once again headed for war. But he never lacked for companionship: "One seemed to see friends everywhere and it would have been difficult to be lonely," he observed, adding wryly, "and anyway the Americans had not yet arrived."

But marriage to the Honorable Rosalind Cubitt, daughter of the third Lord Ashcombe at St. Paul's Church, Knightsbridge, on the second day of 1946, followed swiftly on his return to England. Both individuals brought a private income to the marriage, but future employment was always going to be necessary. The couple settled into a rented home, the Manor House at Westdean, set high in the Sussex Downs above the English Channel.

Camilla was four months old when the nation finally shook off the burden of war in order to celebrate the marriage of Princess Elizabeth to Prince Philip of Greece. In London, such was the frenzy of excitement over the forthcoming spectacle—somehow an embodiment of all that the nation had been fighting for—that seats on the processional route were being resold for the modern-day equivalent of £35,000. At Buckingham Palace, a series of glittering parties, the like of which had not been seen for a decade, took place. At one, an Indian maharajah became belligerently drunk and physically attacked the Duke of Devonshire, and Field Marshal Smuts, casting his eye across a sea of tiaras, turned to Queen Mary and enthused: "You are the big potato; all the other Queens are small potatoes." At another, Princess Juliana of the Netherlands, dancing with Elizabeth's uncle, the Duke of Gloucester, slipped to the floor "large and plump and gasping" so that everyone froze, including the royal family, until she was hauled into a vertical position once again.

In Sussex, the population celebrated at a rather more sedate pace, with a telegram from the mayor of Lewes, Alderman Whittington, deemed most fitting to mark the occasion. A thousand local schoolchildren crammed into the Town Hall for tea; and near The Old Manor a celebratory bonfire was lit, though in the aftermath of war there was some difficulty in finding material worthy of the occasion. Gabriel, the ancient bell in the Market Tower, was rung for an hour during the wedding, distracting the denizens of the Crown Hotel who were trying to watch the proceedings, without too much success, on a prototype television set.

The royal wedding, which so instantly set the nation aglow after the long dark years, had been engineered by Lord Mountbatten, who, a generation later, was to play a part in providing sanctuary for Queen Elizabeth's unborn son and the blond-haired little baby yet too young to recall any of these heartwarming events. Yet from the obscurity of rural Sussex, thirty-four years later, this child would share the bed of another future sovereign in the hours running up to an even more famous royal wedding.

When Camilla was sixteen months old, the nation celebrated the birth of an heir to the throne. Prince Charles arrived on a cold, raw, moonless November evening in the Buhl room of Buckingham Palace, in marked contrast to the efficient but overcrowded and under-resourced surroundings in which Miss Shand had been born. But like Camilla, as a citizen of the Welfare State, he received his ration card, free milk allowance, Ministry of Food orange juice and cod-liver oil—and he was inoculated against diphtheria.

Barely had the nation settled down from the excitement of a future king's birth than another baby girl, Annabel, was born to Bruce and Rosalind Shand, again at King's College Hospital in London. A few weeks later—after the birth had been registered—another name was tactfully remembered and added, so that she became Sonia Annabel Shand, the first name after her grandmother, King Edward VII's daughter. Two years on a brother, Mark Roland (named after Lord Ashcombe), was born. The family was now complete.

Pretty and with long blond hair, Camilla was a lively child who made friends easily. Her first school—Dumbrells, at Ditchling—was three miles from the Shands' new home, a former rectory at Plumpton called The Laines.

The regime at Dumbrells corresponded with the age: tough, resolute, unswerving; yet its driving force was Victorian. And with good reason. Its co-founders, Edith and Mary Dumbrell, who started the school in 1885, were still omnipresent sixty-five years later when Camilla was first pushed through its doors. Their protégé, Miss Knowles, was now headmistress, but their indelible presence was everywhere. Nothing had changed—the place was a time capsule, frozen in the days of Queen Victoria, grimly hanging on to values and virtues which had long since perished. One of Camilla's teachers, Miss Vera Clarke, chillingly summed up the school and its pupils: When the children came at four and a half, she averred, the first thing they had to learn was the meaning of the word "No."

Today's children, vouchsafed Miss Clarke soon after Camilla had fled the school, were more independent, much noisier, and lacked consideration. They were inclined to be superficial, lacking in depth of thought, and, living in a perpetual rush, tended to act on impulse. They spelled badly, were unable to retain knowledge, and on no account was one ever to curry favor with them.

"Discipline was strict," recalled one old girl. "It was decreed that any possession found lying about must be worn by the culprit for a whole day, including mealtimes. One of the older girls came to lunch wearing three hats; a younger one was sadly hampered by a large sewing basket tied to her waist."

The five-year-old Camilla was terrified by a large "crucified" bat with wings outstretched which had pride of place in the entrance hall of the school, which was furnished with a wide variety of stuffed animals in glass cases. Old girls talked with the bravado of the escapee of the days when they were turned out of bed at 6:30 and forced to take a cold bath. There was no central heating in the bedrooms, on winter mornings the ice had to be cracked in water ewers, and chilblains were a regular event. At 7:30 the bell would ring for "some violent exercises," which continued for twenty minutes until there was a respite for prayers.

Spartan is an insufficient description of this kind of regime for young girls newly away from home; but instantly the young blonde showed her mettle. Contemporaries particularly recall the cold and her ability to withstand it. Because of the lack of heating, pupils wore wellington boots all year round—a youthful fiction at the time was that this was because snakes permanently infested the orchard.

A fellow pupil from that period remembers: "A school inspector

44

came and was dumbstruck. He never knew such a place could exist. The school was so harsh I used to say that a child who could cope with Dumbrells could cope with anything."

Back at home, life at The Laines revolved around horses. Bruce Shand had lived up to his cavalryman's calling in the years leading up to the war, owning a chestnut horse called The Bashaw, upon which he hunted with the Cottesmore. Indeed, his regiment was filled with ardent huntsmen. By the time Camilla was nine, Major Shand had sufficiently impressed the members of the Southdown Hunt with his dedication to the pursuit of the fox that he was made joint master. Camilla had her own pony and very soon was introduced to the debatable pleasures of fox hunting over some of the most beautiful countryside in the whole of the south of England. The Southdown Hunt's highly individualistic master, Norman Loder, was commemorated in Siegfried Sassoon's "Memoirs of a Fox Hunting Man."

But at the age of ten, at the same time that Prince Charles was making his first tortured steps into boarding-school life at Cheam in Berkshire, it was decided that Camilla—now she had mastered the brutish hair-shirt regime which characterized so much of the country's postwar private education—should be allowed to continue her schooling in London.

This rather unusual choice for an aristocratic country-based family—boarding school in the Home Counties would have been a more obvious choice—was made easier by the Shands' possession of a second home in South Kensington. The decision had little to do with her aversion to the excesses of Dumbrells for, from the start, it was clear that she shared Bruce Shand's courage under pressure—and if her stay at Dumbrells seemed to resemble his own sojourn in Spangenburg a decade earlier, it only served to bring father and daughter closer together.

This was in marked contrast to Prince Charles who, made of altogether different stuff, hated Cheam. One biographer noted: "The Queen remembered him literally 'shuddering' with terror on the journey there. For nights after she left him he cried himself to sleep—quietly, into his pillow, hopeful that no-one would hear him—in his wooden bed which, as his mother had observed before she left him, was too hard to jump on. The memory still hurts; it was, he said many years later, the unhappiest time of his life."

These two contrasting experiences give an early indication of the nature of the relationship which was to develop in adulthood between a resolute woman and a shy, self-questioning man; the one confident in her capacity to cope and make friends, come what may; the other forced by his position to lack spontaneous reaction or friendship. In addition, the warmth of Camilla's homelife, where she enjoyed a close and loving relationship with both her parents, contrasted sharply with the emotional wilderness Charles endured during those formative years, when he would greet his mother with a bow or a handshake, and would bitterly observe in later life that sometimes a whole day and night would pass before he could see the queen or she asked to see him.

So, at the age of ten, with Charles miserably installed at Cheam, Camilla Shand set off for the fashionable Queen's Gate School in South Kensington, described at the time as "an establishment which provides wives for half the Foreign Office." Smart, but not the sort of place from which you might expect to meet a prince. Her father would take the bus from their South Kensington house to South Audley Street, Mayfair, where he had become a partner in the blue-chip wine merchant, Block, Grey and Block.

The sixth-form English teacher at Queen's Gate was Penelope Fitzgerald, later a Booker Prize–winning author. "When I arrived the school was changing," she recalls. "It had been a place where girls were taught how to write checks and play bridge, but by then academic standards were improving."

The ever-sporty Camilla—now known as Milla—excelled at fencing and improved well on horseback. London was an open door, and as the new decade of the 1960s approached she started to taste the daily freedoms which are available only to upper-class metropolitan children: tea at Fortnum's, a stroll with friends to Harrods, a walk on summer days through Hyde Park to watch the Household Cavalry ride by, their breastplates and medals gleaming in the sunlight.

By comparison, Charles was now stuck in Gordonstoun, of all the brutish public schools in an age of brutalism, the worst. Ross Benson, a contemporary at the Scottish public school near Elgin, recalls: "He was bullied. He was crushingly lonely for most of his time there.

"One coterie of ruffians hanged the cat belonging to their housemaster Major 'Hebbie' Downton, in retaliation for his attempt to curb their unruly behaviour. At another house the seniors made a practice of greeting new boys by taking a pair of pliers to their arms and twisting until the flesh tore open. In all the houses boys were regularly trussed up in one of the wicker laundry baskets and left under the cold shower, sometimes for hours."

While Charles may have escaped falling victim to some of these wilder excesses, he was by no means inviolate, and often psychological torture replaced the more customary physical torture the boys inflicted upon each other.

In one other respect, too, Camilla's and Charles's schooling differed. From the moment she arrived at Queen's Gate it was clear that the spirited Miss Shand had an eye for the boys; and they for her. Though it was a girls' school, it was perfectly possible in the course of the day to bump into boys from Westminster School or St. Paul's, let alone those who did not attend London day schools. Camilla may not have been the most conventionally pretty girl in her class, but she possessed "an inner glow," as one of her contemporaries described it. "When a boy hove into view she could turn on the headlights—and how!" In this, Camilla shared something with another royal mistress, Wallis Warfield. Fifty years earlier, noted her biographer Charles Higham, fellow schoolgirls of the Baltimore belle "asked each other how she, the least pretty of them all, had managed to hook the handsomest boy they knew. Her secret was that she researched her prey. She knew how to praise, to build the adolescent male's ego." Here, indeed, was an eerie echo.

But at a time when teenage thoughts turn to the opposite sex, Charles found himself in an establishment where the very idea of sex was treated as a perversion. The philosophy of Gordonstoun's sexually repressed founder, Kurt Hahn, was "to kindle on the threshold of puberty non-poisonous passions which act as guardians during the dangerous years."

A contemporary of Charles recalled: "There was little homosexuality at Gordonstoun . . . but there was very little heterosexuality either, and the school gave the prince no experience of dealing with women. Quite the contrary: to keep the royal virtue intact the usual sources of female companionship had been carefully closed off."

That included visits by younger sisters to the still all-male establishment; visits to or from nearby girls' schools; or permission to visit places with a promising female population. While Camilla was in London practicing, as all adolescent girls do, their charms on the opposite sex, Charles was three hundred miles away in a cold and cheerless community with not a girl in sight. In retrospect, it was a disastrous way of going about trying to raise a well-rounded, balanced, and socially gregarious child.

Back in London, Milla Shand was turning into what one former classmate described as "a bit of a tearaway." Another contemporary, later to rise to prominence as the sixties pop star Twinkle, recalled: "I always thought she was the coolest girl in the school. I remember her best when she was fifteen and a half. She was a very hoity-toity little madam, and she always looked great. She was what you would have called a Sloane Ranger type. We didn't get on that well because she was very into hunting and shooting and that kind of thing. We used to have mammoth rows about all that because I was totally against it.

"She knew that I wanted to be a pop star—she didn't have to say what she wanted to be. She had a confidence that I envied. She was someone who didn't need to be anything other than she was."

While some of the pupils were destined to become debutantes, traditionally virgins at that time, others took off on the hippie trail down the King's Road, eating in the Chelsea Kitchen just opened by a man called Terence Conran or trying, and usually failing, to score some hash—as the phrase went—in The Picasso.

But despite her undeniable sex appeal Milla wore un-hip twin sets and tweed skirts and appeared thoroughly conventional. She was not in the vanguard of girls excitedly pushing through the magenta doors of Biba's clothes shop in Kensington. "She didn't seem to mind being different from the others. It was odd, in a way, because girls can be cruel, but there was an inner something in Milla that others recognized as stronger," recalled a friend from that time. "She was looked up to by the other girls—a lot of them wanted to be her friend. She had a certain magnetism—I think simply because she knew she was going to be a success in life."

Compare that experience with Prince Charles's. He found himself followed wherever he went at Gordonstoun by boys making slurping noises—anyone who socialized with him was accused of "sucking up" and therefore he found himself despised, and cocooned in isolation—

and it is plain to see who at the end of their secondary education was equipped for adult life. "She would live the life that she wanted," said a Queen's Gate contemporary. "That's what Milla exuded."

Her brother, Mark, like his father before him, should have gone to Eton but did not. Instead he attended Milton Abbey, a public school in Dorset, reserved, in contemporary parlance, for "rich thickos." However, like his sister, he found an instant rapport with the opposite sex, which, coupled with outstanding good looks, transcended the delights of a bookish partner.

In the summer of 1964, as Charles grappled with his O levels—he scored passes in English language and literature, Latin, French, and history—Camilla prepared to leave Queen's Gate. As academic careers go, it was not an outstanding one, and she would not be staying on for her A levels. Instead, the plan was for her to travel, to Switzerland and to Paris, a city her father and paternal grandfather adored, to be "finished."

Though despised by educationists as an upper-class cop-out, to persons of an inquiring mind, international travel and exposure to foreign languages and culture was a valid learning experience. Paris in the mid-sixties was a hotbed of revolution. The OAS, the right-wing Secret Army Organization led by outlawed French generals and colonels of the failed putsch in Algeria, started a bombing campaign against leading intellectuals. Their purpose was to blame the subsequent protests and demonstrations, which came in wave after wave, on the Communists. Once the atmosphere of protest was triggered, demonstrations became the fashionable thing—cars were burned, pavements ripped up. On the Boulevard Saint-Michel one morning, a student coolly directed the traffic while the CRS riot police sat helplessly by: The students had gained control.

As Camilla traveled back to England, the protests followed her—there were riots in Grosvenor Square, and the Rolling Stones captured the spirit of the age with their song "Street Fighting Man." The Beatles wrote "Revolution," but it transpired the song was against, rather than for, radical change. Bob Dylan played the Royal Albert Hall, round the corner from Camilla's house, and was booed hysterically when he put aside his folk songs, strapped on an electric guitar for the first time, and crashed into the first chords of his anthem "Like a Rolling Stone."

Camilla's return was followed, inevitably, by her debut in the London season. This strange, complex, and once courtly ritual had diminished somewhat in status since its heyday in the Edwardian era. The fact that the debutantes were no longer received at court by the queen had taken away some of its prestige, yet if there was a focus and a purpose, it was toward the House of Windsor and the continuity of the class system. Whatever reduced status it may have enjoyed in the new egalitarian Britain of Socialist premier Harold Wilson, those white-clad virgins who trooped the large, wheeled cake into the ballroom of the Grosvenor House Hotel in Mayfair on the occasion of Queen Charlotte's Ball would have thought themselves a cut above the debutantes who, fifty-one years before, attended the Bachelors' Cotillion at the Lyric Theater in Baltimore. But they were wrong, for from both events emerged into the world a mistress, and more important, a lasting love, for an emotionally deprived Prince of Wales.

Camilla's official introduction to society occurred on a chilly March day in 1965, when her parents gave a cocktail party for her at 30 Pavilion Road, Knightsbridge, just behind Harrods. These hired rooms were a popular venue for parents whose London house was insufficiently large to cater for the 150 or so debutantes, "debs' delights," relations, and friends who traditionally attend this stepping-stone in a time-honored ritual that starts with tea parties, then progresses through cocktail parties, dinners, dances, and balls. These continue through until the early autumn, when it is considered that the girls are sufficiently "out" to cope in the adult world.

A contemporary account, giving a flavor of the age, survives of this first step into the outside world. Mrs. Betty Kenward, the social diarist of *Harper's,* under her awesome nom-de-plume of Jennifer, intoned: "The Hon. Mrs. Shand's cocktail party for her attractive debutante daughter Camilla, was another successful party.

"This was one of the very first of the debutante cocktail parties and might have been a bit sticky as, at the beginning of any season, the young people have not yet got to know each other, but both the hostess and Camilla did plenty of introducing and it went with a swing."

Outside, in the real world, India and Pakistan went to war over Kashmir. General Franco, pressing Spanish claims to Gibraltar, enforced a landward siege of the Rock. Ian Smith, the new prime minister of Rhodesia, issued a Unilateral Declaration of Independence from Britain and its Commonwealth, and American forces became even more deeply involved in the war in Vietnam, initiating a series of bombing attacks on North Vietnam. In America, Malcolm X, the extremist black leader, was shot dead in New York, and civil rights agitation took hold with outbursts of violence in Watts, the Los Angeles suburb.

But in gentle Knightsbridge, champagne was poured and Camilla Shand came out. Among her guests were Rupert Hambro, of the banking family, who was shortly to become her lover, and a host of girls who, in the fashion of the time, wore scoop-neck dresses, pearls, and too much mascara. Lady Mary Gaye Curzon, the drop-dead blond daughter of Earl Howe, who was generally agreed to be Deb of the Year, was there too. That year, 311 girls took part in the London Season, dressing themselves in Mary Quant and making their miniskirted presence felt in the King's Road and Carnaby Street. They danced to the old-fashioned music of Confrey Phillips and (down in the discos which were now *de rigueur* at every deb dance) to the headier sounds of the Beatles, the Stones, and the Walker Brothers.

But 1965 was the end of the old world. Sir Winston Churchill died; so too did T. S. Eliot and Somerset Maugham; the Beatles were made MBEs, collecting their medals from Buckingham Palace and smoking a joint in the lavatory while waiting for their moment with the queen, and Russian and American astronauts met in space.

The contraceptive pill became more generally available, and the sexual habits of a generation changed virtually overnight. According to the diarist Nigel Dempster, it was during this debutante year that Camilla lost her virginity to Kevin Burke, an independently wealthy nineteen-year-old who was then a handsome fixture on the debutante scene. "She was terrific fun, immensely popular, and although she wasn't a beauty like Mary Gaye Curzon, she was attractive and sexy," Burke, son of the aviation chief Sir Aubrey Burke, recalled. "She was never tongue-tied or shy, and she always had something amusing to say."

He added: "I remained with Camilla all that year. I suppose we were in love. Then she ditched me."

It may well be Mr. Burke was the first, but a friend from Sussex wryly observed: "Camilla had been fooling around from an early age," and in any case it was time to move on from her first steady relationship. The next person she saw was the one she really wanted.

The Royal Horse Guards, commonly known as the Blues, were an integral part of the Household Cavalry—one of the great tourist attractions of London as they mounted guard in Whitehall on their black chargers. Alongside Bruce Shand's 12th Lancers, the Blues had fought valiantly at El Alamein in the Second World War, but their battle honors went back to Waterloo and beyond.

Among their blue-blooded officers were numbered Viscount Somerton, shortly to become the Earl of Normanton, Lord Chetwode—and Lord Fermoy, whose sister Frances was about to divorce her husband and lose a bloody battle to keep her four children, who included a four-year-old called Diana Spencer.

All these soldiers, and others in the regiment, had been educated at Eton. But one who, by virtue of his being Roman Catholic, had not was Andrew Henry Parker Bowles, a twenty-seven-year-old lieutenant, recently promoted to the rank of local captain.

Possessed of striking, almost beautiful, looks, Andrew may not have been an Etonian but his credentials were impeccable. His father, Derek, who had also served in the regiment and lived at Donnington Castle House near Newbury, was said to be the closest male friend the queen mother had. Certainly, when it came time for her daughter to be crowned queen in 1953, a place was found for the fourteen-year-old schoolboy as a page to the lord high chancellor, Lord Simonds: a deft genuflexion, at the queen mother's behest, to his ancestry.

The Earls of Macclesfield emerged in the reign of King George I when Sir Thomas Parker, lord high chancellor of Great Britain, was first made Lord Parker, Baron of Macclesfield. He then advanced five years later in 1721 to become Viscount Parker and Earl of Macclesfield—though this success was later tainted when he was tried by his peers on charges of corruption, and found guilty.

The sixth earl's son Algernon married the daughter of Lord Kenyon, who had the distinction of being a lord-in-waiting to Queen Victoria, King Edward VII, and King George V. Their son Eustace married in 1913 an heiress called Wilma Bowles, daughter of Sir Henry Ferryman Bowles, upon whose death the Parker Bowles name emerged. But by bloodlines and marriage, Andrew Parker Bowles was also connected to other great families—the Earls of Derby and Cadogan, the Dukes of Marlborough, and, indeed, to the queen mother herself through the

Earls of Strathmore. His mother, Dame Ann, was a close friend of the queen and chief commissioner of the Girl Guides, and through her family, the de Traffords, Andrew was able to trace his ancestry back to the twelfth century.

All this was handy for a serving cavalry officer in a senior regiment and was in marked contrast to Bruce Shand's humbler—though more interesting—ancestry. It also helped when it came to the London Season, for only young men of gentle birth were admitted to the parties given by parents of each year's three hundred debutantes.

By the time he met Camilla, Andrew Parker Bowles was a little long in the tooth to be doing the rounds of the deb circuit again, and in the normal course of events would never have bumped into his future wife. But while he had been in New Zealand serving as an aide-de-camp to the governor general, Sir Bernard Fergusson, his younger brother Simon had escorted Camilla to several parties—he had been working for Bruce Shand at his wine merchants, Block, Grey and Block. Simon and Camilla were friends, but when Andrew met his brother's date it was a *coup de foudre.*

Nigel Dempster recorded: "In London, Andrew lived in a small bachelor apartment in Portobello Road in Notting Hill, and it was there that he and Camilla began what friends remember as 'a very hot affair, indeed.' Andrew was already an accomplished lover and quickly proved himself to be an unfaithful one, too. He had a penchant for beautiful titled women, including Lady Caroline Percy, who was already the steady girlfriend of a baronet, and pursued Lady Amabel Lindsay."

This aristocratic merry-go-round was a very sophisticated world indeed, far removed from the icy wastes of Gordonstoun where Prince Charles labored on in numbing isolation, desperate to escape the cheerless and antisocial environment into which his father had plunged him. Indeed, by the beginning of 1966, he had had enough. Despite much acclaim for his starring role in the school's production of *Macbeth,* he had done averagely or badly in virtually all other spheres, failing to make any of the school sports teams and promising little hope of an outstanding academic success when it came to A levels. His escape to Timbertop, an outstation of Geelong Grammar School two hundred miles north of Melbourne, was a welcome relief. As Camilla Shand and Andrew Parker Bowles made their name as a dazzling couple around "swinging" London, the heir to the throne, still only seventeen, was living in the Australian outback, learning for the first time in his life how to fend for himself. His chores included chopping and splitting wood, feeding pigs, cleaning out flytraps—and sheep shearing. Had Camilla met him in this passage between boyhood and manhood, there is little doubt she would have dismissed him from her mind: he was no match for a dashing cavalry officer and man of the world who was ten years his senior.

And yet, and yet . . . Kevin Burke, the jilted lover, remarked that during their yearlong association he was struck by how much store Camilla placed in the fact that her great-grandmother had been Edward VII's mistress. "She was always mentioning it, as if it were something almost talismanic," he later recalled.

But all that was in the future. Parker Bowles, a gifted amateur jockey, took the same devil-may-care attitude toward his love life as he did toward his racing. Soon he was to break his back in a fall at Ascot, but as much damage might have befallen him from the way he conducted his love life.

Once he and Camilla became entangled in 1966 he ran her against his current love, Lady Caroline Percy, and everybody knew it. "I certainly knew I wasn't the only person being taken out by Andrew at the time," Lady Caroline said. "There were always other girls and older women. I never knew Camilla very well when we came out, but when I was with Andrew she would come up to me at parties and ask me what I was doing with her boyfriend. She was always doing this to girls at parties. But I got fed up with it and said to her, 'You can have him back when I've finished with him.' "

Nigel Dempster, in his book *Behind Palace Doors,* shines considerable light on the army officer's helter-skelter love life, whose complexity and variety meant that the couple had been lovers—on and off—for seven years before they finally married. While Camilla wore white for the wedding at the Guards Chapel, followed by a reception at St. James's Palace, she had participated in a love imbroglio worthy of a French farce or a cheap sex novel, depending on the reader's tolerance of those times. For it truly was the era of free love; and while its more vocal advocates tended to come in kaftans and long mustaches or miniskirts, it was not their province alone. In the Age of Aquarius, anyone could join in.

Certainly Andrew Parker Bowles, no hippie he, breathed the scented air of the sixties with relish. Possessed of a dazzling charm, outstanding looks, a brave athleticism, and private means, he found that few women could resist him. Before being seconded to New Zealand, he had been engaged to Sue Morley, the daughter of a brigadier, but it was a short-lived arrangement. Now he dropped Camilla Shand and picked her up at will, and she was powerless to do anything about it.

"Andrew behaved abominably to Camilla, but she was desperate to marry him. When I was with him I discovered he was also having an affair with a married woman," recalled Lady Caroline Percy. Camilla responded by bedding banking heir Rupert Hambro. "Rupert knew that their affair was futile because of Camilla's obsession with Andrew, but he liked her and knew they would always be friends," wrote Dempster. "He still remembers the masochistic glee she took in telling him about tricky situations Andrew's unfaithfulness sometimes caused. But she often saw the funny side of things afterwards; her girls' talk always had the funniest lines and the best anecdotes."

In 1969 Parker Bowles was posted to Hobart Barracks near Hanover in Germany, which gave Camilla time to draw breath and look around. On his brief returns home over the next couple of years, he was off again—this time in hot pursuit of Princess Anne, who at nearly twenty was eleven years his junior and currently involved with Brian Alexander, the son of war hero Earl Alexander of Tunis.

Anne, with a libido which matched the cavalry officer's, caved in to his charm and enjoyed a torrid relationship which gave both much cause for pleasure. But Parker Bowles's absence in Germany on duty and the fact that, as a Roman Catholic, he knew that he could never marry Anne without creating painful turmoil within the royal family put a dampener on the relationship.

With time on her hands, Camilla started to spend her days at polo. A friend from debutante days, Carolyn Gerard Leigh, was the daughter of Colonel Gerard Leigh, the chairman of the Guards' Polo Club at Windsor, and encouraged her to come along to matches.

Shortly before going up to Cambridge, Charles had played in his first polo tournament at Smith's Lawn, his side beating Ronald Ferguson's in the final. While an undergraduate he joined the University Polo Club, as much out of his combination of reticence, natural introspection, and remoteness of position as because his father dictated it. He gained his half-blue, and by the time he graduated, his handicap had gone from minus two to plus two.

He once explained: "I love the game. I love the ponies. I love the exercise. It's the one team game I can play. It's also a very convenient game for me—you can't just nip out of Windsor Castle and enjoy a soccer game."

What he omitted to add was that polo is an aphrodisiac, that the sport itself heightens sexual tension in the participants, that the women who follow it are fully cognizant of this, and that a secret language develops between player and spectator at the close of play which, fueled by Pimm's or champagne, has provided for many memorable encounters.

In addition, polo was something at which the prince almost instantly excelled, and for once he was allowed to show off without inviting criticism from the press—indeed, such was the recondite nature of the sport that at Smith's Lawn, certainly in the early days, the prince was pretty much left alone by a puzzled Fleet Street, who did not understand the rules and weren't interested enough to find out.

One further factor brought Charles to love the polo field. The women who watched were the right sort: well-bred, tight-lipped, admiring, discreet. After the hamfisted fumblings of his undergraduate days, when he felt too embarrassed by the thought of who he was to proceed in a way that young men should, suddenly he was admired by beautiful women for himself, for his body and his horsemanship. Being Prince of Wales was just the icing on the cake—what the women were looking at was a fit, tough player in tight jodhpurs who clearly had a taste for danger.

And one of the women who was looking, and looking hard, was Camilla Shand.

Chapter 4

$\mathcal{T}$HE BOY BECOMES A MAN

WHEN CHARLES AND CAMILLA FINALLY MET, AT SMITH'S LAWN IN THE shadow of Windsor Castle, it was as if they had known each other forever. Certainly they already knew a lot of people in common. For example, Charles's first-ever "date" was with Marilyn Wills, the daughter of the queen's cousin Jean Wills, when they went to see *The Sound of Music* at the age of fourteen. Marilyn went on to be one of the principal guests at Camilla's coming-out party at 30 Pavilion Road in 1965, and the pair remained close friends.

On taking up fox hunting, Charles had become devoted to the remarkable Ulrike Murray-Smith. This redoubtable huntress was the wife of one of Bruce Shand's closest friends at Sandhurst, George Murray-Smith, and between them this couple managed to foster a consuming passion for hunting in two generations—Shand *and* the Prince of Wales. (Charles had a chance to return the compliment in 1989 when Mrs. Murray-Smith, by now eighty-two, was thrown from her horse and knocked unconscious while hunting with the Quorn; royal detectives were instantly ordered to her assistance.)

Another connection between Charles and Camilla was Nick

Paravicini, a swashbuckling former Life Guards officer who was a towering presence on the Smith's Lawn turf and a friend of the prince. He was stepping out, ironically, with Andrew Parker Bowles's sister, Mary Ann, who, while the cavalryman was abroad, had become good friends with Camilla. These were just three obvious connections—conversation came easily because of the many other friends and acquaintances they had in common, and it took very little time for the mutual attraction to grow. In addition to all this, Bruce Shand had made his own way to the fringes of the royal family by being nominated as a member of the Queen's Body Guard of the Yeomen of the Guard, the ancient group of stalwart former soldiers whose nineteenth-century uniform forms a colorful backdrop for the sovereign to liven up many a state occasion.

It was a fallow time in the prince's love life. After Lucia Santa Cruz and Sibella Dorman, there had been nobody very much. Since graduating from Cambridge in 1970, he had been pressed into service by a delighted queen, who at last felt she could show him off to the world—a visit to Ottawa was followed by a tour of Canada; then he was dispatched with Princess Anne to be guests of President Richard Nixon in Washington. A tour which included Fiji, the Gilbert and Ellice Islands, Bermuda, and Barbados was followed by a trip to Paris to represent the Crown at the funeral of President de Gaulle. A brief trip to Kenya on safari with his sister was followed by further single-sex incarceration in the RAF at its Lincolnshire officers' college, Cranwell—so that by the summer of 1971 the young, fit, handsome prince was desperate for congenial and obliging female company. He was twenty-two and had less experience of the opposite sex than the majority of males his age.

"For the prince, real life began with Camilla," says another Smith's Lawn fixture from that time, the Argentinian polo player Luis Basualdo. "He either met his girls at polo or took them to polo. A favorite place was the Guards' Polo Club."

With Charles's active support, polo was enjoying an upswing. Though still a fledgling spectator sport with a heavy emphasis on the military, it was, during the next decade (and particularly with the arrival of the Princess of Wales) to turn into a champagne-drenched sponsored jamboree, adored by people who have never had the slightest intention of climbing onto horseback; but in the early seventies it was still the child of Earl Mountbatten, his nephew Prince Philip, and a few postimperial devotees.

But its popularity was growing. Within a couple of years polo would become an unofficial arena where the queen and her family could mix in informal circumstances with relatively ordinary people—at least those with a penchant for equine pursuits who could follow the more esoteric aspects of the game—and it was at Smith's Lawn that Captain Mark Phillips was to make his debut as a future member of the royal family.

Charles made a creditable show on the turf, encouraged by his father and Major Ronald Ferguson (ultimately to rise to prominence as father of the future Duchess of York), and in 1972 was made captain of the Young England polo team. It was a consolation prize for Prince Philip's losing his place on the England polo team because of a wrist injury that put him permanently out of the game. The pressure was on Charles to perform on the polo field, and he obliged. The girls loved it.

One of the stars of Smith's Lawn was the accomplished horseman Andrew Parker Bowles. Often he would find himself drawn against Prince Charles's side in low-goal matches. A habitué of the Guards' Polo scene from that time recalls: "Andrew would often come to Smith's Lawn—he was an excellent player. About once a week he'd bring Camilla down by car. If Andrew was playing against Charles, she'd watch; otherwise she'd just go and watch Charles. She wasn't that interested in the game. She was interested in hanging round Charles.

"What was astonishing was that he took any notice of her. There were plenty of glamorous women around, but she had holes in her jeans and looked a mess. Not exactly an oil painting."

"The relationship developed almost straightaway—it took no more than a casual glance to see that something was going to happen," says another friend from that time. "There was an electric magnetism between them, and even if they were standing some way away, you could tell from the intensity of their conversation and the way they looked at each other what the upshot would be. It was like watching two steam trains heading towards each other at full pelt."

Ironically, the British press, determined to find a future bride for the prince, missed it completely. Charles's exploits in the saddle were covered sporadically, but so much was going on in his life at that time that the hallowed turf at Smith's Lawn was quite often given a miss. "And there was no one there who was going to call up the *Daily Mail* and tell them, 'Come quick. Charles looks like he's got himself a woman,'" said

one polo regular. In addition, royal coverage, as opposed to court reporting, had yet to develop as a tabloid art and its greatest exponent, the
Daily Mirror's James Whitaker, had only just come on the scene.

But even before the 1971 polo season came to a close, Charles was
forced back to duty. The regimen his father had worked out as preparation for kingship—which, as all recognized, was only a heartbeat away
and could come soon or late—was tough, demanding, leaving little
room or time to woo. As Whitaker reported: "[Charles] is a man who
courted with flowers, tender words, a lot of hand holding and soft can-
dlelight. At the end of the evening he would drop off a girl at her flat and
then get on the telephone to her as soon as he returned to his own
apartment at Buckingham Palace. For the next hour he would talk softly
and lovingly to the girl. He would say how much he loved her, how
much he savoured the colour of her eyes, the smell of her hair." All the
things, in fact, he found impossible to say to the person directly—an
unfortunate trait that would expose itself two decades later in the
Camillagate tapes.

But for now, there was no time for wooing. In the autumn of 1971
as he faced his twenty-third birthday alone and, he thought, unloved,
he set out on the next stage of his hair-shirt career preparation. In the
autumn he joined the Royal Navy as a sublieutenant, and after a six-
week induction course at the Britannia Royal Naval College at Dart-
mouth in Devon, he set off for Gibraltar to join HMS *Norfolk.* For the
next nine months, if his thoughts were of Camilla Shand, they had to be
shared with the incessant noise and grinding turbines of the 5,600-ton
guided-missile destroyer.

The following May he earned a brief respite, being allowed by his
senior officers to accompany his mother and father on a state visit to
France. And coinciding with the start of the polo season, Charles found
himself ashore again undertaking courses at HMS *Dryad,* a shore establishment at Portsmouth. From there to Broadlands, the stately home of
his "honorary grandfather" Earl Mountbatten, was a fifty-minute drive
in his Aston Martin Volante. Throughout this period, in reaction to his
father's persistent questioning about navy life, he preferred to seek refuge with Mountbatten—himself an Admiral of the Fleet—and it was
during this time that their relationship, adult to adult, flourished.
Charles was able to discuss his love life (or lack of it) with Mountbatten,

and though the old seadog had an eye on a self-aggrandizing dynastic alliance with one of his Knatchbull granddaughters, she was still too young and Charles had had no chance to sow his wild oats.

The polo season of 1972 allowed Charles further respite, and it is where the relationship with Camilla Shand was at last allowed to develop. But it was short-lived. Within months of his return from Germany Andrew Parker Bowles realized that there was no future in his relationship with Princess Anne, and by the autumn she was seeing Captain Mark Phillips, an officer in the 1st Queen's Dragoon Guards. Charles's affair with Camilla, when it finally happened, was short, vigorous, and a dazzling revelation. "It finally made him a man" was the comment of one of Camilla's friends.

But despite all the lengthy telephone calls and whispered *tendresses* it became eminently clear that there was no future in it. Camilla's seven-year on-off affair with Andrew Parker Bowles was too well known ever to remain a secret for very long, and the questionable mores of the time would not allow for a Princess of Wales who was "secondhand goods." That, almost single-handedly, killed the idea of their having any future together; but in addition there was the question of Camilla's pedigree to be considered, even if that first apparently insurmountable hurdle could be overcome.

Though, in the New Elizabethan Age, there were no apparent hard-and-fast rules about whom the young royals should marry—King George V had relaxed them sufficiently during his reign to allow his daughter to marry into the aristocracy rather than to some foreign prince, and the Duke of York did similarly, bringing the blood of the Earls of Strathmore into the royal line—it was assumed that if Charles were to marry an English girl, she would be high-born.

Though Camilla Shand was an aristocrat by virtue of her mother's lineage, there were discrepancies along the way, not least the rabid lesbian Violet Trefusis. And Bruce Shand's wayward ancestors, not least his four-time-married father, would inevitably prove an embarrassment upon discovery.

These factors, together with the rather crueler matter that though possessed of a magnetic charm, Camilla was unphotogenic, meant that there was little future in the affair at that time. Camilla was aware of it from the moment she invited the prince into her bed—and in any event, Andrew Parker Bowles, now putting all thoughts of Princess Anne from his mind, was ready for marriage.

"There was a school of thought at that time which said that Camilla only seduced Charles because Andrew had seduced Anne," one polo source said. "She was determined to show him that she could do as well in the royal pulling-stakes as he'd done. There was always that element of pursuit by her, the feeling that she was determined to show him that she was as good as him, in no matter what."

If the affair between Andrew and Camilla, which had started so many years ago, was a battlefield, then a truce was called on March 15 when the couple announced their engagement. Andrew spent the day in a Berkshire nursing home, hobbling around with the aid of a walking stick after a riding accident.

Four months later the couple were married in what one society magazine described as "the wedding of the year." The Guards Chapel in Birdcage Walk, a stone's throw from Buckingham Palace, was so crowded that three hundred extra chairs were added to the chapel which normally seats five hundred. Even then, late guests were forced to stand at the back. The groom appeared to have recovered from the effects of his stag night at White's, the supra-exclusive St. James's gentleman's club. "I've paid the damages bill," Andrew's brother, Simon, revealed nonchalantly. "The party got slightly out of control—there was a lot of broken crockery and glass, and chairs."

Princess Anne, now infatuated, however briefly, with Captain Mark Phillips—they would marry four months later—was present to see her former lover marry. If there was a twinge of regret, she would in the fullness of time ease its pain by returning to Parker Bowles's side after the collapse of her marriage.

Present at the ceremony too was the queen mother, Andrew's distant relation, and though Princess Margaret missed the service, she attended the reception across the park at St. James's Palace. On a boiling hot summer's day, Camilla looked cool and self-possessed as she finally achieved what she had waited seven years for. "She was wearing lashings of tulle, and diamonds in her hair," recalled one guest. "She sparkled as much as they did."

For the time being at least, it was over between Charles and Camilla. "There was never any question then of Charles marrying Camilla," recalled her friend the former Carolyn Gerard Leigh. "He was much younger, simply a nice boy. . . . Camilla was conscious of her select status but she never wanted to be queen."

The one interested person not present at the wedding was Prince Charles himself. By early July he was aboard HMS *Minerva,* a Leander-class frigate, cruising the waters of the West Indies. If his thoughts dwelt on his lost love—and despite other versions of this tale, it was Camilla who dropped him, not vice versa—they could not do so for long. At one stage *Minerva* called at Hamilton, Bermuda, and Charles strolled on the lawn of Government House with Sir Richard Sharples, the British governor. Within a week Sharples had been assassinated by terrorists on the same spot, and with *Minerva* due to call again for repairs, Charles was transferred briefly to the survey ship *Fox.*

The voyage went on to the Bahamas, where the prince represented the queen at the independence celebrations, and he put all thoughts of love from him by deep-sea diving in the shark-infested waters of the Caribbean or dancing until 5:00 A.M., with his ship due to sail at 6:00 A.M., in the nightclubs of Caracas, Venezuela.

While the newlyweds honeymooned, plans were being made at the Admiralty for Charles, which were likely to prove the prince's greatest alibi in the years to come, when a scurrilous and potentially damaging rumor emerged at the Guards' Polo Club.

In 1990 Charles's polo manager, Major Ron Ferguson, embarked on an ill-starred love affair with a charity polo organizer, Lesley Player. Ferguson became obsessed by the woman who, it emerged, had had an affair with Texas millionaire Steve Wyatt—who had had an affair with Ferguson's daughter, the Duchess of York.

Three years later, the affair over, Lesley Player published her version of the affair in a book, *My Story: The Duchess of York, Her Father and Me.* From the completed text was missing the rumor which had been told to her, she said, by Major Ferguson: that Prince Charles was the father of Camilla's son.

"He is, but for the grace of God, the future King of England," Ms. Player reported Ferguson as saying. "Charles pays the boy's school fees at Eton. But it must never come out."

If true, the story would have a terminal effect on the future of the monarchy. Other kings and princes had fathered illegitimate children—

only two generations before, both the Duke of Kent and, less convincingly, the former Prince of Wales were supposed to have fathered bastards. Even the godson of Prince Philip, the Maidenhead-born Max Boisot, was rumored for over forty years to be the prince's natural son—a rumor that swirled along unchecked until 1988 when, with her son now forty-four and a professor of economics at the Euro-Chinese Business Center in Beijing, Philip's wartime girlfriend, the former nightclub owner Hélène Cordet, issued a denial. She said that although Philip had paid Max's fees through Gordonstoun, it was simply because at the time she was virtually destitute.

But it was unthinkable that such a thing could happen now (though why, it is hard to fathom: The bastard descendants of King Charles II currently sit perfectly respectably in the House of Lords as the Dukes of St. Albans, Grafton, and Richmond & Gordon). Nonetheless, according to Lesley Player, in conversation on different occasions with various individuals, Major Ferguson—who during a lengthy career as polo manager to both Charles and his father spent long hours between chukkas in intimate conversation with the young prince—had repeated this allegation several times, and was convinced of its veracity.

To those with a nose for scandal, it was perfectly possible.

Camilla—as everyone at Smith's Lawn knew all along—had an affair with Prince Charles before her marriage. Before too long, she was once again engrossed with the prince, and since royal bastards are such a part of the fabric of British history, it seemed hardly surprising to their sophisticated thought, barely worthy of note. Cloaked with the veil of enforced secrecy, the rumor spread and took wing. Once the prince's lasting love for Camilla had been exposed, anything, it seemed, was possible.

Except this. It is true that Camilla gave birth to her son, Thomas Henry Charles (that last name another clue for the rumormongers), on December 18, 1974, seventeen months after her wedding. It is also true that Charles agreed to be the boy's godfather. But that is where the connection ended, for exactly nine months before the child's birth, while Camilla was making Bolehyde Manor in Wiltshire a home for herself and her new husband, Lieutenant the Prince of Wales was halfway through a tour of duty as communications officer on HMS *Jupiter* on the other side of the globe. There is no evidence, in a period when he also accompanied the queen and Prince Philip to the opening of the Commonwealth Games in New Zealand, to support the notion that he found time to fly halfway around the world for a secret tryst with a woman who had rejected him for an older man—any more than there is evidence that she flew out to Australia and New Zealand to meet him at the various ports of call made by the *Jupiter*. But just because it wasn't true didn't mean the rumor went away—by the time it emerged, the public was ready to believe anything about Charles's relationship with Camilla.

The truth was that Charles was dismissed, if not entirely, then to a large extent, from Camilla's mind as she made her life with an army officer who, she was told, would go far. Was he not the prize she had striven for over seven long years? Most of her contemporaries from the debutante season all those years ago had married and had their children. Camilla was way behind and needed to catch up.

The prince was to become the "moving target" suggested by the man he increasingly turned to for advice, Earl Mountbatten. The honorary grandfather had already chided him about getting too serious about Camilla, according to his private secretary, John Barratt. It has been suggested that in order to increase his power over the prince, Mountbatten set up a "slush fund" in Nassau to take care of any difficulties arising from unfortunate entanglements with women—a fund that was called upon two or three times between late 1974 and mid-1979. While this cannot be entirely discounted—students of British royal history will recall similar arrangements made for Charles's wayward, bisexual great-uncle, the Duke of Kent—it is unlikely that Mountbatten would have raised the hundreds of thousands of dollars himself. In this late period of his life he was strapped for cash, with holes in his bedroom carpet and a rusting and dangerous car to transport him about.

Whatever the arrangements, Charles was now about to move into a restless period where his preparation for kingship was at the cost of personal happiness. From the insecurity of his own refugee childhood, Prince Philip was determined his son should be perfect in his appropriateness for kingship—that all matters, including personal happiness, should be put to one side in pursuit of this goal. In many senses this was an admirable ambition, despite its merely being fueled by the memory that a dilettante monarchy, such as the one into which he was born, is a short-lived monarchy. The fear that his son could turn out like some of his Greek royal relatives drove him on, and in the end Charles, though at the cost of mutual friendship and respect with his father, came to see his point of view.

The rootless years between 1972 and 1980, looked at with the advantage of hindsight, bear witness to the lack of care and understanding devoted by parents and advisers to Charles's personal happiness. Some observers say that his haunting search for alternative philosophies and remedies was simply an outlet for his feeling of being unloved.

Between 1972 and 1980 Charles had a number of identifiable girlfriends, and sexual relationships with a few other women. None of them, ultimately, were satisfactory. Those he felt strongest about sexually he cared less for personally. Those who seemed more on his spiritual wavelength failed to entrap him sexually. His relationships were a sorry mess, but instead of earning sympathy from his family, each new failure (described paradoxically by the press as a conquest) brought increasing irritation from his father, who was anxious that the royal line should multiply without delay.

One woman who knew him well at that time reported: "He was excruciatingly shy [with women]. I don't think he was happy doing what he was doing. He was using women, and he knew it."

Another woman who knew the prince then said: "He was a gentle melancholic soul. There seemed to be such a loneliness, a strange desolation trapped inside him." It did not stop him from falling in love—an acknowledged reaction by those who feel themselves unloved. He had a nine-month relationship with Georgiana Russell, the daughter of Sir John Russell, Britain's ambassador to Spain and a kinsman of the Duke of Bedford. Georgiana had a certain exotic quality by virtue of her mother's Greek background—she was contemporaneous with Prince Philip, though, being a commoner, lasted longer in her homeland—and Charles was attracted by her sophistication. She was eighteen months older and worked for *Vogue* magazine.

This relationship was doomed to failure because Charles had yet to learn that women required more than an early declaration of love, followed by an unswerving march down his own particular path. He may have told them he loved them, but Charles had been alone so long he had lost the art of unselfishness. Georgiana Russell went missing after a freezing fishing trip to Balmoral where Charles carried on with the routine he had developed for himself over the years, one that he saw no reason to vary.

Stephen Barry, Charles's valet, recalled: "She was freezing cold and eating scraps because the Prince was on one of his economy drives. I think she thought the week would be rather glamorous—a romantic interlude in the Highlands with her Prince. Nothing of the kind. He was standing with his feet in icy water all day, while she was bored out of her mind. I thought then she was not going to last the course and I was right."

Georgiana was followed by Lady Jane Wellesley—a likely princess if ever there was one, or so Fleet Street thought. She was beautiful and poised and had known Charles since childhood. Her father was suitably grand, being the eighth Duke of Wellington and a direct descendant of Britain's most valiant soldier. The duke and the queen were close friends; Lady Jane had all the outward and visible hallmarks of a future Princess of Wales.

While this relationship endured, over three years or so, Charles's star remained in the ascendant with the nation. It looked as though he would be making his marriage vows before his thirtieth birthday, the period of grace he had ordained for himself before tying the knot. But in the end the relationship failed, despite the turnout of a crowd of ten thousand at Sandringham for the New Year of 1975 when an announcement seemed imminent.

"She appeared to pass muster on most counts, being aristocratic, lively, attractive and thoroughly discreet, but Charles was never entirely sure about her," wrote his biographer Alan Hamilton. "He found her emancipated, tough and radical in her views; indeed, she went on to work in the highly competitive world of television, and combined her BBC researcher's job with being her office representative of the National Union of Journalists. For Charles, in the end, she was too outspoken, too articulate, and too unwilling to accept a subsidiary role, although had she married the Prince of Wales her effect on his outlook would have been fascinating to behold."

Lady Jane's attitude was best summed up when she was subjected to the same kind of press interest that was to characterize Lady Diana Spencer's entry into public awareness five years later. Instead of a demure smile, a bashful lowering of the eyes, and a helpful pause for the photographers before getting into her car, Lady Jane snapped when asked if she was to marry Charles. "I don't want another title," she said. "I've already got one, thank you." And with that, she was gone. Some thought Charles had proposed marriage and this had triggered her departure.

If, during this sojourn in the emotional wilderness, Charles harbored thoughts of that brief and passionate affair with Camilla Parker Bowles, it is less likely she was thinking of him. By the time his relationship with Lady Jane Wellesley was over, Camilla was caring for a toddler son and thinking about another addition to the family. For the time being at least, her life at Bolehyde Manor was uncomplicated and focused on domestic issues—not for her the demoralizing chase after love.

And none came more demoralizing than Laura Jo Watkins. In March 1974 HMS *Jupiter* paid a courtesy visit to San Diego, home of the U.S. Pacific Fleet. Laura Jo was a tall, blond, stunning-looking part of the welcome committee, the daughter of Admiral James Watkins, an acquaintance of Earl Mountbatten, whom he had met in Malta while serving with the U.S. Sixth Fleet. She fell for the prince and he for her. Mountbatten decided to improve the shining hour by inviting her to London to accompany Charles to the farewell party for Walter Annenberg, departing U.S. ambassador.

Charles then went on to invite her to hear his maiden speech in the House of Lords—a milestone for him, in that this would be where he put down his marker for history. The speech was about the better coordination of leisure facilities across the land. Apparently noncontroversial and certainly avoiding the major issues of the day, it actually dealt with a reasonably important long-term problem to which successive governments had applied neither policy nor resources. It was tailor-made for Charles's burgeoning philosophy of looking after the nation's spiritual well-being.

But whatever effect he hoped to achieve was wrecked by the presence of the delectable Miss Watkins in the Gallery of the House of Lords. Leisure facilities do not make headlines, but a stunning blonde, and an American at that, does. And so the newspapers turned their magnifying glasses on the admiral's daughter, and before too long she was being described as "an unmarried Wallis Simpson"—a not very accurate parallel which stressed her nationality and the fact (which was left unsaid) that she was sleeping with the Prince of Wales.

This kind of crude analogy drove the queen mother, a lifelong foe of Mrs. Simpson, into paroxysms of rage. She blamed Mountbatten.

By now, nothing was going right—until Charles met another spectacular blonde, Davina Sheffield. If the nation was to have a chocolate-box Princess of Wales, this must surely be the one. From whichever angle she was photographed, she was stunning. During the first nine months of 1976 she came increasingly to be seen on Charles's arm, after meeting the prince at a dinner party at Jane Wellesley's Fulham house in the summer of 1975.

A few weeks later, Charles invited her up to face the "Balmoral test" and she passed with flying colors. "Jane and Davina had been close friends, but they have not spoken since," said a friend at the time. Between that summer meeting and the New Year, Davina flew to Vietnam, where she worked hard looking after sixty orphaned boys until Saigon fell to the Communists.

When she reemerged on Charles's arm, she was about as eligible as they came: always beautifully dressed, always ready with a smile for the cameras. But then, in September, came the crash—her former boyfriend, Old Harrovian powerboat designer James Beard, with whom she had lived in a cottage near Winchester, opened his mouth. He confessed they had had a full sexual relationship, then added disingenuously: "I think Prince Charles is a very impressive man and I am sure they will be very happy. I think she will make an extremely good Queen and a magnificent wife."

With this last, Beard destroyed a nation's irrational hopes for a virgin bride, and the relationship was over. It is worth noting in passing that Davina had enjoyed the same circular relationship with Charles and his sister, Anne, as the Parker Bowleses: Her former boyfriend, Old Etonian Robert Rodwell, also used to escort Princess Anne. It was not enough to save her.

And so the escorts came and went. Those logged by an increasingly bewildered press included Lady Leonora Grosvenor and her sister Lady Jane, both sisters of the Duke of Westminster; Lady Victoria and Lady Caroline Percy, daughters of the Duke of Northumberland; Bettina Lindsay, daughter of Lord Balneil; Lady Cecil Kerr, daughter of the Marquis of Lothian; Lady Henrietta FitzRoy, daughter of the Duke of Grafton; Lady Charlotte Manners, daughter of the Duke of Rutland, and her cousin Libby Manners; Angela Nevill, daughter of Lord Rupert Nevill; Louise Astor, daughter of Lord Astor of Hever; and Lady Camilla Fane, daughter of the Earl of Westmorland.

Though, at the time, these women must have seemed startlingly different from each other, they were drawn from one section of English society only. They were all public-school–educated scions of aristocratic families, all imbued with the same conservative values, and all, ultimately, dull. The only exception was a brief tangle with Fiona Watson, daughter of the Yorkshire landowner Lord Manton, who, it subsequently emerged, had revealed all of her glorious 38-23-35 figure in *Penthouse* under an assumed name. It would not take a royal expert long to calculate her fate once the news came out.

All through this long period Charles had seen little of Camilla Parker Bowles—"though he used to telephone her all the time," said one friend. "They had that shared intimacy which people who were lovers once do. Andrew was playing the career army officer and was away from home a lot—and anyway Camilla preferred the country to London now she had the children."

But those early nights of passion had not been forgotten, and by now both parties were more mature, with a greater understanding of life's pitfalls. With Camilla, who was absolutely to be trusted, he could share the intimate details of his failed love affairs. Some of the women he escorted were known to Camilla, and she was able, once the affair was over, to tell Charles what everybody had been saying—what the bookies had been offering on this or that one ending up being Princess of Wales.

"In a sense, because she was beyond that pressure, she could laugh and joke about it in a way that no one else could—and he needed that because frankly, it was becoming an embarrassment all round, this inability to find someone to settle down with," said the friend. "And of course the further down the road he went, the more the pressure to settle for this one or that one, the more resistant he was becoming. It wasn't getting any easier for him."

He rewarded this intimacy with Camilla by inviting her and Andrew Parker Bowles to his thirtieth birthday party. He danced with her, with the Countess of Lichfield—a former date when she had been Lady Leonora Lichfield—and another former flame, Lady Jane Wellesley. It seemed that *all* the people he danced with that night were old flames; except one. She was the actress Susan George, who subsequently enjoyed candlelit dinners with the prince at a secret address in St. James's, and though on at least one occasion she stayed all night, this was merely the fulfillment of one of Charles's fantasies. Albeit perfectly charming, she had already had a number of male partners, and in any event the nation would never countenance as their queen an actress who had had her clothes ripped off and been raped in Sam Peckinpah's *Straw Dogs*. It didn't last long.

The years were rolling on. By now it was 1977, the year in which, Charles had predicted for himself, a bride would come along to be wed. There was no one in sight, though for a moment the matchmakers held their breaths when Charles attended a charity event in Monte Carlo and was seated next to Princess Caroline of Monaco. They loathed each other on sight, and dreams of a great dynastic match dissolved amid claims from both sides—he "bored" her and she "irritated" him. In a rare and frank aside, Charles added acidly: "Before I arrived the world had me engaged to Caroline. With our first meeting the world had us married—and now the marriage is already in trouble."

In July, playing polo at Cowdray Park in Sussex, Charles was introduced to a beautiful Colombian socialite, Cristabel Barria-Borsage. His official companion that day was yet another sprig of English aristocracy, Lady Sarah Spencer, sister of his future wife. "But," said one report, "although Sarah was Charles's date that evening, it was clear he fancied Miss Barria-Borsage tremendously and had no hesitation in exercising his princely rights. They danced together for hours and Sarah wasn't very happy."

The prince drove back to London. In the front of his car was his Colombian firecracker; in the back a very disconsolate Sarah Spencer, jammed up against the detective. A few days later the not entirely gallant Miss Barria-Borsage confessed to a friend that Charles had seduced her. "As they got into bed she asked the prince: 'What shall I call you— Sir, or Charles?" went the report. "As he started to make love to her, he replied 'Call me Arthur.' "

Sarah was treated more seriously. Picked "out of the blue" to attend the traditional Windsor Castle house party for Royal Ascot week, she drove herself there in trepidation: She was suffering from anorexia nervosa. Unlike his chilly response when later faced with Diana's bulimia, Charles showed sympathy and understanding, but then the girl he saw before him was in poor shape. A few months earlier, standing five feet seven inches tall, her weight had gone from 112 pounds to 77 pounds. She confessed her figure had gone down from 34-24-34 to 27-20-28. "I looked like something out of a concentration camp—I couldn't find any normal clothes to fit me, and I did my shopping in the children's department of Marks and Spencer—the bit for ten-year-olds."

She went on: "In such circumstances you behave like an alcoholic; you just will not admit there is a problem. Worse, you end up believing you are beautiful, looking so thin." It was a forerunner of what Charles could expect, in a different form, from his wife. The girl who had been thrown out of her school, West Heath, for drinking ("I used to drink because I was bored. I would drink anything: whisky, Cointreau, gin, sherry, or most often vodka because the staff couldn't smell it") had lost the enamel from her teeth because of the slimming disease.

But Charles persisted, taking her skiing to Klosters that winter, where they shared a bedroom. Next summer, however, Sarah overplayed her hand when Charles planned a polo trip to Trouville on the northern French coast. As the week approached, she more and more obviously let it be known that she wanted to be taken along. "She kept going on and on about how she would love to go, how she could speak almost perfect French, and how she knew so many people who'd be there," said a friend. But Charles opted for a French girl called Chantal—"*not* the kind of girl who was likely to become the Princess of Wales," remarked a seasoned royal watcher dryly, as he watched the couple bop the night away at a discotheque in Trouville—and once again Sarah was on the back burner, this time for good.

There were a couple of flirtations and a grand passion left to come. After the death of Lord Mountbatten, killed by a terrorist bomb in Ireland in 1979, all the old sea dog's hopes of a dynastic match between Charles and his granddaughter Amanda Knatchbull evaporated, and the prince went on to romance Jane Ward, a pretty and well-born assistant manager at the Guards' Polo Club. She was briefly followed by a scion of the brewery clan, Sabrina Guinness, who had been friendly with Jack

Nicholson and Mick Jagger and was hated on sight by the queen and Prince Philip when she turned up at Balmoral. When she remarked that the vehicle that brought her from the station reminded her of nothing so much as a Black Maria, Prince Philip barked: "You'd know all about Black Marias." And when she sat down in a chair and the queen snapped: "Don't sit there—that is Queen Victoria's chair!," she realized the futility of the whole exercise—particularly since her stay went unconsummated. Nonetheless, before she went on to become nanny to the young Tatum O'Neal, Sabrina made an attempt to revive the relationship by writing twice to the prince. He did not bother to reply on either occasion.

Increasingly during this period Charles had taken to visiting Bolehyde Manor, the Parker Bowles country home. He would do so when Andrew was there, and he would do so when Andrew was not. "He was eating there regularly," recalled a friend. "This was before he'd set eyes on Highgrove, and outside the royal houses he had no place to call home.

"He was very conscious about his public image, and even at that stage, if the affair hadn't been rekindled physically, he just wanted to hang around Camilla. And Camilla certainly didn't mind that. Often he had nothing else to do and he'd hang round the kitchen while she was cooking for a dinner party—then when the guests turned up, he'd disappear upstairs and have his supper on a tray. When they went, he'd come down again and carry on where he'd left off."

Andrew Parker Bowles became used to finding Charles in the house, accepted the situation, and in doing so lost points among his colleagues at the Guards' Polo Club over his keenness to be hospitable to the prince. One member complained: "When he was asked to umpire after he had played himself, he would often say: "Terribly sorry, I am needed by royal appointment,' and off he would go to pour Charles's drinks."

But still the prince was single, apparently pursuing no active course to find himself a wife—until along came Anna Wallace.

Anna, daughter of a Scottish landowner, was at twenty-five both beautiful and clever. In addition, she was a passionate horsewoman, well-born, discreet, and with an iron will of her own. In their extended romance she was accorded special treatment, as if Charles knew he was now on the home straight, coming to the end of his bachelor days.

"But it was a complete nonstarter. She'd had boyfriends like Davina Sheffield had boyfriends—she had a track record," recalled a friend. "And she would speak up for her rights."

Nevertheless, Charles, by now more than a little desperate to marry and under intense pressure from all sides to show willing to an increasingly impatient nation, did offer his hand in marriage to Miss Wallace. She was rich enough and old enough and wise enough to refuse. The oft-told story of their row at a party given for the queen mother's eightieth birthday—where having been abandoned in favor of other guests she lashed out at the prince: "Don't ever, ever ignore me like that again! No one treats me like that, not even you!"—was followed by an equally vicious exchange at a polo ball at Stowell Park, the Gloucestershire estate of Lord Vestey. Anna walked out of his life forever.

For that night, Charles had spent all evening dancing with Camilla Parker Bowles.

It was on again.

WEB OF DECEIT

*I*N FACT, IT WAS AS IF IT HAD NEVER STOPPED. UP UNTIL NOW CHARLES AND Camilla had convinced themselves they had been discretion itself, but for some time the mask had been slipping.

In early 1980 Andrew Parker Bowles, by now a lieutenant colonel, had been posted to Rhodesia, where, in the run-up to independence, the situation had become volatile. Lord Soames, son-in-law of the wartime leader Winston Churchill, had been appointed governor, and the ambitious Parker Bowles, newly promoted, was posted to the colony as chief liaison officer.

In early March, there was the first public sighting of Charles and Camilla together since that night in Annabel's nearly eight years before. The *Daily Mail* reported:

WHILE HOUSEHOLD CAVALRY OFFICER LT. COL. ANDREW PARKER BOWLES, 40, IS HELPING KEEP THE PEACE IN RHODESIA, HIS WIFE WAS AT PLUMPTON YESTERDAY CHEERING ON HER OLD BOYFRIEND PRINCE CHARLES.

CAMILLA, 32, WAS BROUGHT UP NEXT TO THE RACECOURSE, AND SHE HAS BEEN BACK HOME WITH HER PARENTS FOR CHARLES'S VISIT.

ANDREW, PERSONALLY SELECTED BY GOVERNOR LORD SOAMES, HAS BEEN ONE OF THE GREATEST SUCCESSES OF THE BRITISH PRESENCE IN THE FORMER REBEL COLONY—SO MUCH SO THAT HE IS KNOWN TO PREMIER-ELECT ROBERT MUGABE AS "COMRADE PARKER."

Soon the satirical magazine *Grovel* and its gossip columnist were on the scent:

NO SOONER HAD LORD SOAMES BEEN APPOINTED GOVERNOR OF RHODESIA THAN THE SUBJECT OF JOBS FOR THE BOYS AROSE. AMONG THE LUCKY ONES, MAJOR ANDREW PARKER BOWLES, NOW A COLONEL AND IN CHARGE OF BRITISH LIAISON WITH THE GUERILLA FORCES.

ANDREW, 39, IS MARRIED TO A FORMER (?) PRINCE CHARLES FANCY, CAMILLA SHAND, AND IF I SHOULD FIND THE ROYAL ASTON MARTIN VO-LANTE OUTSIDE THE PARKER BOWLES MANSION WHILE THE GALLANT COLONEL IS ON DUTY OVERSEAS, MY DUTY WILL BE CLEAR.

The word was out, yet—the libel laws being particularly ferocious in England, and with no direct evidence beyond the constant wagging of well-born tongues that the prince was once again bedding his old love—it was left to the cognoscenti to read between the lines and learn what was going on in Charles's life, even while he was still supposed to be in love with Anna Wallace and still trying to make her his wife.

The subtle digs had not escaped Anna Wallace. Maybe she was ready to put up with the charade; maybe she was prepared to entertain the idea of becoming Princess of Wales despite all this—particularly since Charles had pressed his case so convincingly, though, it has to be said, so dispassionately.

For she can have been left in very little doubt what the deal would be. In a relationship lasting the better part of a year—and one that seemed to have a purpose, after all—they had never once slept together. Anna may have made her own arrangements on that score, but so had Charles. He was utterly satisfied in that department.

It was an abnormal relationship for two grown adults, though suc-cessful marriages have been built on less. But that night at Stowell Park was more than any self-respecting woman could take. "Dancing with Camilla Parker Bowles at Stowell Park that night—I mean, *Camilla*

Parker Bowles!" uttered a friend. "Anna wasn't stupid, she knew how Camilla vetted all his women. Camilla dangled him like a trout—HRH knew that Anna would never put up with that."

Another story appeared in the newspapers during the period when Charles was wooing Anna Wallace—one that would have given her even more cause for alarm. The *Daily Mail* reported on April 11, 1980:

PRINCE CHARLES CAN EXPECT A MIXED WELCOME IN RHODESIA NEXT WEEK WHEN HE PRESIDES OVER THE ZIMBABWE INDEPENDENCE CELE-BRATIONS. FORMER PRIME MINISTER IAN SMITH, WHO ONCE VOWED THAT "NEVER IN 1,000 YEARS" WOULD BLACKS RULE HIS COUNTRY, IS SLIPPING OFF ABROAD TO FULFIL A "LONGSTANDING ENGAGEMENT."

BUT THERE WILL BE A FAMILIAR FACE FOR THE HEIR TO THE THRONE—OLD FLAME MRS. CAMILLA PARKER BOWLES, 32, IS EXPECTED IN SALISBURY TO ACT AS AN OFFICIAL ESCORT FOR CHARLES.

The report went on:

PARADOXICALLY [ANDREW] PARKER BOWLES IS NOW BACK IN ENGLAND AFTER MAKING A GREAT SUCCESS OF HEADING THE LIAISON FORCES UNDER SOAMES AND WILL NOT BE RETURNING WITH HIS WIFE, NIECE OF LORD ASHCOMBE.

BUCKINGHAM PALACE OFFICIALS HAVE ALWAYS BEEN HAPPY TO SEE CHARLES IN THE COMPANY OF HAPPILY MARRIED WOMEN, BECAUSE SUCH SIGHTINGS CANNOT GIVE RISE TO RUMOUR.

This last sentence was another warning shot across the prince's bow, but he was not to be deterred. Camilla had let him back into her life, and he was besotted.

Their rekindled passion was dangerous and, for a time, out of control. Despite the well-timed press report—no informed person believed the "official escort" tag for a second—Charles insisted that she should still accompany him to Zimbabwe. This drove senior officials into paroxysms of rage. "The hauling down of the British flag was a humiliating enough circumstance without everyone knowing the royal family's envoy had brought his popsy along with him," a Foreign Office source said later. "The lack of tact was indescribable. It just made a joke out of the whole thing."

Lord Soames, the most successful postwar ambassador to Paris and a diplomat as seasoned as they come, reacted with horror at the thought of sharing a table with Charles and Camilla, together with Andrew Parker Bowles and his own daughter Charlotte—with whom the soldier had fallen in love during his tour of duty in Africa. Eventually Charlotte was persuaded by her parents to fly home to London and her place was taken by another. Calling for assistance from the Almighty to overcome the dinner party from hell, Lady Soames added dryly: "And pray God may the claret be good."

Back in London, and with the Anna Wallace affair apparently going strong, the matchmakers were now pinning their hopes on an early engagement announcement. But now the relationship with Camilla, sealed in the heat and dust of Africa, was on again, the prince could hardly care less. "He was aware that something would have to be done sooner or later about finding a wife, and the person he turned to for advice was Camilla," says a former courtier. "It was most bizarre.

"Camilla felt that, now her family life was established, she could act in pretty much the same way as her great-grandmother. All that stuff about Alice Keppel was coming true for her."

She slipped into the role with consummate ease. With time on her hands and her husband away for long periods, she could devote herself to Charles and his problems. Often they would meet in Sussex, and it was at this stage that Camilla's parents became aware of their daughter's double life. Major Shand, though himself happily married for nearly a quarter of a century, took an urbane view of this accident of history. After all, he had seen his own father fall victim to a fickle heart several times. Friends say the relationship worried Mrs. Shand far more. But they were able to see for themselves that after so many years in the wilderness, without a friend and helpmeet, Charles had finally found a safe haven—someone to whom, for the first time, he could unburden himself. The relief was indescribable, the consequences unthought-of, but those who knew and cared for Charles thanked providence for his having found someone who could help him shoulder the burden of life.

Charles and Camilla's interests—apart from their new and overwhelming passion for each other—were manifold. Both were accomplished on horseback and enjoyed the thrill of the chase; Camilla insisted he should come to hunt in Gloucestershire. Both were fascinated by architecture—and Camilla was able to draw on the life of her grandfather Philip Morton Shand, the lively proponent of the Bauhaus movement and friend of Walter Gropius. Both were amateur watercolorists seeking to improve their technique, and both had developed a passion for Italy, its architecture and art. Later critics derided Camilla for her lack of academic qualifications and her addiction to the hunt; they sought to delve no deeper to discover what else lay there for Charles to adore. But there was plenty.

To most of the population, theirs was a passion which simply did not exist. But a privileged few were witness to an astonishing display of the almost animal attraction that the two now had for each other.

The Cirencester Polo Club Ball was, as always, a private affair, with no members of the press or public allowed. A biennial celebration, it was remarkable that year only because it was the club's centenary. A marquee was built on the lawns of Cirencester House, a large Cotswold-stone edifice set in fifteen thousand acres belonging to Earl Bathurst, and around 350 black-tied and bejeweled guests were expected.

The guest of honor would be the Prince of Wales, a man who adored the turf of the Cirencester ground and played there regularly. Among the other guests were Andrew and Camilla Parker Bowles. It was a glittering occasion, where the wine flowed and the hot summer evening raised the temperature of all but the dullest guest.

"But what happened was quite astonishing," recalled one guest that night. "Charles and the Parker Bowleses shared the same table, and Charles spent the whole evening dancing with Camilla. They were kissing passionately as they danced—on and on they went, kissing each other, French kissing—dance after dance.

"Andrew wasn't quite sure how to react—he sat there smiling and saying to people: 'HRH is very fond of my wife. And she appears to be very fond of him.' He was not uncomfortable with what was going on, but other people were, especially the older ones. Some were embarrassed and shocked and upset because the whole thing was so blatant," went on the guest. "It's bad enough, in such company, to monopolize one woman all evening. It's worse if it's someone else's wife. But the way they were behaving was completely beyond the pale."

This episode does more than anything to illustrate the difficult line Andrew Parker Bowles chose to tread, and the decorous manner in which he attempted to overcome the difficulties (if indeed they were difficulties) he faced in his marriage. In common with Alice Keppel and her husband, George, neither partner was faithful to the other, and yet an intensely strong bond held them together. If, as seems clear, Andrew was prepared to tolerate the *liaison dangéruse* between his wife and the Prince of Wales, he was having to pay a very high price in terms of public esteem. Later he would have to endure the public jeers from the godfather of his son at Royal Ascot when he was publicly dubbed "Ernest Simpson"—a reference to the man who so willingly allowed himself to be cuckolded by the previous Prince of Wales; but by then he was inured to the whispers and cackles that followed him wherever he went.

It is impossible to ascribe motives to this kind of behavior, but the fact is that at the *very latest* from 1980 onward, Andrew Parker Bowles was aware of the rekindled sexual relationship between his wife and the Prince of Wales, which had begun some time before. When that relationship finally started to break surface in the press, a friend commented: "Andrew's not that unhappy. He's got his own fish to fry."

For some years the prince had been looking for a home of his own. In 1974, while still serving in the navy, he had been offered—and accepted—a redbrick pile in Kent called Chevening. It had 115 rooms and 3,500 acres of Kentish downland and he hated it. His visits were rare and got rarer.

With his heart and mind now very firmly in the West Country and encouraged by an imploring Camilla, he ordered his Duchy of Cornwall staff to start looking for a proper home for him. It had to be in Gloucestershire or Wiltshire—in other words, not too far from Bolehyde Manor—and before too long, they came up with a suitable suggestion, the home of a Conservative minister, Maurice Macmillan, son of the former prime minister.

Highgrove, a distinguished though comparatively small Georgian house, had nine bedrooms and was set in 347 acres. It was charming, but hardly befitting the status of a Prince of Wales who might want to raise a dynasty there. Some saw the choice of Highgrove as his future home as a demonstration to the world of his "small is beautiful" philosophy; others saw a natural symmetry in his choosing an area near his sister, Anne, at Gatcombe Park and his cousin Prince Michael of Kent, thus creating the "royal triangle."

Nothing could be further from the truth. Highgrove—near a main road, and with a worrying footpath meandering past its door—was a poor choice, but it was there and it was available. Charles plumped for it, later saying: "It was a challenge to create something and I did rather fall in love with it. The big cedar tree in front and the walled garden finally made up my mind."

Possibly. But what is beyond dispute is that the royal-triangle factor was an irrelevance. Charles at that time saw very little of his sister, who was less than complimentary about his private life and who basked in the love and approbation of their father—something Charles had long ago reconciled himself to live without, but the lack of which galled him nonetheless. No more did he see of the Michaels of Kent—though he was devoted to his cousin Prince Michael, his initial enthusiasm for the prince's wife had turned to a chilly contempt. She was never to be allowed to visit Highgrove—indeed, Charles begged the security services to point out to Prince and Princess Michael that it would be too much of a burden on their resources to have three such obvious terrorist targets living in close proximity.

It was Camilla who made up his mind. The house was a few minutes' drive from Bolehyde Manor, and that was all that mattered. Not for the first time, Charles allowed his heart to rule his head. The purchase—the house cost a shade over £800,000—was made in August 1980, several long months after the affair had spun into top gear. And now that the prince had a house and the heart of "the woman I love," he could concentrate on thinking about marriage.

It was that cold and calculating a step.

New Grove, the home of Commander Robert de Pass, near Petworth in Sussex, was one of Charles's "safe houses." During the long and lonely years since his first fling with Camilla, he had taken several girlfriends there—though often they would be accommodated elsewhere and suffer the indignity of being bused in by a detective, made love to by the prince, then bused out again. One particular girl, well-born and with high expectations of an evening of courtly love, had been driven away in tears at the brutal reality of Charles's neglectful technique.

It was at New Grove, however, that another young hopeful was first entertained, apparently at the behest of the de Passes' son Philip, one weekend in July 1980. The pair had become acquainted through Rory Scott, a handsome Guards officer who had the distinction of having his shirts ironed by Earl Spencer's daughter and had responded by inviting her for weekends to his parents' home near Petworth. Only as Diana was packing her bags in London to travel south did she discover that a fellow houseguest would be the Prince of Wales.

They met, according to legend, on a hay bale. "You're a young blood," Philip de Pass had told her. "You might like him." During that weekend she drove to the nearby Cowdray Park polo ground to watch Charles play with his team, Les Diables Bleus, and at the end of the game the house party drove back to Petworth for a barbecue. The bale of hay was where they first had an opportunity to speak.

Some have painted her opening conversational gambit as a spon-taneous message of sympathy which touched the prince's heart to the core. Speaking of his role at the murdered Earl Mountbatten's funeral at Westminster Abbey, Lady Diana Spencer told the prince: "You looked so sad when you walked up the aisle at the funeral. It was the most tragic thing I've ever seen. My heart bled for you when I watched it. I thought, it's wrong, you are lonely, you should be with somebody to look after you."

But James Whitaker, who already knew Diana and in the coming months was to become her confidant, argued that from the time of her sister Sarah's estrangement from the prince, there had been a concerted campaign by all three Spencer sisters—Sarah, Diana, and Jane, wife of the queen's private secretary, Sir Robert Fellowes—to get Diana "in the frame." Thus her conversational gambit could be construed as a guileful ploy to attack Charles's Achilles' heel. If so, it was a success.

The prince left the house party early and insisted on the eighteen-year-old accompanying him back to London. Aware from her sister that instant compliance to his wishes tended to downgrade a woman in Charles's eyes, she held out, saying it would be rude to their host and hostess. Charles returned to London alone, to telephone Camilla and tell her of his latest find.

The wooing process started, in typically backhanded fashion. At the last minute Charles asked Diana to accompany him to a performance of Verdi's *Requiem* at the Royal Albert Hall. So little advance warning was Diana given that her flatmate, Carolyn Bartholemew, recalled: "I walked in about six o'clock and Diana went: 'Quick, quick, I've got to meet Charles in twenty minutes.' Well, we had the funniest time ever, getting the hair washed, getting it dried, getting the dress, where's the dress. We did it in twenty minutes flat. But I mean, how dare he ask her so late."

There was also an urgency about it all, which, given the lack of love ("Whatever you mean by love," delivered by Charles on the day of their engagement, was a phrase that haunted the couple for all their married life), could mean only one thing—Charles had found the solution to the problem.

It would not be long before he would be taking Lady Diana Spencer to be vetted by Mrs. Camilla Parker Bowles, but first came a whirlwind round of backbone-testing royal engagements—Cowes Week aboard the Royal Yacht *Britannia,* the traditional voyage north to Scotland, then Balmoral. It took less than a month from her first meeting Charles to her being considered, privately at least, to be the future Princess of Wales. "The haste was positively indecent," said one of Diana's friends, while Diana herself felt "fairly intimidated" by the atmosphere on board the royal yacht. Not only were his friends so much older than herself, but they seemed aware of the royal strategy toward her. Diana found them too friendly and too knowing—"They were all over me like a bad rash," she told her friends.

Determined as she was to grab Charles, it was if she had stepped into a boat with the intention of heading downstream, only to discover herself borne along on a raging torrent, which was pushing her toward the rapids. "She started it, but he took it over," said a friend.

Having passed the Balmoral test, Diana headed back to London accompanied by Charles's friend Nicholas Soames. There was one other escort on the flight to Heathrow from Aberdeen—Andrew Parker Bowles. He and Camilla had been part of the Balmoral house party, and Camilla had had her first glimpse of the future princess. Then Andrew headed south, leaving Camilla and Charles alone together in Balmoral. The bliss of their lovers' tryst was not wholly unalloyed—Camilla came down with mumps and was carted off to the hospital.

Whether by now Andrew Parker Bowles cared about his wife's relationship with Charles is open to debate. Certainly he had not shaken off his feelings for Lord Soames's daughter, and for some time after it was debated among his friends whether he would leave Camilla for her—not because of Camilla's affair with Charles, but because of his own feelings. In the end his indecision was his undoing: Charlotte Soames met and married Earl Peel, a Yorkshire landowner, in 1989.

There can be no doubt that Diana was aware of Camilla's relationship with the prince from the outset, for within weeks of the affair restarting it was common knowledge throughout Buckingham Palace. Among those he knew and trusted, Charles made no secret of his joy at rediscovering Camilla—and at a lowlier level, royal detectives had the evidence of their own eyes. All this very soon came to the attention of Robert Fellowes, at the time the queen's assistant private secretary. Fellowes was of course married to Lady Diana's sister, a woman well placed to give her kid sister some much-needed advice.

Thus the apparent love affair between Charles and Diana that was played out to the world at large was a sham from the beginning, a cruel hoax upon those who believed that even in the new, hard-nosed age of Thatcherism, there was still room for a fairy-tale royal romance.

Charles and Diana both wanted to marry, for entirely their own reasons. Common to both was a barely veiled ambition—on her side, to become Princess of Wales and ultimately queen; on his, to secure a wife who would be acceptable to both himself and the populace and who would provide an heir.

Things moved at such a pace between the first meeting and the first rumors of an engagement that a normally cynical Fleet Street lost its head and went with the myth. No single commentator or investigative journalist took heed of the still small voice repeating Mrs. Parker Bowles's name in their ear. The idea of a royal wedding, of the laying to rest of the specter of the previous Prince of Wales, was too seductive.

On the inside, the reality was harsher. Lady Diana found herself pursued by adoring newshounds, and though she took to the novelty with commendable humor, the wear and tear on her nerves grew increasingly unbearable. In desperation she contacted the press office at Buckingham Palace to seek advice, only to be told in no uncertain terms that she was on her own. Her equilibrium was not improved when

Prince Charles telephoned to discuss at length the enormous stress Camilla was being forced to undergo, with three or four reporters outside her door. Diana, fourteen years her rival's junior and not toughened by worldly experience, habitually had ten times that many.

Nor was her humor improved when, a month later, she and Prince Charles emerged before the public gaze at a race meeting at Ludlow, in the West Midlands. Charles, then attempting to make his mark as an amateur jockey, brought Diana along to admire his prowess in the saddle. Charles finished second on his horse Allibar, but though Diana shouted her support for him, there was a marked reticence in her appearance. Only later did people realize that Charles had brought along as chaperone none other than Camilla Parker Bowles. At the end of the day the trio managed to give the pursuing press photographers the slip—whereupon Charles ordered the car to be driven to Bolehyde Manor, where they all spent the weekend. Diana's mood was not improved when she was informed they would be back the next weekend as well.

But there was virtually nothing she could do. Camilla appeared to be holding the reins and Charles was content with that. "Diana had to swallow her feelings," said a friend at the time. "She had to bide her time—she wasn't even his fiancée yet."

Another friend described the courting couple's relationship as being warm enough, but almost master-and-servant: "She had to keep going in the way she did, fitting in with everything that Charles—and Camilla—suggested. The alternative, as she saw it, was that she would be ditched. Can you imagine how awful it was for her?"

It became clear that Diana's mother, conscious of Camilla's omnipresence, was unimpressed by Charles's pursuit of her daughter, urging caution to Diana without seeking to bring the fledgling relationship to a halt.

Andrew Morton, in his watershed book *Diana: Her True Story,* characterized those early days thus:

"As the romance gathered momentum, Diana began to harbour doubts about her new friend Camilla Parker Bowles. She [Camilla] seemed to know everything that Diana and Charles had discussed in their rare moments of privacy and was full of advice on how best to handle Prince Charles. It was all very strange. Even Diana, an absolute beginner in the rules of love, was starting to suspect that this was not the way that most men conducted their romances."

This information, accepted by Morton in good faith, is disingenuous in the extreme. There can be no doubt whatsoever that Diana was completely aware of the situation from the outset. She had learned on the grapevine what had happened to her predecessor Anna Wallace, and was privy to the reasons for the breakdown of that relationship. It is even said that Miss Wallace issued a warning to Diana through a third party, alerting her to the Camilla problem.

So to suggest that a bewildered young ingenue had been bamboozled by an aging Bluebeard was stretching things, to say the least. There can be no doubt, however, that in the early stages Diana believed that she could win her future husband's love, and set about doing so with youthful gusto.

As September moved into October, Diana dined at Buckingham Palace with Charles; the Parker Bowleses came too. Charles took her to Highgrove and asked her to decorate it for him. Camilla's helpful comments after this invitation made it all too clear to Diana that the older woman knew the house intimately. It did not take long for the penny to drop: Camilla had helped choose it.

But even if there was a doubt left in Diana's mind as to the nature of Charles and Camilla's relationship, it was about to be shattered in a most spectacular way.

On November 16, 1980, the *Sunday Mirror* carried a story which alleged that, ten days before, Diana had secretly joined Charles on the royal train, parked for the night in a siding at Staverton in Wiltshire. She was alleged to have stayed on board for several hours—and the implication was clear. There could be no other interpretation than that she had slept with Charles, who was not then even betrothed to her.

In Britain, at that time, the story caused a furor. The country was basking in the belief that Charles had found himself a well-born, good-looking, charming, and fresh young thing for his future bride, a woman who was a virgin and would remain so to the altar. However passé that notion might seem in the present climate, it was what the public wanted.

But the evidence was there. A blond-haired woman had entered the train at night after Charles had finished giving dinner to three Duchy of

Cornwall officials. The telephone log subsequently showed that a call had, a little earlier, been made to Bolehyde Manor.

What happened next, some might suppose, was a deception that could only be described as conduct unbecoming a future king. Both Charles and the queen feigned anger at the *Sunday Mirror*'s supposed invention, and the queen's press secretary, Michael Shea, was instructed to write to the newspaper's editor. He protested in the strongest terms about the story, which, he said, was "totally false" and a "total fabrication." No doubt in all innocence of the true circumstances—for he was only acting on information supplied to him by the Prince of Wales himself—Shea demanded a printed apology in a prominent position in the newspaper at the earliest opportunity.

The newspaper's editor, a respected journalist called Bob Edwards, was shocked by the vehemence of the Palace response. On the one hand, he could understand their anger at his printing a story that could derail the much longed-for royal engagement; on the other, it appeared that their complaint came from the utter belief that Diana had *not* been on the train.

But the evidence said differently—a woman *had* boarded the train, *had* stayed for hours, *had* left clandestinely. What no one could believe, because Fleet Street had fallen in love with Diana and had allowed its guard to drop, was that if there was a woman on board, it was someone else.

Diana herself was caught off guard. Thinking herself to be in grave danger of falling in the public's esteem, and with Charles's proposal of marriage not yet uttered, she hastened to put the record straight. "I am not a liar," she told the *Daily Mirror*'s James Whitaker. "I have never been on that train. I have never ever been near it.

"I stayed in all that evening with my three flatmates, Virginia [Pitman], Carolyn and Ann [Bolton]. Please believe me, I am telling the absolute truth. I had some supper and watched television before going to bed early. I had been at Princess Margaret's party at the Ritz the night before, and I was feeling very frail and hung over. I didn't feel like going anywhere and I never moved out of my flat. My flatmates will testify to this."

This was an extraordinary outburst from a girl who had quickly learned, some months before, the virtue of saying nothing to the press.

But Diana went further: "These allegations have not put me in a very good light," she told Whitaker. "It is all very upsetting."

In Diana's mind there was no doubt that the woman in question—and by now it was clear that evidence had come from the security services guarding Charles that there *was* a woman—was Camilla Parker Bowles. It was a shattering thought that, four months into their relationship, Charles could dance the night away with her at the Ritz, only to sneak away to have sexual relations with his mistress the following night, while she, Diana, bathed in the afterglow of the most romantic evening she had ever experienced in her short life. Worse still was the thought that her own ambitions could be thwarted by Charles's infidelity.

The row did not go away. A protest was made to the Press Council; it was clear, said the complainant, that in the light of Buckingham Palace's outright denial, the *Sunday Mirror* should be censured. But by now wise to what had happened, Palace officials, in an apparent gesture of magnanimity, said they had no wish to pursue the matter. The *Sunday Mirror*'s editor, still unaware of the true circumstances surrounding his story, met Prince Charles personally; the matter was not alluded to.

Six years later, in recognition of his outstanding services to journalism, Bob Edwards was made a Commander of the Order of the British Empire, only a step away from a knighthood; it appeared he had been forgiven by the Palace. Generously, in his memoirs, Edwards had written, "How awful if I had been wrong about the whole silly thing." But he had not. Those privileged to be invited to the editor's home that Christmas could have discovered, among the welter of seasonal cards and greetings, one from a former politician and close friend of the royal family. The card, inscribed with a short message, simply said: "It was Camilla."

That was in the future. In the aftermath of the Royal Train Scandal, as it became known, Charles flew out to India on a prearranged visit. In New Delhi he made a speech in which he took the opportunity, several thousand miles from home, to swipe at those who had questioned his behavior on that fateful night. He hit out at what he described as the "sensationalism" of the British media, and the lack of moral values in reporting. Speaking to members of the Indian Institute of Technology he said: "Honesty and integrity are vital factors in reporting and often get submerged in the general rush for sensationalism." Insofar as personal integrity goes, this was a low watermark in Charles's life.

In the ensuing rush to see who could capitalize most on the press's discomfiture, Diana's mother, Mrs. Frances Shand Kydd, wrote a letter to *The Times* complaining about the "lies and harassment" Diana was forced to endure. Certainly she was right about the lies, though on this occasion it was not the press who were being economical with the truth. Then sixty members of Parliament took up the cudgels, drafting a motion "deploring the manner in which Lady Diana Spencer is being treated by the media." There was an urgent meeting between Fleet Street editors and the Press Council—and all because the Prince of Wales had telephoned Mrs. Parker Bowles and invited her to spend the night with him.

At this distance Charles's behavior, in particular his New Delhi response, must seem unworthy of his status as future king. But by now he was not acting entirely of his own free will. The nation wanted him to marry, so too did the queen, and more especially so did his hectoring father. A possible bride had been found, and he was doing his duty—unlike his great-uncle—working his way toward what was required of him. It was tough luck that fate had decreed he should fall in love with a married woman who came quickly to understand his problems, and learned how to comfort him in the way he needed most.

As his need for marriage receded, so he was being pushed into it. He had been caught virtually *in flagrante delicto* and his relationship with a married woman all but uncovered. It was a frustrating and bewildering experience, and he did not respond well to it. Diana did not spend Christmas with him, nor New Year's Eve. It was not until New Year's Day, 1981, that she was invited to join him at Sandringham.

Whether through compassion for her granddaughter, or the desire not to see the family name besmirched, Ruth, Lady Fermoy, sounded a warning note, cautioning Diana about the difficulties of marrying into the royal family. "You must understand that their sense of humour," she said, "and their *lifestyle* are very different. I don't think it will suit you."

It made no difference. Having once again consulted Camilla, Charles decided to propose to Diana on his return from a skiing trip to Klosters. Yet his approach was leisurely. Though he had flown back to London on February 3, it was not until three days later that Diana was summoned to Windsor Castle for the historic proposal. She accepted, saying, "Yes, please." That, at least, was the official version; a more popular one is that he proposed in Camilla's kitchen garden at Bolehyde Manor. When Diana accepted, Camilla raced away to get the champagne.

How much of the decision to go ahead with the betrothal was his, and how much Camilla's, is a matter for speculation. But having now had plenty of opportunity to size up her protégée, Camilla made a fundamental miscalculation. When asked by friends what she thought of Diana, she replied: "She's like a mouse."

The mouse was not yet ready to roar, and took the silence of her future husband, when she flew to Australia for a ten-day respite, meekly enough. As the days wore on, he made no attempt to telephone her, and when she finally plucked up the courage to call Buckingham Palace from New South Wales, she was told the prince was not there. He finally returned her call, and upon her arrival back in England, she was greeted by a member of Charles's staff with a large bouquet of flowers. There was no card.

Things were moving at an alarming pace. Within six weeks, on February 28, 1981, the formal announcement of the royal engagement was made. Charles and Diana made their debut together before the television cameras and were asked the fateful question: "Are you in love?" Was it because he knew that Camilla would be watching that all he could stammer was: "Whatever 'in love' means"?

The royal machine took over, and Diana was swept out of her Colherne Court flat forever. She was given a suite of rooms at the queen mother's London home, Clarence House, and within twenty minutes of arriving she discovered, on her bed, an invitation to lunch from Camilla.

Ironically, it was the warmest gesture of welcome she received. No one from the royal family was there to greet her, and she had no idea where her future husband was. Camilla's note had been written several days before the announcement of the engagement, making it clear that she had prior knowledge; but then, that came as no great surprise, for in the six months since Diana had entered this extraordinary love triangle, Camilla had been omnipresent. What galled Diana was that Camilla knew where she would be staying—at Clarence House, not Buckingham Palace—whereas Diana herself was informed only a few hours before she left Colherne Court.

➤ The lunch with Camilla was the high point of her first few days in royal custody. With unerring female instinct, she knew what Camilla meant when she asked Diana whether she proposed to hunt when she was at Highgrove. The mouse, compliantly, said no. ➤

 MARRIAGE MADE IN HELL

IANA'S ROYAL CAREER BEGAN IN THE STATELY ROOMS OF CLARENCE HOUSE, the queen mother's eighteenth-century mansion situated in The Mall, a five-minute walk from Buckingham Palace. It was to Clarence House she returned in the early hours of Tuesday morning after the nuptial ball, leaving behind Prince Charles—and Camilla Parker Bowles.

It is fair to say that having first questioned whether he could go on with the marriage—as Diana had done—Charles then committed himself to it, in just the way he committed himself to all aspects of his duty.

If, then, he took Camilla Parker Bowles to bed in those last hours leading up to his wedding, he saw it as no act of betrayal. Rather, it was in the belief that he must now dedicate himself to his wife, and to married life. This, he told Camilla, was the last time they would make love.

And they did. Charles's valet, Stephen Barry, later told James Whitaker: "Sir had always been infatuated with Camilla since they first knew each other in the early 1970s. But when he took her to bed in the very week of his wedding it seemed incredible. Certainly incredibly daring, if not incredibly stupid."

Perhaps. But if this was a passionate farewell, delivered in the dark hours after Buckingham Palace had stilled and the guests had gone, it was indeed poignant; a full stop to a passion and understanding that had grown and flourished in the past two years, and whose origins stretched back the best part of a decade. The intensity of their relationship was heightened by the constraints imposed upon it, creating a greater excitement by the ever-present knowledge that it was *verboten*.

But it was an act of betrayal, nonetheless, not only to his future wife but to the queen and the waiting country, all of whom might have expected him to still his ardor on the eve of his wedding vows. Within hours, he would hear the Archbishop of Canterbury, Dr. Robert Runcie, ask a packed and hushed congregation: "If anyone can show cause or just impediment why these two people should not be joined together in holy matrimony, let him now speak, or else hereafter for ever hold his peace." One person—Stephen Barry—could show such cause, or at the very least open a debate as to the wisdom of Charles's actions; but he wasn't talking.

The night before the wedding Charles sent an emissary to his fiancée with a prenuptial present, a signet ring engraved with the Princess of Wales's feathers. The man had to fight his way through the crowds standing crushed against the Buckingham Palace railings; with voices hoarse with emotion they raised them in song, serenading the prince in his sitting room with "Rule Britannia." "I found myself standing in the window with tears pouring down my face," he recalled; but what were the tears for? In gratitude for the genuine affection of his subjects? In sorrow for his lost love? In fear of the life to come with a wife he could not love? Or was it because this essentially decent, hardworking, honorable, and dedicated man felt he had let himself down?

Meanwhile, over at Clarence House, Diana opened Charles's present and read the accompanying card, which said: "I'm so proud of you and when you come up I'll be there at the altar for you tomorrow. Just look 'em in the eye and knock 'em dead." Diana, for a moment deliriously happy at this uncharacteristic romantic gesture, went down to dinner with her sister Jane, ate everything she could, and was promptly sick.

There was a brief moment of sweet revenge. After the wedding, 120 guests were invited to Buckingham Palace for the wedding breakfast.

Camilla Parker Bowles's name was struck off the list, along with that of another close friend, Lady "Kanga" Tryon. Camilla responded by hosting a luncheon party herself for friends, content in the knowledge that her wedding present to Charles was packed in his going-away luggage. But perhaps sensing Charles's determination to put the past behind him—and his acceptance that Camilla and Lady Tryon should not be his guests on that important day was the first step—Diana began to relax. "I had tremendous hope in my heart," she said.

But Camilla never went away. Days into their Mediterranean cruise on the Royal Yacht *Britannia,* which they had joined at Gibraltar, and after an unhappy consummation, the royal couple were comparing engagements in their respective diaries when two photographs of Mrs. Parker Bowles fell out from the pages of Charles's diary. A tearful row ensued, stoked up by the unreleased tensions from the wedding days before. A cornered Charles, embarrassed at being caught, angry that his new wife, so many years his junior, should have the moral advantage over him, simply refused to discuss his relationship with the older woman. Diana was distraught.

Several days later the couple entertained the president of Egypt, Anwar Sadat, and his wife, Jihan, to dinner aboard the royal yacht, by now anchored at Port Said. Sadat favored a lounge suit, Charles a form of naval mess kit with bow tie and starched white shirt. Diana, who had been instrumental in rejuvenating Charles's sartorial appearance and who took a close interest in what he wore, noted that in his starched cuffs he was sporting a new-looking pair of gold cuff links.* They bore two entwined Cs, deftly symbolizing the bond between Charles and Camilla, and yet again Diana challenged her husband about Mrs. Parker Bowles. He finally admitted they were a gift from her, but rather than admit his boorishness in wearing them in front of Diana, he resorted to a "So what? She's been a friend of mine for years" argument.

The fragile truce, it appeared, was over.

---

*After a quantity of jewelry and personal effects was stolen from the Prince of Wales's apartments at St. James's Palace in 1994, inquiries about these cuff links were met with the Palace response: "They never existed in the first place." But this statement was made without apparent conviction and not repeated. If there is one instruction above all others the denizens of that office are told to obey, it is that they must not be caught out in a lie.

Yet by now, and against all odds, there seemed a determination to make things work; after all, in the short term there was nothing else they could do. There may have been mutual suspicion, but both the young ingenue and the older, experienced man knew what they were in for. They had seen the expressions on the faces of the crowds, knew what they owed them.

And a growing bond of affection, manifested in exchanged letters which touched on the topic of love, demonstrated that there was still hope. "When you are young," Diana said later, "optimism keeps breaking through."

Those who support the Prince of Wales believe there was an absolute determination on both sides, after that last night of love in Buckingham Palace, that Charles and Camilla would go their separate ways. She had a young family and, though she could never be categorized as an "army wife," had certain responsibilities toward her husband in terms of entertaining and being entertained. Charles had a public life and now, at last, a private one.

But, incarcerated with Diana at Balmoral on the return from their honeymoon, Charles found that he was sharing his life with an alien being. Diana was losing weight at a quite alarming rate, though no one—apart from servants who occasionally had to clean up after her—was aware of her bulimic condition. She was isolated at Balmoral, separated from friends and family and the London life she knew, finding herself the most junior member of the royal family, who, in any conversation, was the last to be spoken to by members of that xenophobic clan. There were no familiar reference points, no moments of respite, and no escape. She crumbled.

"Inexorably," wrote her apologist Andrew Morton, "her thoughts turned to suicide, not because she wanted to die, but because she desperately wanted help."

In early October she flew to London for professional counseling, seeing doctors and psychologists at Buckingham Palace; their collective opinion was that she should be put on a course of tranquilizers. All this appalled Charles, a man who at best was an innocent unprepared for the buffets of the married state, at worst a man who hardened his heart at any sign of weakness.

In his wife's absence, confused, bewildered, desperately unhappy,

The greater love . . . portrait of the only woman ever to capture the heart and mind of Charles, Prince of Wales (*Joan Wakeham*)

Royal mistress: Alice Keppel with her daughter Sonia, whom many supposed to be King Edward VII's daughter—St. Moritz, 1920

Royal mistress: Alice's great-granddaughter, Camilla Parker Bowles (*London News Service*)

The first sighting of Camilla Shand, four, at the wedding of her uncle, the Hon. Jeremy Cubitt: St. Mark's, North Audley Street, January 1952. Holding her hand is sister Annabel, three. (*Hulton Deutsch Collection*)

First home: The Old Manor, Westdean, East Sussex (*Helen Scanlon*)
The Laines, Plumpton, East Sussex (*Helen Scanlon*)

After seven years' courtship, Miss Camilla Shand and Captain Andrew Parker Bowles marry to royal approval: Princess Anne witnesses her former boyfriend wed. Guards Chapel, July 1973 (*Hulton Deutsch*)

Where love began: Flat 1, Stack House, Cundy Street (*Helen Scanlon*)

Magic moments: the newly married Mrs. Parker Bowles and the Prince of Wales at polo in 1975 (*Rex Features/Haydn Jones*)

Just the three of us . . . Camilla, Andrew, and Charles enjoy a night out on the town, 1976. (*Rex Features*)

He proposed marriage to her, but their relationship remained unconsummated: Diana's predecessor as future Princess of Wales, Anna Wallace (*Rex Features*)

Who comes second in Charles's affections? The two women in the prince's life at Ludlow races, 1980. Diana was dismayed to discover she had to spend the weekend at Camilla's home. (*Rex Features*)

and at a loss as to what to do, he broke all the promises he had made to himself and telephoned Camilla.

Whatever her determination at this point to stay away from Charles, there can be no doubt that the call came as a blessed relief. Despite their row over Diana's suitability as a future Princess of Wales—and, it must be acknowledged, Charles's reservations were by now seen to be justified—there was a magnetic attraction, forged in secrecy and tempered in adultery, which would not go away. They arranged to meet again.

Thus it was that three days before Buckingham Palace announced to the waiting world that the Princess of Wales was pregnant, her husband was to be found out riding with the Vale of the White Horse Hunt. The hunt was not one with which he had previously been associated, preferring the superior country (and breeding) of the Quorn, the Belvoir, and the Beaufort.

However, on November 2, 1981, four months after his marriage and immediately after his return from his extended Scottish sojourn, this obscure pack suited the Prince of Wales's purpose. There had been some hope that he might turn out with the Beaufort, but while he was keen to return to the saddle, he chose the remoter charms of Ewen, near Cirencester, where the Vale of the White Horse met that day.

His presence in the field remained undetected for some hours until a fox led hounds out of a wood toward a main road where about forty people had gathered. The fox went to ground and the prince turned back and rode away as the hunt regrouped, finding his only path was down the empty main street. As he turned the corner, he met the hunt followers and a pack of Fleet Street photographers. Flushing bright red, he bellowed at them: "When are you going to stop making my life a total misery?" His vehemence stunned the witnesses to this scene, but as he spurred his horse back toward the regrouped hunt, a blond woman on horseback joined him and they rode away together. The woman looked suspiciously like Camilla Parker Bowles.

After that encounter, which went unremarked in a press now reaching fever pitch at the prospect of the birth of a future king, Charles and Camilla relaxed. They started to hunt regularly together, often with the Beaufort but sometimes farther afield in Leicestershire, where Charles's old friend—and Bruce Shand's—Ulrike Murray-Smith was to be found. Camilla had hunted from an early age, Charles started when he was older, but both derived the same breathtaking satisfaction from the chase. Royal author Suzy Menkes observed: "I believe that Charles gets a tremendous sexual thrill and charge from hunting, which many people do."

He adored to see Camilla in full flight on horseback. "She's a ruthless horsewoman, aggressive, shouting in the hunting field," said a member of the Beaufort who has ridden with her. "To use the word assertive would be an understatement. You should hear her screaming as you approach a fence. She's shouting, "Bloody hell, get out of the fucking way!' She steamrollers people and it can be quite frightening."

Compare this red-blooded, sexual, athletic being with the painfully neurotic and bulimic Diana, and it is suddenly easy to see why Charles broke the vows of abstention he had made himself. For four long months he had nurtured his desperately unhappy wife the best way he could, had been subjected to her temper tantrums and had heaped even more opprobrium upon himself by being a less than competent liar.

Camilla was normal. She was grown-up. She was womanly with voluptuous curves, not a bag of bones. She could listen for hours without having to counter Charles's litany of woes with a list of her own troubles. She was sexually adventurous. And she was, in all truth, a very nice woman.

She had also come to the realization that there was room in her life to cope with the prince and his problems—and the prospect, now he was married, of truly following in her great-grandmother's footsteps as La Favorita was an enticing one.

The couple were pushed closer together by the now alarming behavior of Diana, who had the burden of pregnancy to add to her miseries. John Bowes-Lyon, a co-godfather with Prince Charles of Camilla's son Thomas, reported: "She had fits which would last just a few minutes, during which she would go crazy and become uncontrollable. Then it was all over as quickly as it began."

Whether, as some claim, Diana's tumble down the stairs at Sandringham that Christmas was a manifestation of this rage, an attempt at suicide (if so, a risible one; the stairs are very shallow), or simply a desire to be noticed, it was depressing for Charles to find himself being called for, to help pick up his pregnant wife and order a gynecologist to be sent from London.

"At first doctors thought her outbursts might have been epilepsy," John Bowes-Lyon reported. "But that was discounted because she didn't swallow her tongue or have other epileptic symptoms. Apparently what she suffers from can be hereditary and there have been other instances in the Fermoy family, so the royal family have been told."

With—as he saw it—a lifetime's marriage still in front of him, Charles offered an olive branch to Diana. Conscious of her irritation that Highgrove had been chosen in part by Camilla, and of her desire to be rid of the house, he suggested they look for an alternative base in the country. Diana took up the suggestion with alacrity, but made the proviso that it should be as far away from Camilla as possible—no more Gloucestershire, no more West Country—and nearer to her own family seat, Althorp.

On March 4, 1982, the *Daily Express*'s prescient diarist William Hickey recorded under the headline DIANA FALLS OUT OF LOVE WITH HIGH-GROVE:

THE PRINCE AND PRINCESS OF WALES ARE LOOKING FOR A NEW HOME. DESPITE EXTENSIVE REFURBISHMENTS TO HIGHGROVE, IT IS SAID THE PRINCESS IS "UNHAPPY WITH THE CHARACTER OF THE PLACE" AND WANTS TO MOVE.

HAVING BEEN USED TO THE PALATIAL SURROUNDINGS OF HER OWN FAMILY HOME, ALTHORP, THIS IS QUITE UNDERSTANDABLE. ALTHORP HAS 15,000 ACRES, HIGHGROVE JUST 348.

THE COUPLE HAVE SPENT VERY LITTLE OF THEIR SEVEN-MONTH MARRIAGE IN THE PLACE, AND COUPLED WITH THIS COMES WORD FROM BELTON HOUSE, THE STATELY HOME OF LORD BROWNLOW IN LINCOLN-SHIRE, THAT CHARLES AND DIANA ARE INTERESTED IN BUYING.

Belton was, in many ways, ideal. It was grand, unlike Highgrove: an impressive foursquare house built originally in the seventeenth century and containing carvings by Grinling Gibbons. It also boasted priceless tapestries and paintings by Titian, Rubens, Raphael, Rembrandt, and Van Dyck, as well as a *Mona Lisa* by Leonardo da Vinci similar to the masterpiece hanging in the Louvre. Equally attractive was the fact that, though situated in prime hunting country, it had no associations with Camilla. Charles had stayed there on many occasions while training as an RAF pilot at nearby Cranwell, and it was within striking distance of Sandringham. It had royal associations—the present incumbent's father, Perry Brownlow, the sixth baron, had been a lord-in-waiting during the brief kingship of Edward VIII and one of the closest friends of the Duke and Duchess of Windsor. And from Diana's point of view, it was a short drive from her sister Sarah's house.

The royal couple visited Belton on at least three occasions in 1982 and came close to making the decision to move there. Diana, desperate to shake off Highgrove, pressed ever harder. But for Charles two factors weighed against it—the seventeenth-century house, with its 4,792 acres, would be costly to run and was too far from Duchy of Cornwall land for resources to be shared; and it would mean abandoning Highgrove. So many of the prince and princess's wedding presents, including the gift of a swimming pool and some ornamental gates, were associated with that particular house that it would be taken as a monumental snub if they walked away from it, leaving the (immovable) presents behind.

But as his critics have ever been ready to point out, Prince Charles is indecisive; and he continued to toy with the idea of Belton for the next year. Only in the summer of 1983 was the house finally put on the market, and the official reason why Charles and Diana did not move in was because Belton's grandeur was out of keeping with the royal family's new line in frugality. Diana was furious at being forced to stay at Highgrove—even though, with the help of interior designer Dudley Poplak, she had lavished £100,000 of her husband's money redecorating the place, rubbing out any vestige of Camilla's influence.

The relationship between Charles and Camilla, hinted at and gossiped about in the newspapers since the days of Anna Wallace, now went underground. Even columnists who had kept a close watch on the pair found themselves starved of information, and by May 1982, with Diana's pregnancy nicely on the way, a woefully wide-of-the-mark piece appeared in one tabloid newspaper. It revealed that Camilla, along with her friend Rose Pitman, was selling secondhand frocks from Bolehyde Manor. Referring to Camilla's exclusion from the wedding breakfast the previous year, the piece concluded: "This step into trade is a far cry from the ways of the royal family, and serves to confirm Camilla's status—on the outside."

If she read it, she must have laughed. But it served her purpose. Fleet Street's article added neatly to the smokescreen which had been laid around the couple: They were finished, a dead letter, if anybody asked. Increasingly, people did not—they were too distracted by the excitement of the forthcoming royal birth.

With the arrival of Prince William of Wales on June 21, 1982, Charles found himself even more alienated from his wife. He attended the long and often painful labor and was present when his son was born. It was a rare moment of reunification for the couple, and they shared that sense of joint pride which all young couples enjoy at the arrival of their firstborn.

But Diana was not a well woman when she gave birth. Her body had suffered from the recurrent bouts of bulimia and she was in a weakened state. Once the initial euphoria passed, it was replaced with postnatal depression. This, once again, triggered the bulimia. Charles was aware of the problem; in fact, he was not allowed to forget it—Diana's depression evinced itself most often in a series of attacks on him for his continued relationship with Camilla. Although the princess could not have known the details, somehow instinctively she was aware of the situation. There were tears and panic telephone calls when he did not arrive home on time, and nights without sleep when he was away. Charles's telephone calls to Mrs. Parker Bowles became more urgent, and it was only a matter of time before Diana overheard one—the prince was in his bath and talking on the telephone. His words echoed out of the bathroom and ran a dagger through Diana's heart.

The man who, when asked about his feelings for his future wife had said, "Whatever love is," raised his voice above the splashing water. "Whatever happens," he said into the telephone to Mrs. Parker Bowles, "I will always love you."

Love, of the physical variety, was not high on the royal couple's agenda after the birth of William. After their move to Kensington Palace a servant confirmed that the couple rarely slept in their four-poster bed together. Often Diana would go to bed early, while Charles preferred to stay up late: "When he had finished what he was doing each night, the prince would creep upstairs and without disturbing his wife slip into his dressing-room, which adjoined the master bedroom, from an outside door leading off the corridor. There he would get into the bed

which was always made up for him. Whether this was out of consideration for his wife or because he just wanted to be on his own I couldn't
say. But it did happen frequently."

The servant could not know it, but these nights near, but not with,
his wife gave considerable ease to Charles's vexed state of mind. He was
married—inescapably, it seemed—and there was, even now, a warmth
between him and Diana. But Camilla was Charles's greater love; with
her he had found peace and serenity, the hope and right of all lovers,
and the nights spent in his dressing room allowed her into his dreams.
The unbearable life which he and his wife were leading was already
doomed, yet he did not know it; and he clung to the belief that as long
as he had Camilla in the background he could soldier on.

But it was hard. On the eve of Remembrance Day, 1982, the year of
the Falklands War, Charles and Diana were due to join the queen at the
annual British Legion service of remembrance at the Royal Albert Hall in
London. Coupled with the following day's homage at the Cenotaph in
Whitehall, this event recalls to the nation those who died in defense of
their country and is considered to be at the top of the royal family's list
of annual public engagements.

Minutes before the ceremonial was due to begin, a doorman was
told that Diana would not be attending. There had been a monumental
row, and she was in no state to be seen in public. There was a frantic
rearrangement of chairs in the royal box as the queen was informed of
her daughter-in-law's intended absence. Fifteen minutes later, with the
queen already in her seat, Diana appeared, looking "grumpy and fed
up," according to an eyewitness. This latest intransigence was yet a further embarrassment to Charles, particularly when it was picked up by
the newspapers the following day.

"No one is ever late for the Queen," wrote the indefatigable James
Whitaker, "so I set out to find what was the matter.

"A month or so before, Diana had swept out of Balmoral in a fury,
leaving Charles and their three-and-a-half-month-old son behind. She
just wanted to get out of Scotland. Most particularly she objected to the
way that Charles would always side with his mother in any disagree-
ment. She was also beginning to be extremely irritated with the Queen
Mother continually 'helping' her. She had been given no assistance by
the Queen Mother on her introduction into royal circles, despite popu-

lar myth, and she felt that by now she could cope perfectly adequately without little lectures."

Whitaker also discovered by talking to Diana's press officer, Vic Chapman, that there was, indeed, "a little problem." Chapman vouchsafed that the princess had become obsessive in her behavior, citing as an example a preoccupation with her shoes—when cleaned, they should be put back in precisely the straight lines they were in when taken away. "She is obsessed that everything and everybody around should be perfect," Chapman explained.

The resulting article by Whitaker suggested, for the first time, that the Princess of Wales was behaving irrationally, and that this could be because of an eating disorder. He described her painfully thin body, and the fact that she would needlessly stress, on meeting members of the public at official functions, that she had to watch her waistline.

The publication of the article created a furor. There was an angry denial from a Buckingham Palace spokesman, who added the desperate rider: "For God's sake, leave her alone." The BBC's Brian Redhead criticized Whitaker's article on the air as "outrageous"; but the reporter had the information correct, and from the best possible source—Diana's deeply concerned sister Sarah.

That the public prints were now discussing his wife's dietary abnormalities was a further humiliation to Charles, who had to answer to his still-critical father every time something damaging about the Waleses appeared in the newspapers. He started taking lunch with Diana "just to make sure she eats properly."

Andrew Parker Bowles had been recently promoted to commanding officer of the Household Cavalry. The regimental headquarters, a vulgar high-rise block which blights the south side of Hyde Park, became home, since his duties became increasingly social as well as military. Camilla was not, as has been noted, an army wife; she was content to live her life at Bolehyde Manor, just a short drive away from Highgrove. Soon the couple were to move to another home, Middlewick House near Corsham, just twelve miles from Highgrove—even closer. Diana faced this prospect with deep unhappiness, but for form's sake attended the housewarming party without apparent demur.

Charles's enthusiasm for the hunt increased. His official workload had gone down and he was allowing himself more time for personal pursuits—and the fox came high on that list. He would turn out with the Beaufort once, twice, and even three times in a week, which necessitated his staying behind at Highgrove while Diana traveled to London. Followers of the Beaufort noted that Charles would carefully avoid the meet, then join the field once the chase was under way. Mrs. Parker Bowles, a respected member of the Hunt, would at some stage fall back in the field and the couple would walk their horses into the woods, catching up with fellow members later in the day.

Though she was never present on these hunt days, Diana was only too aware of what was going on. In November 1983, soon after she had suffered a miscarriage while staying at Balmoral, a monumental row broke out at Highgrove when Charles left for a day's hunting; Diana was under the impression he had said he would stay behind. There was another screaming match, in front of witnesses, as he left the house to join the Beaufort and Mrs. Parker Bowles. As he drove off, Diana collapsed once again in tears—but by this stage, Charles was immune. He had had enough.

Their conjugal life was not yet quite over, however, and in September 1984 Diana gave birth to Prince Harry. This time the joy of a new life made was savored separately, not together. In his perpetual quest for knowledge Charles had become something of an expert on baby care, so much so that Diana was heard to snarl: "My husband knows so much about rearing children that I've suggested that he has the next one and I'll sit back and give advice."

That was not to be, for the gap had widened so considerably between the two that now, three years after the wedding, they rarely slept together. Charles had greeted Harry's arrival at St. Mary's Hospital, Paddington, with an airy: "Oh, it's a boy" (he had wanted a girl) "and it's even got rusty hair"—and with that he set off for polo. According to some, this single act signaled the end of the marriage.

But not yet: Though they often attended official engagements together and between the rows had established a not unendurable truce, the royal couple pursued their leisure hours separately. Charles would go to the opera—and Camilla would go too, sometimes bringing along a perfectly content Andrew Parker Bowles, who would sit smilingly behind them in the royal box.

For Charles these outings were an oasis of calm in a turbulent domestic life; he would return to find Diana seething with indignation. "Her temper grew worse as the hours passed and by the time Charles arrived home she was often in a towering, door-banging fury," revealed one source. Charles's reaction, more often than not, was nonconfrontational; he would simply shake his head and walk away. It drove Diana into even greater paroxysms of rage.

Outwardly, the couple made a great show of togetherness. Public duty was the one point where they saw eye to eye, and indeed, Diana's love affair with the public was still extremely hot. Wherever she went, she could, on her exit from the official car, create an electric charge through a crowd of thousands. Her early faltering steps on the fashion ladder were gone. She was now a supreme dresser, both daring and modest, and there could be no questioning her success in her public role, both at home and abroad. She possessed in public a heady cocktail of formality and informality which somehow maintained her position as Princess of Wales, yet made her accessible to all.

Analysts at that time who detected a certain reserve in Charles's welcome for this success put it down to jealousy. On joint outings he would apologize to the public: "I'm sorry it's me you've got, not my wife." Or: "It's me you've got, I'm afraid. Better ask for your money back." It was an inescapable fact that it was *her* face that appeared on magazine covers wherever they traveled in the world, not his; that on joint outings the cameras pointed only at her; that when flowers were waved in his direction they were destined for Diana. It was initially confusing, for Charles had devoted his whole life to the idea of service and thought that his people should be able to sense it and tacitly, by their attention and applause, thank him for it. Even as late as April 1994 he had still not reconciled himself to the impact Diana's arrival on the scene had had on the revival of interest in royalty and, in an interview with former Labour Cabinet minister Roy Hattersley, repudiated the idea of a "showbiz monarchy." "The media helped create the showbiz idea," he accused. "They invented it, we didn't." But the truth lay somewhere in between, for in the last quarter of the twentieth century the media were very lukewarm about the House of Windsor until Diana came along. Notwithstanding the inner turmoil she created in that great dynastic house, she helped put it back on the map.

Yet Charles could never voice—except to Camilla—his dismay as to how the public could get it so desperately wrong. Surely they didn't fall *that* easily for a pretty face? Surely they could sense that there was no substance to her, that indeed there was something wrong with her?

But the adoring public could not. The only person who knew of Diana's instability was Charles. The only person who could share the burden was Camilla. He took his problems to her at Bolehyde Manor, the house where he had proposed in the kitchen garden and where Camilla had opened the celebration champagne—and was, for a moment, diverted by the good news in Camilla's life.

She had found a new house in the village of Pickwick near Corsham in Wiltshire, called Middlewick House. Built in Cotswold and Bath stone sometime in the eighteenth century, the beautiful manor house, complete with ghost, came with five hundred acres—plenty of room to exercise her horses and to escape the unwelcome, though not yet intrusive, attentions of the press. Middlewick was the quintessential English country house and Camilla lost her heart to it—and there was no disadvantage in its being only fifteen minutes' drive from Highgrove.

The Parker Bowleses sold Bolehyde for around £500,000—no special mention was made of the historic kitchen garden in the estate agents' literature—and unexpectedly found the purchase of Middlewick eased by an inheritance, for on August 16, 1986, Sonia Cubitt died.

The daughter of Alice Keppel took with her to the grave the secret of whether she was King Edward VII's illegitimate daughter or not, and thus whether her granddaughter Camilla was a blood relation of her love, Prince Charles. What she did leave behind, however, was a handsome legacy. Camilla was said to have received over half a million pounds from it. It almost put an end to the rumors among a wider circle that Middlewick House had been paid for by Prince Charles, but few people wanted to let a good story like that go without examining all the possibilities.

Such rumors were of no consequence to the prince, however, who had greater problems on his mind. The bulimia was still there, an increasing embarrassment to Charles as commentators started, at last, to write about how pitifully thin the princess had become. On a trip to Vancouver to open the Expo exhibition, her wasted figure gave cause for excited comment, but the worldwide media went on red alert when she fainted as she reached the California stand. She put her hand on her husband's shoulder and whispered, "Darling, I think I'm going to disappear," and promptly collapsed. She had not eaten for days.

With some justification, Charles was furious. He had a job to do; she was simply providing a distraction that took away from the purpose of the whole trip. But then, his friends argued, Diana had long ago discovered how to upstage the family she had come to hate. Arriving at the State Opening of Parliament as a supernumerary to the queen, whose historic role it is to lead her Lords and Commons into the next parliamentary session, she ordered that her hair be turned up into a chignon. It altered her whole appearance—as she knew it would—and drew all attention away from the queen. Everyone was furious, including her strongest ally, Princess Margaret, who asked her sister: "How could you let her make such a *fool* of you?"

In recent biographies there has been criticism of the prince for neither containing Diana's rages nor investigating their root cause nor seeking a solution to them. His refusal, except under extreme provocation, to be drawn into rows with his wife has been dismissed as uncaring and churlish behavior, whereas his friends argue that Charles simply sought to end what he considered to be irrational rantings by defusing the situation. That, to him, meant walking away and giving his partner time to cool down. No great psychologist, he did not realize he was simply making matters worse by refusing Diana her full say. On more than one occasion, doctors brought in to deal with the difficulties facing Diana and her relationship with Charles offered advice on this, but the prince was dealing with an irrational being and, it must be borne in mind, was only human himself.

Soon after Charles resumed relations with Camilla, he and Diana had traveled to Althorp, her family home, where they stayed in a specially redecorated suite. On their departure it was left, revealed Earl Spencer, in a "somewhat damaged" state—an antique mirror was smashed, so too was a window, and the leg of a priceless eighteenth-century chair shattered. Later, Lord Spencer, showing others around the house, admitted there had been "an almighty row" between the married couple. Yet Diana, when quizzed by the valet, Stephen Barry, vaguely dismissed the devastation. "There was no air in here," she said. "It was an accident."

By 1987 the marriage was over, but no one was yet ready to admit it.

From Charles's point of view, he could remain married to Diana for the rest of his life—it did not matter. He had the one person on whom he could rely, Camilla, safely at his elbow, and with her undiminished support he was now confident he could withstand most of life's buffets.

From Diana's point of view, she had achieved what she had set out to do—become Princess of Wales. She had borne two children in pursuit of her husband's dynastic ambitions. She had become a world icon, a very important person in her own right. She lacked love—whatever love is—but most other things were in place. For a moment it looked as though the bulimia that had dogged her these many years was on hold.

But then the whole thing started to become unglued. On their skiing holiday at Klosters that year, Charles and Diana were accompanied by the newly married Duke and Duchess of York. The duchess had been asked to bring along a couple of extra men: One was Philip Dunne, a merchant banker, son of the lord lieutenant of Herefordshire and godson of Princess Alexandra. One night Diana went to the local disco and spent the evening chatting sociably to Dunne; on another she and Fergie stayed in the chalet and played an idiotic après-ski game, which ended up with the princess lying in the bottom of a large chest of drawers pretending to be asleep. One observer reported that she called out that the first person to kiss her would become a prince; Dunne was the one to step forward.

Dunne has always maintained that their relationship was entirely innocent, and there is little evidence to support a contrary view. But what happened next drove a greater wedge between the Waleses than anything that had gone before.

Dunne invited members of the skiing party back to his parents' house, Gatley Park. Soon it emerged that while Charles had not been there, neither had Dunne's parents. When this appeared in the tabloid press in its original form, only one conclusion could be drawn. The Waleses were having a bumpy patch in their marriage, Diana had found someone to comfort her. An almighty scandal looked ready to blow, until Dunne pointed out—extremely forcefully—that a dozen friends had also been present in the house over that weekend.

But Charles, deep in his own adultery, misread the runes. Certainly he could tell there was an attraction between the younger man and his wife; maybe for a moment he found reason to ascribe his own motives and actions to Diana. Whatever the cause, by the time the marriage of the Duke of Beaufort's son the Marquess of Worcester came around in June 1987, relations between the two were at an all-time low, with mutual suspicion and disregard the order of the day.

At the wedding reception Charles first danced with the woman he had once proposed marriage to—Anna Wallace—then sat down with the woman he had been aching to see, Camilla Parker Bowles. The couple talked to the exclusion of all others for the rest of the night. Diana, infuriated by what she saw, started to dance with Philip Dunne. She danced and she danced, long and hard and frenetically, "pausing only long enough to wipe her forehead with the hem of her gown," one guest reported, until at six the next morning the music stopped. Charles and Camilla had, by this stage, slipped away hours before.

That display, and the publicity surrounding the weekend at Gatley Park, convinced Charles that his wife had been unfaithful to him, and it struck a mortal blow to his *amour propre*. It does not take a liberated man to identify the dual standards employed here by the prince, but he was a man who had grown up bolstered in the belief that as the future king, all things were his for the asking. And that included a faithful wife. If she had been to bed with Dunne, writhing on the dance floor in front of him with this man was simply rubbing his nose in it—and in front of a wide cross-section of the aristocracy, to boot.

Almost certainly this assumption of Diana's infidelity was based on a false premise, but he did not stop to consider that. Gathering Camilla up, he headed for Scotland and Balmoral, arriving on September 22.

There began his longest exile, a quite unprecedented gesture, which no amount of comment in Parliament and the press would do anything to shake him from. He was not to see his wife for the next thirty-seven days, nor did he see his children. No explanation was forthcoming—he seemed not to care what interpretation was put on his actions. He spent long days alone with Camilla, talking his way through the past six disastrous years, reminding her of her pledge that Diana was "a mouse" and that she would be perfect for the job of princess; he reminded her of their broken pledge of abstention, and talked long and hard about the future. He had come to love Tuscany, and saw a future for himself and Camilla there, away from the humiliation and criticism and away from the duty which kept him locked to Diana's side.

Three years later, Charles came close to a nervous breakdown, but it was here, in the purple hills of Balmoral, that the first seeds were sown. Other friends, including Lord and Lady Tryon, came to stay, and they passed the days in a mechanical observance of the Balmoral round—fishing, shooting, stalking, painting—but it was here that Charles started to question, possibly for the first time, what it was all for, and whether it was worth it. Even the warmth of Camilla's love did little to stop his downward spiral into depression.

Meanwhile, back in London, the newspapers were counting the days the couple were apart in bigger and bigger type. Diana's relationship with the merchant banker came under the microscope, and another member of that fateful Klosters ski party, Major David Waterhouse, was forced to spring to his defense. "There has been a lot of talk about the princess and Philip," he said. "It is absurd to say they are having an affair. The allegation is totally untrue."

Whether this reached Charles, as it was designed to do, and whether the prince took any comfort from this reassurance, it was difficult to tell. Certainly there was no early reaction from north of the border, no indication that he intended to return home to his wife and children.

Enter, stage left, the most unlikely character in the whole lexicon of British celebrities, to propose himself as an honest broker in the Waleses' marriage: Jimmy Savile. A disc jockey whose trademark was fat cigars and a line in death-defying banality that makes all but the lion-hearted cringe at its triteness, he had become a TV personality through his can-do TV show for the BBC, *Jim'll Fix It*. This, indeed, was his finest hour—because if he could fix the Waleses' marriage, he would have done the nation a service worthy of the knighthood that was shortly to be his.

Savile suggested to the estranged couple that a way out of their present impasse would be to make a joint appearance in Dyfed in Wales, which had been devastated by flooding. There was a nice symmetry in their coming together again in public on the very soil whose name they both bore. For whatever reason, though probably spurred by Camilla, who saw Charles's credibility ebbing with each day he continued to stay away from his family, both made their way to RAF Northolt for the flight to Swansea.

* * *

The trip was a disaster from the very start. Diana arrived first, in an extremely agitated state, but she was clearly unprepared for the naked hostility Charles showed toward her on his arrival—a hostility he took no trouble to conceal from the numerous members of staff foregathered in preparation for their departure.

Unlike Charles, who had been cushioned from world media attention during his exile, Diana had suffered from the spotlight that was turned on her during those thirty-seven lonely, and increasingly dramatic, days. Her outward appearance had remained calm as she continued her duties under intense pressure. Some of these matters she tried to explain to her husband on the short flight to Wales, but Charles could barely bring himself to listen. As she described how difficult it was to be in the continued glare of publicity caused by his self-imposed exile, he groaned: "Oh God, what *is* the matter." For much of the flight he completely ignored his wife, and the tour, designed to raise the spirits of the unhappy Welsh, did nothing more than draw attention away from their plight and concentrate on the Waleses.

The Times, for example, considered this sighting of the estranged couple of such significance that it devoted part of its front page to report: "The Prince looked concerned as he heard accounts of the deluge; the Princess scowled when she saw photographers, no doubt suspecting that they were there only to record the Waleses' first public appearance together since September 16."

The brief encounter in Carmarthen lasted six hours, during which time their several duties allowed little opportunity for the couple to speak to each other. They flew back to London, and Charles returned to Balmoral. Meanwhile Diana, realizing that nothing lasting had been achieved beyond a fence-mending public-relations job with the people of Wales (despite the observation of one flood victim, Mr. Darrel Reynolds: "I would rather have had £2,000 compensation than a royal visit. There is nothing they can do"), gamely set off for a charity auction at Christie's. She was described by one newspaper, whose reporter was not admitted to the proceedings, as "looking happy and relaxed." But evidently the hoped-for reconciliation was a task too Herculean for even this TV personality with a superabundance of self-confidence.

The pressure on the two participants in this cynically arranged marriage was getting worse. At that stage, friends of Diana and of Charles agree, there was no question but that the marriage was for life. It was a question of both of them buckling down and agreeing on a formula whereby they could live together, but apart. But neither, psychologically, was up to making that accommodation. After the threat of exposure by her well-meaning former flatmate Carolyn Bartholemew, Diana submitted to the ministrations of Dr. Maurice Lipsedge, a specialist in eating disorders at Guy's Hospital. One of his earliest questions, put directly, was how many times Diana had attempted suicide. The princess, startled, answered: "Four or five times."

Lipsedge's dedication ultimately stilled the bulimia, though there were recurrences whenever Diana was forced to return to Highgrove. Indeed, her hatred of the place had continued to grow since the day when Charles finally announced that they were not to move to Belton in Lincolnshire. But while she fought to contain the bulimia, she found she now had the strength to tackle Camilla.

Early in 1989 there was a party to celebrate the fortieth birthday—on February 2—of Camilla's sister, Annabel Elliott, wife of Dorset landowner Simon Elliott, which was held in a house on Ham Common near Richmond. "There was," recorded Andrew Morton, "an unspoken assumption among the forty guests that Diana would not appear. There was a frisson of surprise among the assembled company when she walked in. After dinner, Diana, who was chatting to guests in an upstairs room, noted the absence of her husband and Camilla Parker Bowles. She went downstairs and found her husband, Camilla, and other guests chatting. The princess asked the others to leave because she had something important to say to Camilla."

What Morton failed to report is the manner in which the two rivals squared up to each other. When the room was cleared, Diana marched over to Camilla and bellowed: "Why don't you leave my husband alone?" Mrs. Parker Bowles, unblinking, shrugged her shoulders, and then, as a further verbal blast was fired in her direction, she opened the door for Diana to leave. The princess, losing the initiative, did so. Guests at the party said later that as she turned, Camilla gave the merest hint of a mock-curtsy before returning to her friends, her face registering no emotion whatsoever.

According to Morton, one of the factors that forced Diana into this useless and ultimately self-defeating confrontation was the fact that whenever she was at Highgrove, she routinely pressed the "last number redial" button on the telephone only to find herself connected to Middlewick House, the Parker Bowleses' home. While this may not be inconsistent with the facts, it is presented as though Diana might expect otherwise; but by 1989 it would come as no surprise to the princess to discover that her husband was in daily contact with Camilla.

Charles, portrayed as the churlish, uncaring husband, succumbed to the pressure too. In the autumn of 1990 he was, according to friends, on the verge of a nervous breakdown. Initially it was dismissed as a "midlife crisis," but in private there was concern that he was suffering from clinical depression. "It was the sense of guilt—of having failed his family and himself—with which he found it so difficult to come to terms," wrote his biographer Ross Benson. "It took four months before he was willing to undertake any official engagements, and for some considerable time afterwards his friends continued to worry about his mental health."

This mental ailment developed from a physical one—a terrible fall from his pony while playing polo at Cirencester in the summer of that year. The prince's right arm was broken in two places; indeed, so bad were the breaks that the bone could be seen sticking out of the flesh of his arm at the elbow. The break was a complex one, and though originally left to set itself in the normal way, it had to be rebroken when it was discovered that the break had failed to heal properly. At the second attempt, a metal pin was inserted into the arm, and bone from Charles's hip was grafted on to speed the mend—but it was a drawn-out and painful process. Added to this, it was suggested that, in the initial operation, part of a tendon was caught in the fracture, which then started to heal around it, creating almost permanent pain. The delayed shock from this, it was said, was enough to produce severe depression.

On the prince's exits from these two operations—first from Cirencester General Hospital in July, then from the Queen's Medical Centre in Nottingham in September, he was accompanied by Diana, who on both occasions escorted him back to Highgrove to recuperate. But she did not stay long. As a royal protection policeman, Police Constable Andy Jacques, was later to reveal, she left almost immediately. "It was a complete sham," he said.

Jacques was to play an important part in providing missing pieces to the jigsaw of Charles, Camilla, and Diana, for by now the nation's suspicions were aroused to the nature of the "close friendship," which was the only reference Fleet Street would make to the relationship. It took two years for his eyewitness account to surface, but the police constable's recollection of life at Highgrove in the aftermath of Charles's polo accident was clear and graphic.

"Diana sped off back to London almost as soon as they arrived back at the house," he said. "When she'd gone, Charles sent his detective to collect Camilla Parker Bowles, who lived nearby.

"Later I was patrolling outside the house when I noticed a light on in Princess Diana's private sitting room. There should be no one in there when the princess is not at home.

"The curtains were closed, but through a chink between the drapes, I spied Charles and Camilla dancing cheek-to-cheek. Though the Prince had his arm in a sling, they were smooching to very romantic music. Eventually they disappeared down on to the sofa, out of my sight.

"I moved away, but when I returned 15 minutes later, the light was still on. I saw Camilla emerge from behind the sofa and shake her dress. Then Charles stood up. He looked down and intimated that, because one arm was in a sling, he couldn't readjust his clothes."

Another version of his testimony, published in the United States in *Globe* magazine, described his witnessing "a dishevelled Charles and Camilla stand from behind the sofa, doing up their clothes."

This Peeping-Tom evidence was said to have shocked Diana on its publication, but as usual it was the press's hyperbole that provided the shock element: Diana was all too conscious of the depth and longevity of his husband's relationship with Mrs. Parker Bowles, even if its increasing visibility appalled her. She enjoyed a particular friendship with the Highgrove butler, Paul Burrell, and his wife, Maria, and even though no direct information as to Camilla's comings and goings may have emerged from Diana's conversations with Maria, by a process of osmosis the princess was able to construct a fairly accurate picture of what went on while she was in London.

For during that long summer the prince allowed only one person to nurse him: Camilla. Diana went to Highgrove from time to time, but the joke among staff was that as she drove in one entrance, Camilla was driving out of another. James Whitaker reported: "Camilla was now regarded by their friends as Charles's official hostess in Gloucestershire.

She boasted about the roses she was growing in the Highgrove garden, she threw dinner parties for Charles, and she sunbathed in the grounds in a bikini while Charles pottered in the garden nearby. Set against the standards of most civilised people, this behaviour was outrageous. A neighbour told me: 'It was as if neither cared who saw what was going on. They were, to all intents and purposes, living as man and wife.' "

He flew to Balmoral—and Camilla went too. They took with them Patty Palmer-Tomkinson, whose closeness to Charles had deepened after the 1988 Klosters ski accident which killed the equerry Major Hugh Lindsay and seriously injured her. Diana was not invited—indeed, her by now traditional ritual of taking the princes to school neatly precluded her being there. As September moved into October, he showed no signs of returning from Royal Deeside, or of wishing to see his wife and children, even though the boys were said to be missing him. It was a repeat of the 1987 Scottish exile after Charles supposed his wife had been unfaithful. Then, his very visible exile could be put down to misapplied jealousy and hurt pride. Now, it was because he was suffering a very real depression.

"At this time he underwent a major reappraisal of his life," said a friend of the Parker Bowleses. "In general, he was getting a bad press. He felt tortured by his marriage, and angry at the unqualified adulation his wife attracted wherever she went. Part of this was a selfish jealousy, of course, but mostly he was suffering a tremendously hurt pride: he was doing his damnedest, and nobody really cared. Although he has always had this inner sense of destiny, for the first time in his life he could not see the way forward.

"Wherever he turned it was Diana, Diana, Diana—yet the woman was a nightmare.

"Charles's difficulty then, as now, is his inability to blame himself. But it's hard to avoid the conclusion that he made a mistake not only in his choice of bride—and the choice was his, no one else's—but the method by which he chose her.

"It was an arranged marriage, no doubt of that, but it was poorly done. It was as if once he'd found Camilla again, he didn't give a damn who the hell he married. He knew he *had* to get married—his father was perpetually on at him to do something about it—but Charles didn't care. Anyone might have done."

At Birkhall on the Balmoral estate, a decade after plighting his troth to a teenage ingenue, these nightmares came back to haunt him. No one, not the Palmer-Tomkinsons nor the Parker Bowleses (Andrew made fleeting appearances) seemed able to pull Charles out of his depression. On top of the psychological pressure, he was still in great pain from his polo injury. He donned walking boots and tweeds and spent hour upon hour sketching, painting, shooting, and fishing. He was digging deep into his spiritual resources to try to find some solution to what seemed an insurmountable problem. For even at this stage, there was no question of separation or divorce—all Charles could see ahead was a long, cold, lonely road in a loveless marriage with a woman whose company he could no longer tolerate, even for short periods.

Meanwhile, back in London, Diana was suffering. Charles's solution to her continued rages was to avoid speaking to her; now he was six hundred miles away, they had no need to talk at all, even by telephone, he reasoned. Diana had no idea what he was doing at Birkhall, how many people were with him or who they were, or how long he intended to stay there. Starved of information, she was trying her hardest to put on a brave face, while knowing that he was with Camilla. She paid an official visit to Edinburgh in mid-October, but lacked the nerve to turn up at Balmoral to ask her husband when he was coming home. Having completed her engagements, she simply turned around and came home again.

One Kensington Palace servant vouchsafed at the time that Diana had been "desperate with worry" over Charles. She added: "She's normally one of the most pleasant and easygoing people you could ever imagine working for. But this past week she's been a right cow—you can see this situation is getting under her skin. It's like working in a place where a bomb is about to go off."

Toward the end of October Charles returned briefly for a weekend with his wife and children, but then just as abruptly turned around and flew back to Scotland. It was not until the very end of the month that he finally came south for good, heading for Highgrove and his children. It was no coincidence that Diana was in London on duty when he returned, attending a reception with the president of Italy at an art gallery.

One report of his movements ran thus: "Charles arrived at Highgrove at around 7:00 P.M. on Thursday. He dined alone after working on official papers in his study.

"Around 11:00 P.M. the prince slipped out of the house in a plain Ford estate car. He headed for Camilla's house near Corsham with just one police bodyguard—and did not return until the early hours of Friday morning—while Diana was still in London."

The prince and princess finally met up that night in time for a formal photographic session, the results of which were to be considered, ironically, for the couple's tenth wedding anniversary pictures. But the session, with the newly qualified India Hicks—Lord Mountbatten's granddaughter and a bridesmaid at the royal wedding nearly a decade before—behind the camera, was gloomy and fruitless.

Within days Charles found that Highgrove was proving too suffocating; he had become restless, irritated by both the constant pain and his inability to do much more than sit and read. After three months of aches in his arm, he now had the additional burden of pain in the hip from where bone was grafted for the second operation. After consulting surgeons John Webb and Christopher Colton, who pronounced him fit to travel, he flew on Camilla's recommendation to the south of France, where the Baroness Louise de Waldner had offered the use of her Château le Barroux at Caromb, near Avignon. He took with him a physiotherapist and a detective and forced himself to start painting again, but despite the restorative powers of the sun, the breathtaking landscape, and the regional cherries, peaches, and wine, the mental anguish he was suffering on top of the physical pain did not abate. It was made plain in a haunting photograph which caught the prince, arm in sling, hair disheveled, staring out of a window into the distance. After a week he flew back, in a jet of the Queen's Flight, to Camilla. Diana stayed in London.

And as time went on, Charles sought less and less to conceal his involvement with Camilla, reasoning that it was demeaning to lie to his wife when she was aware of, if not exactly happy about, the situation. In May 1989 Charles and Camilla had celebrated their first decade of continuous relationship by taking a holiday in Turkey.

While Diana carried out official engagements at home, Charles and Camilla set out to enjoy a sun-kissed tour of the great archaeological and historic sights around Ephesus as guests of the millionaire businessman Haldun Simavi. Ostensibly in the country on official business—he met President Kenan Evren and Prime Minister Turgut Ozal in Ankara—this was the couple's most daring public adventure to date, having been flagged by at least one newspaper unaware of Camilla's presence as "a cultural trip to Turkey." Charles felt that the country was sufficiently obscure for the omnipresent royal ratpack not to follow him, out of sheer indifference to the venue; but even so his presence did not go unnoticed. Almost immediately he sparked a security row by refusing to reveal where he was going on day trips, and with good reason.

The *Sunday Mirror* sounded a warning note: "Prince Charles made waves on a sunshine cruise by keeping his blonde companion Camilla Parker Bowles under wraps," gritted the newspaper. "Speculation grew about the mystery beauty in a pink swimsuit who cavorted with him on a millionaire's yacht.

"The playful pair were pictured swimming, sunbathing and water-skiing off Turkey. Everywhere Charles went on his eight-day trip to see archaeological sights, civic leaders asked: 'Where is your wife?' "

The intense interest caused by Charles's visit, not least by a for-once-untrammeled Turkish press, caused the prince to declare: "I will come to Turkey again—this time with my wife." It was a promise he was unable, and unwilling, to keep.

For on his return he found that nothing had changed in his marriage. The imperfections of both partners in this ill-starred marriage served, in the end, to provide evidence to each that the other was to blame for its gradual disintegration. Charles's dedication to Camilla, unswerving over a decade, was sufficient for Diana to think him an unworthy spouse. Despite all the talk of Philip Dunne, and later James Gilbey and Captain James Hewitt, few who were close to her were in any doubt that she had remained physically faithful to her husband.

Charles's complaint was that his wife was an irrational being, that she had understood the ground rules before he proposed to her, yet was unable to live tolerantly within the framework he had laid down for the marriage. "A contract is a contract," he told friends bewilderedly, but Diana refused to see their marriage as a business arrangement. Her critics argued that, stupidly, she believed what she read in the newspapers and magazines and sought to turn their fantasies of a "fairy-tale marriage" into reality.

As she felt her grip slipping on her husband, she made a concerted effort to breathe new life into the failing marriage on a personal and public level. Buttressed by the advice and support of friends outside the Palace, she piled on public appearances and wooed the press with a series of svelte new outfits. The irony did not escape her that while at home she was unwanted and unloved, the moment she set foot outside the portals of Kensington Palace, her personal popularity rating rose ever higher.

She made attempts to win her husband back: "There was enormous pride at stake. Her sense of rejection, by her husband and the royal system, was apparent," recalled her friend of that time, James Gilbey. Under pressure from her own family and from concerned members of the royal family to rejuvenate the marriage, she agreed that another baby—Charles had always wanted a girl—might help pave the way forward. But that was, of all solutions, the most improbable; for the couple had ceased to enjoy conjugal relations in the summer of 1986, just five years after they had married, on their return from a Balearic holiday with King Juan Carlos of Spain. Charles had quit the holiday two days early to fly to Balmoral, where his beloved Camilla was waiting. From now on they would have separate bedrooms.

In public, Diana held the line. At a reception for journalists in Madrid in 1987, she made an attempt to paper over the cracks: "When we first got married we were everybody's idea of the world's most perfect couple; now they are saying we are leading separate lives. The next thing is I'll start reading that I've got a black lover," she joked, with gallows humor.

She attempted an explanation of why people misunderstood their separate lives. "It's very simple. My husband and I get around two thousand invitations every six months. We can't do them all, but if we split them up, with him doing some and me doing others, we can fulfill twice as many." As she spoke, she was acutely aware that Charles would be flying off to Bologna to collect an award for his children's book, *The Old Man of Lochnagar*, which would be followed by a painting tour of Tuscany. He would stay in Florence and Padua; his companion would be Camilla.

It was becoming increasingly obvious that despite Diana's gallant defense of their marriage, the couple were spending less and less of their free time together. The *Daily Mirror*'s James Whitaker calculated that Charles had, in recent months, taken off on seven apparently partnerless jaunts, and the *News of the World* kept a score sheet of how often the couple met. The newspaper's reckoning was that in a ninety-day period the royal couple spent thirty-five apart, and while royal duties were responsible for some of the absences, Charles actually chose to be away from his wife for twenty-six nights. The following April Charles was back in Italy, again with Camilla by his side. He confessed to Major Ron Ferguson: "I just want to be with her all the time."

Diana's frustration and anger now became an awesome thing. According to one version: "When he walked out of a room, she would follow him screaming hysterically. She would slam any handy door, then open it and slam it again. She would walk the length of a bookshelf, punching the books and shouting at the top of her voice, 'No, Charles, no, no, I won't. Charles, no, no!,' and members of staff remarked that virtually any decision Charles would make she would seek to countermand. "There was hysteria and tears," recalled one. "Almost everything he wanted to do at that stage, she didn't want to do. She actually seemed to *enjoy* rowing."

Charles's reaction was, simply, to spend less time with his wife. Prince William was at school at Wetherby's, a £785-a-term pre–prep school a short drive from Kensington Palace in Notting Hill, which required his and his mother's presence in London all week during term time: Diana would habitually deliver and collect William, giving press photographers an almost daily photo opportunity as she varied her outfits. During this period she appeared a great deal in British newspapers, establishing herself in the national consciousness as a devoted mother, winning the mothers' race at one school sports day while Charles chose to deliberately come last. His ploy—to show that he did not have to compete with his wife in public—backfired badly when newspapers ran pictures of the two races, captioning Diana's "The Winner" and Charles's "The Loser."

The prince increasingly began to base himself at Highgrove, but even when Diana came down at weekends he would rarely see her. Verbal communication had all but broken down and Charles, always one to avoid demeaning himself by an outright confrontation, would devote his Saturdays to polo or hunting. Diana would return with the princes to London on Sundays, having barely spoken to her husband—"He couldn't bear to sit with Diana anymore," said one member of staff—

and as Diana left, Charles would go to see Camilla, whose husband also had to return to London on duty.

But Charles's sanguine behavior, his unstated attempt to establish in his marriage what the French would call an *arrangement,* all served to drive Diana into further paroxysms of rage. In the years from 1987 to 1990 these rages, according to those who witnessed them, were frightening: "Her face turned bright, bright red."

According to Andrew Morton, one particularly ferocious exchange ended with Diana telling her husband that unless he altered his attitude toward her and acknowledged her virtues, she would have to "reconsider her position." With this, she ran upstairs in tears to the bathroom; while she regained her composure, Prince William pushed a handful of paper tissues under the bathroom door. "I hate to see you sad," he said.

She learned to hit back where it hurt. In May 1988 Charles was on another visit to Italy; Camilla was said by friends to be accompanying him. On his way to Paris he was informed that Prince Harry, then not quite four, had been taken into the hospital for an emergency hernia operation. He immediately offered to fly home, but was told it would not be necessary. It did not take him long to learn that Diana had refused to go home after the operation at the Great Ormond Street Hospital, and had instead spent the night curled up in a chair watching over her little boy. The following day's headlines labeled her a saint: Charles was furious. She made a speech on AIDS on the day he made one on education: She stole the headlines again. She had mastered the art of upstaging him, and she began to enjoy it. On a trip to Australia they paid a visit to a music college where Charles was persuaded to play the cello, an instrument which was part of his history but which, in truth, he had barely mastered all those years ago. He made some faltering passes at its strings, but as he did so, Diana walked across the room, sat down at a piano, and struck up the opening theme of a Rachmaninov piano concerto. All eyes—and cameras—swung round to witness this great event, and Charles's photo opportunity was quickly and brutally brought to a close.

Inevitably, the atmosphere of mutual suspicion increased between man and wife, with Charles constantly complaining to Camilla that Diana's was a "rowdy act"—lots of noise and not much substance. One of Diana's closest friends complained: "It's time he started seeing her as an asset, not as a threat, and accepted her as an equal partner. At the moment her position within the organization is a very lonely one."

This perceived inequality was a fact that evaded Charles, enlightened freethinker though he claimed to be. With the support of Camilla, now ferociously anti-Diana, he now viewed his wife as nothing more than a royal aberration, a low-class music-hall turn by comparison with his own intellectually superior stage act. By virtue of the splendid isolation he had lived in most of his life, he failed to recognize that his wife had forged a powerful bond between herself and the nation, and had done so without his help.

And yet his own attempts at popularity could be staggering in their banality. As he made a self-conscious return to public life after breaking his arm, he proposed that he should make a statement regarding the speculation which had attended his injury and his subsequent state of mind. According to Diana's friends, he ordered that a false arm with a hook on the end should be found, so he could appear like Captain Hook while delivering his statement. One was found, then "lost" on Diana's instructions, in order to preserve the prince's dignity.

With the battle between them now as disconcertingly visible as his broken bones a year before, Charles wilted before his steely wife, and Diana was able to take the upper hand from time to time. When Prince William was hit on the head with a golf club by a fellow pupil at Ludgrove, his prep school, Charles was in Gloucestershire with Camilla while Diana was in London. The royal couple hurriedly arranged to meet at the Royal Berkshire Hospital in Reading, but it was Diana who took control as Charles dithered about sending his son on to the Nottingham hospital where his arm had been operated on the previous year; the consultants recommended the Great Ormond Street Hospital in London. "You heard what was said," she barked at her husband. "Fix it!"

The day ended with another propaganda coup for Diana, for while William underwent surgery, Charles left Diana at the hospital to fulfill a long-standing engagement at the Royal Opera House. The headlines next morning trumpeted: "What sort of Dad are you?"

And yet Charles had learned how to hurt back. Their rows were no longer conducted behind closed doors, and all personnel in the prince's and princess's offices were witness to the venomous attacks they would launch on each other. According to people who worked for the Waleses, Charles now responded in kind to Diana's onslaughts. One Kensington Palace employee reported that he would spit at Diana: "You stupid woman," or "You silly young girl," over and over again. He added: "It was awful. I felt so sorry for Diana. But it was obvious that the two hated each other and I knew they were bound to separate—I could tell by the way they talked to each other."

Another employee witnessed arguments that would culminate with Diana telling Charles to "shut up," to which he would reply: "I can't stand living with you." The employee added: "He told her he didn't like the way the children were being brought up—that she was far too casual with them and didn't respect their positions in life. And he said that he thought her encouragement of the boys to go go-karting all the time was stupid."

But at the root of all these arguments lay the stumbling-block of Camilla Parker Bowles. In April 1991 Diana was forced to take the two young princes skiing by herself; Charles had cried off at the last moment and was heavily criticized for having done so. Buckingham Palace officials and members of his household agreed that a public split of this nature would cause adverse press comment, and so it proved, but Charles was in no mood to compromise, or spend leisure time with his wife. The excuse that was offered up to the public was that Charles had to go to Scotland that weekend, and had some important speeches to write.

Indeed, Charles did go to Scotland—where Camilla was already waiting for him; Diana knew, and secretly cursed the fact, that the world's royal press photographers were all on the slopes photographing her while not a single one was on the River Dee, where they would find an altogether more intriguing shot.

From having a walk-on part in Diana's life, Camilla Parker Bowles was now moving center stage and beginning to soak up the limelight. Diana professed to be deeply wounded by her husband's suggestion that Camilla attend the memorial service for Leonora Knatchbull at St. James's Palace. The six-year-old daughter of Lord and Lady Romsey had battled bravely against cancer and lost. The nation took the little girl to its heart when, in June, she had been seen on the balcony of Buckingham Palace watching the annual Trooping the Colour ceremony.

Though there was delight in her eyes, she was soon to succumb to the fatal illness; in December, a family memorial service was held in her name. As she left the service, Diana, who had held Leonora close on the palace balcony, was photographed in tears—but they were tears of rage.

"Diana was upset that Camilla Parker Bowles, who had only known the Romseys for a short time, was also present at such an intimate family service," wrote her apologist Andrew Morton, though in truth Lord Romsey's home, Broadlands, had been a welcome retreat for the couple.

"It was a point she made vigorously to her husband as they travelled back to Kensington Palace in their chauffeur-driven limousine. When they arrived at Kensington Palace the princess felt so distressed that she ignored the staff Christmas party, which was then in full swing, and went to her sitting-room to recover her composure. Diplomatically, Peter Westmacott, the Waleses' deputy private secretary, sent her avuncular detective Ken Wharfe to help calm her."

The real significance of this event was that, among a broader group of friends and family, Charles was "going public" with his relationship. That may have been in defensive response to his wife's hysteria, as a reaction against her much-vaunted relationship with James Hewitt, or simply because he believed that with more space in his ailing marriage, nobody would much mind. Diana's outburst came as a huge surprise. After all, she knew about the trips to Italy and Turkey, she knew about Camilla's visits to Balmoral and Sandringham, and she knew that on their much-hyped "family" summer holiday aboard Greek tycoon John Latsis's yacht, Charles had spent hours on the telephone to Camilla. In fact, on that particularly barren piece of failed public relations, Diana had insisted on having her own quarters, had eaten with the children, and had convinced herself that Charles had exchanged more words with his mistress than with her.

Friends also noted Diana's "morbid game" at social events where all three were unavoidably present of eyeing Camilla, then avoiding her, or watching to see the eye contact between Charles and Camilla. In the days before the Salisbury Cathedral spire-appeal concert, Diana learned that her rival would also be present, and was furious. But by the time all three attended she was able to watch the eye contact with something approaching amusement.

Sometimes Diana's frustration at this ménage-à-trois reached breaking point. Pedestrians around Marble Arch witnessed an extraordinary scene one night as the royal couple passed by in their official car; a clearly vicious exchange of words culminated with Diana trying to force open the door of the moving car to throw herself out. One witness, a road sweeper, recalled that the princess was hysterical and crying. He said, "She was clearly saying something like 'I've had enough of this' and then I watched as a man in front, who I presumed was a detective, held her back."

But by this time, Charles's relationship with Camilla Parker Bowles stretched back in an unbroken line for well over a decade. The queen mother knew, and approved, of the relationship, encouraging the couple to stay at Birkhall, her house on the Balmoral estate; so too did the queen. The House of Windsor's view, from the other side of the ramparts, is remarkably different from the one enjoyed by the public; their raison d'être is to strengthen the dynasty, not weaken it—and as soon as Diana showed signs of recalcitrance, they closed ranks around their favorite son.

"There is one rule for the royals, another for the rest of us," observed one of Diana's friends. "Unfortunately they don't see her as royal—they see her as one of the rest." No matter that she was wife and mother of future kings—her role ended after the birth of her second son, and if she refused to be compliant over the matter of Charles's great love, then, argued senior courtiers, she must be sidelined.

The queen, agreed observers, was sympathetic to Diana's isolation, but only up to a point. Powerful Buckingham Palace machinery existed to preserve the monarchy at the top of Britain's totem pole, and she would do nothing to interfere with its workings. Camilla understood what was required of royal women—silence, compliance, devotion— and earned the respect of all for her discretion.

The same could never be said about the Princess of Wales.

Chapter 7

CAMILLA:
HER TRUE STORY

FROM THE VERY BEGINNING OF 1992, THERE WAS A WHIFF OF IMPENDING DISAS-
ter in the air. Charles rode out with the Meynell Hunt only to be
faced by a crowd of angry hunt saboteurs, to whom he bellowed with
unusual fury: "Shut up!"—possibly because he felt that one among
these subversives might spot the figure of Mrs. Parker Bowles on horseback.

The prince and princess were committed to a tour of India—"yet
another foreign minefield for the Waleses to traverse," observed the seasoned royal watcher James Whitaker—and Charles started out as he
meant to go along. Although it was Diana who had "adopted" Mother
Teresa of Calcutta, the prince insisted to his private office that when a
bouquet of flowers was sent to her in Rome, where she was recovering
from a heart condition, it should bear his name alone.

Bidding farewell to Camilla, Charles set out on what was to be the
first of two disastrous tours with Diana, which would signal more
clearly than anything else the end of their marriage. Charles ducked his
promise to the Indian nation, made several years before, that one day he
would bring his wife back to stand in front of the Taj Mahal, the exquis-

ite edifice built by the seventeenth-century emperor Shah Jehan. Diana alone posed for pictures in front of its ornate facade, while Charles was in Delhi unromantically addressing a group of business leaders—and once again misunderstanding the need of the world's media to see a couple reunited in the shadow of one of the world's most romantic buildings.

The media took Charles's absence from his wife's side, a symbolic if historically unimportant picture opportunity, as a snub to Diana—the loss of a lasting image for the tour. "Instead," wrote Whitaker, "the image that is retained is of the Prince of Wales looking a complete idiot."

One the eve of St. Valentine's Day Charles played polo at Jaipur. At the end of the match, he stood in line with his teammates to receive a trophy from his wife. The world's media were waiting for the couple to exchange kisses—as once they had done habitually in such circumstances—simply because they all, to a man, did not want to see an end to the fairy-tale marriage. Would they kiss, or wouldn't they?

"The answer was not slow in coming as I watched one of the cruellest, most public put-downs of any man by his wife, executed in front of a hundred professional cameramen and 5,000 laughing Indians. With triumph in her eyes, Diana waited until her husband's lips were almost on hers, then she turned her head away. Not so fast that Charles would be able to pull back—no, it was much more calculating than that. Instead, she moved her head to the left, slowly.

"Charles, who knew the world would see what happened next—television was there too—politely and gallantly tried to follow Diana's turning head. He chased it all the way round until he could reach no further without falling over. He ended up kissing Diana half in mid-air, half on her gold earring." Seeing the results in the next day's newspapers, Charles was overcome with humiliation and rage: Once again, Diana had upstaged him. But it would be the last time, he told Camilla on his return home.

In March Diana took the children to Lech in Austria for their traditional spring skiing week. But unlike the previous year, when Charles stayed in Scotland with Camilla, the prince warned that he would be flying in at the weekend from Milan, where he (and secretly, Camilla) had spent the week. William and Harry were to be paraded outside the

A summer honeymoon . . . but in Charles's wallet were pictures of Camilla, and that night at dinner he wore Camilla's cufflinks. (*Mirror Syndication International*)

Lull before the storm—Charles and Diana ride out the end of the honeymoon at Balmoral, but already his thoughts are turning back to Camilla. Summer 1981 (*Camera Press/Bryn Colton*)

Britain's first family turn out for a photo call for Prince Harry's first day at school, September 1987. But the marriage was already dead and the portrait of togetherness a sham. (*Syndication International*)

How they played it for the cameras: Fairy-tale princess and rugged prince embrace at Smith's Lawn after another successful polo match. (*Rex Features*)

Turkish delight: Charles, Camilla, and Nicholas Soames soak up the Aegean sun, May 1989. (*Rex Features*)

The only woman in his life to pass the "Balmoral Test"—Camilla and Charles slip away for an afternoon alone in the heather. Autumn 1992 (*Nunn Syndication*)

Another love—Andrew Parker Bowles and his former flame, Princess Anne, at Royal Ascot (*Rex Features*)

The Togetherness Team—Charles and Diana at the end of their tether in 1991 and 1992 (*Camera Press*)

The world's most adored princess finds a new role in life: Diana in Zimbabwe, 1993. But soon her new role as a traveling ambassador was to be dropped. (*Popperfoto*)

Living legend meets one of the wonders of the world—meanwhile her husband is catching a tan with his mistress. Diana at the Pyramids, May 1992 (*Mirror Syndication International*)

The show must go on—a solo Diana at the premiere of *Accidental Hero*, April 1993
(*Nunn Syndication*)

The rehabilitation process begins—Charles and sons in Klosters attempt to present a rounded family portrait. (*Syndication International*)

Arlberg Hotel to await their father's arrival, along with the assembled cameras of the world's paparazzi. Diana, who had been hogging the cameras for the past few days, was to stay out of sight.

It was organized, it was efficient, and it got on the front pages. It was the start of a "No More Mr. Nice Guy" routine for Charles. Next morning he rammed the point home by organizing more happy-family shots with his sons, and gradually, following the public-relations disaster in Jaipur the month before, seasoned hands could detect that some radical thinking had been going on in Charles's camp—for the first time in his life, he was coming out on the PR offensive.

Indeed, it was this modest start, and its relative success, which gave Charles and his protector and private secretary, Commander Richard Aylard, a clue to the way forward which was, in due course, to turn into Charles's so-called "charm offensive" to win back the hearts and minds of the British nation ahead of the twenty-fifth anniversay of his investiture as Prince of Wales. But a return to popularity was not that easily won, as Charles discovered when the news came through that Diana's father, Earl Spencer, had died in the hospital.

The royal couple flew out of Austria on a BAe 146 of the Queen's Flight next morning. The cameras were waiting for the grieving Diana on the tarmac at RAF Northolt. Whatever good Charles had achieved in Lech was suddenly shattered, however, as he stood chatting at the foot of the stairs with Commander Aylard. Suddenly, at the top of the stairs appeared a gaunt-faced Diana struggling with a heavy bag. In this hour of grief, the freeze-frame photographs of that moment seemed to say, no one could be bothered to help the world's most famous woman with her luggage. In the snakes-and-ladders game of royal one-upmanship, Charles had just landed on a snake.

The couple headed for Kensington Palace, where Diana was left with the boys. Charles headed west for Highgrove and Camilla. He told her of the massive row that had taken place in Lech while the couple had been waiting for transport arrangements to be finalized, that he had naturally wanted to fly back with Diana, but that she had wanted to come home alone. "The stand-off lasted several hours before his private secretary called the Queen at Windsor, explained the situation and requested her to intercede," reported Nigel Dempster. "Only then did Diana agree to travel home with her husband." It was a further humiliation for the prince, who—despite being forty-three years old—had to rely on his mother to settle a domestic squabble, albeit of major proportions.

The relationship had reached the breaking point, Charles and Camilla agreed. All that remained was to devise a method of unraveling the marriage with tact and decorum. Clearly the future of the boys had to be taken into account—as well as what to do with Diana, the woman Camilla had dubbed, not so long ago, The Mouse.

Warmed by the succor and comfort from Camilla, Charles prepared himself for Earl Spencer's funeral. A Wessex helicopter of the Queen's Flight was sent down to Gloucestershire to pick him up and take him straight to Northamptonshire. Diana, in disgrace for having embroiled the queen in her travel arrangements back from Lech, was left to make her own way to the family seat. Charles insisted that there should not be a joint wreath from them, but separate ones: Buckingham Palace officials endured a sticky few minutes trying to explain that one away.

Charles briefly returned to Althorp and, with a troubled look in his eye, caught the attention of the new earl, Diana's brother Charles. Upset at his father's death—the two men were estranged at the time and the younger man had yearned for a reconciliation—Diana's brother had some difficulty in focusing on what the prince was saying to him. "He did not seem to appreciate how I felt at my loss," he said later. "We had just buried my father and he kept telling me how lucky I was to have inherited so young!"

"I wish *I* had inherited so young," Prince Charles had said. "My parents don't trust me with anything."

If this was a low point in old Lord Spencer's *envoi*, it was not the only one. An apparent reconciliation in church between Diana and her stepmother, "Acid" Raine Spencer, left Raine's personal assistant, Sue Ingram, decidedly underwhelmed. "The graveside note about missing her 'Darling Daddy' just did not make sense. She hardly ever saw him. She hadn't been to Althorp since her brother's wedding in 1989 and she made very little effort to see him in London," she dryly observed. Indeed, others remember a mournful Spencer arriving at Kensington Palace to see his daughter, only to be told she was too busy. On one occasion, they recall, he was turned away; on another he was allowed in to play with his grandsons but did not get to see his daughter.

Charles helicoptered away from this dismal interment before the proceedings were over, claiming a prior engagement; before long he was in Gloucestershire reporting back to Mrs. Parker Bowles. Once again Diana was left to find her way home; even her father's death failed to forge a truce between her and Charles.

The Princess of Wales, in not a happy state of mind, paused in her return only to agree to having her stepmother evicted from the house and her luggage rifled. At least Charles had the decency to send Raine a five-page handwritten letter offering his condolences.

A month later Charles was holidaying in Turkey without Diana, who had undertaken a solo engagement in Egypt. In Cairo, she let slip her vision of the future in a strange, rather spooky, set of asides made at a dinner hosted by Britain's ambassador to Egypt, Christopher Long. In answer to a question, and speaking just as a lull occurred in the conversation, she said: "I still see myself as Lady Diana Spencer."

One of the guests, Mohamed Salmawy, a playwright and former Ministry of Culture official, pointed out that she had been Princess of Wales for more than a decade. "What about when your husband is crowned?" he asked.

"Oh," said the princess, toying with her coffee cup, "I think I will still be Lady Di." This effectively stopped all conversation in its tracks—for all were aware of the implications of what Diana was saying, even though the momentous announcement of the end of her marriage was still seven months away. But then, she knew where her husband and Camilla Parker Bowles were while she made this official trip, and she was blind with rage.

Older and wiser after his untimely discovery in that country in 1989, Charles, in Turkey, gave floundering pressmen no opportunity to catch him with Mrs. Parker Bowles, though later a photograph did emerge of the couple, complete with a grinning Andrew Parker Bowles, enjoying a picnic out of the back of a Range Rover. Yet the trip was not without incident, since aircraft of the Queen's Flight were used to carry Charles and Diana back individually from their separate, but simultaneous, trips. One newspaper reported that Diana's jet would not stop to pick up Charles, even though it flew directly over Ankara: Buckingham Palace officials said the twenty-seater jet was "too full" to carry Charles as well as his wife, and the plane was forced to make a return journey the following day to pick up the prince. This only fueled speculation that Charles had, indeed, managed to take Camilla on holiday with him once again and was not prepared to share the plane back to Britain with his wife.

On their return to London, Charles and Diana set out together to Seville for the Expo World Fair, their marital ship heading surely and swiftly for the rocks, for within days the royal couple's reputation, and their eleven-year marriage, was to be irreparably holed below the water-line.

In retrospect, the Princess of Wales deeply regrets the publication of Andrew Morton's *Diana: Her True Story*. As the polemicist and popular historian Paul Johnson observed in his book *Wake Up, Britain!*: "Morton's book was the most grievous blow inflicted on the British monarchy since Edward VIII's abdication. It is important to grasp that the damage was essentially self-inflicted."

Indeed it was: Through information parceled out to various friends who relayed it onward to Morton, Diana was able to relieve herself of the massive burden she had carried since first encountering Charles as an adult on that fateful hay bale in Sussex. The perpetual shadow of Camilla Parker Bowles; the emotional helter-skelter that drew her onward toward bulimia; the ever-increasing demands by press and public who had made her a goddess and now wanted to own her; the pressures of parenting children in a natural way, in contravention to her husband's atavistic instincts; the bullshit brigade who make up Buckingham Palace's inner guard and made her life hell; and the sheer bloody loneliness of it all—all came tumbling out in a jumble of confused and sometimes contradictory complaints which, in print, constituted the angriest, saddest, and most damaging wound ever inflicted on the House of Windsor. For a woman who was avowedly pro-royal and devoted to the idea of monarchy, to sanction the dissemination of so much ammunition against the very establishment she sought to uphold was an ill-considered, vain, and utterly stupid act.

If there was one virtue to be found in it all, it was that ordinary people were at last given a glimpse behind the heavy veil that camouflages the royal house—something, given the Civil List monies which they contribute toward the royal upkeep, they may feel themselves entitled to.

Diana: Her True Story was perforce an incomplete portrait, since it dwelt much on her husband's relationship with Camilla Parker Bowles, and rather less on Diana's own questionable relationships with the car salesman James Gilbey and the soon-to-be-redundant army officer James Hewitt.

Her grievances were legitimate enough, but the means by which Diana aired them effectively wrecked all the work she had done over the past eleven years in adding luster to an outmoded, stuffy, and self-obsessed institution and turning world attention away from more mundane matters and back toward the antique delights of British monarchy.

Ironically, Diana's star shone for roughly the same period as that of Mrs. Margaret Thatcher. In the eyes of the world, these two women exemplified what was best about Britain: glamour, compassion, magic on the one hand; verve, courage, steadfast resolve on the other. Neither picture was an exact representation of the woman in question, but these images did serve to bolster Britain's standing around the world, and gave the nation cause to pat itself on the back for being so clever as to be British.

In the end the Thatcher dream—wealth at pernicious cost—and the Diana dream—flawless caring beauty—both turned sour, and for the same reason. Each lost control of her destiny by succumbing to *folie de grandeur*. All the time Diana remained in private conflict with her erring husband, she had the moral advantage: He had cheated on her all his married life, but she had never been unfaithful. But when she believed that the nation would back her against him, she made a grave miscalculation. Her friends had persuaded her that she was more popular than Charles—and after all, the opinion polls said so, in spades—and predicted that she would win the battle, whatever the battle was, once the whole thing came out in the open. It was ineffable nonsense.

For Diana's objectives, beyond venting publicly a justifiable anger at Charles's self-contained life—a life that effectively excluded her—were woolly. While her instincts had never let her down in all her years as Princess of Wales—she embraced AIDS victims and took the nation's sympathy along with her; she could spot a wheelchair-bound pensioner at forty feet and in greeting them make their day—her decision to sanction a book that exposed her private life merely served to demonstrate an inability to sustain a line of thought through to its logical conclusion.

Diana: Her True Story did more than punish her husband for his transgressions. It brought the British royal family to its knees.

Each royal biographer has recourse to Walter Bagehot's well-worn decree: "We must not let in daylight upon magic." Nowhere can it be employed to greater effect than here; for Charles's love for Camilla Parker Bowles—or, perhaps more accurately, the way that it was divulged in Morton's book—doused overnight the nation's love for royalty. Suddenly people felt silly for believing in an institution so palpably misleading and corrupt; they eloquently wreaked their revenge in the subsequent opinion polls.

Those who know Diana claim that this was not her intention; she simply wished to expose the humbug surrounding her marriage, assert her equality within that marriage, and shrug off the growing accusations of her unacceptable behavior. But with *Diana: Her True Story* the whole house of cards collapsed around her, and in the end it is she who must take the blame for the House of Windsor's savage loss of credibility.

The kindest interpretation to be put on it is that she did not know what she was doing. No intellectual, Diana lacked the solid backing of the great and good who surround her husband and mother-in-law. Her friends were to be found exclusively among the upper-class underachievers of this world: the wife of a man who ran a disco; a used-car salesman; an army officer who failed his promotion exams; and an immigrant restaurateur. However marvelous as human beings these people might have been, they lacked the education and the historical vision to be able to construct an attack on a thousand-year-old institution which did not permanently disable it. Largely ill-equipped in their own lives, their succor and advice were worthless, and ruinous.

On June 7 the first extracts of Morton's book were serialized in *The Sunday Times*. The world's press camped on Camilla Parker Bowles's doorstep as the extent of Charles's relationship with her was revealed. There was a world of difference between veiled hints of a "confidante" and the raw facts of adultery with which the public was now being entertained. But those hoping for a sight of the woman now officially branded the prince's mistress were out of luck. Two nights before, she had decamped with her sister, Annabel Elliott, her bags in the back of her sister's car. Breathlessly, the tabloid press reported that she had "vanished."

One added:

WHEN ASKED ABOUT ANDREW MORTON'S BOOK SHORTLY BEFORE SHE VANISHED, CAMILLA SAID: "I HAVEN'T READ IT, BUT I WILL WITH INTEREST WHEN THE TIME COMES."

THE BOOK CLAIMS THAT CAMILLA SPENDS DAYS AND NIGHTS AT HIGHGROVE WHENEVER CHARLES IS THERE. SHE HOSTS DINNERS AND LUNCHES FOR HIM, SITS BESIDE HIM AT THE TABLE, ORGANISES HIS PERSONAL LIFE, CHECKS THE MENUS AND THE GUEST LISTS—AND EVEN ORGANISES THE STAFF KITCHEN AND CHEFS.

FORMER ROYAL BODYGUARD ANDREW JACQUES SAID: "CAMILLA STEPS RIGHT INTO DI'S SHOES. CHARLES IS CLOSER TO HER THAN ANYONE ELSE IN THE WORLD AND SHE IS THE ONLY PERSON WHO IS ALLOWED INTO HIS PRECIOUS WALLED GARDEN."

Brigadier Parker Bowles was sought out at his Kensington house and the facts, such as were known, were put to him. "It's fiction, fiction. I've nothing to say" was his measured response. But if he had nothing to say, plenty of others did. Even the Archbishop of Canterbury felt obliged to offer his opinion: "The current speculation about intimate personal matters has exceeded the boundaries which should be observed in a society claiming to respect basic human values."

Yet what emerged in those early days of revelation was only a partial picture, for Morton's book, based on his briefings from the princess's friends, skirted neatly around a pivotal question: *Why, since Diana knew from the very first of Charles's all-consuming love for Camilla Parker Bowles, did she ever accept his hand in marriage?*

That question has never satisfactorily been answered. But at the time, so many thunderbolts were crashing down upon the House of Wales that there was no time for cool analysis. All hell had broken loose; the public uproar was unprecedented.

In private, in the royal corridors from Windsor to Balmoral, from Sandringham to Buckingham Palace, the atmosphere was grim. From time to time, servants had sold their stories to newspapers and magazines for large sums of money—they were considered to be lower than scum. It was unthinkable that a princess would give away family secrets and jeopardize the entire royal family. Strangely, it was the anger among the servants and retainers that made itself felt most. The courtiers and members of the royal family, too stunned by the magnitude of what had occurred, and the long-term implications of it, said little.

But there could be only one person to blame—Diana. Her protesta-tions of innocence cut no ice, and very soon her early feelings of tri-umph at having redressed the balance, as she saw it, turned to alarm and panic as she realized just how grave the effect of her revenge had been—not on her husband but on the whole royal family and its loyal staff. Suddenly, within the royal compound, she was friendless.

The same could not be said of Camilla. Bravely—some would say foolhardily—she ran the gauntlet of public reaction on the very day the serialization of Morton's book commenced. She arrived at Windsor Great Park for the Queen's Cup Polo Tournament and was greeted with a warm and friendly smile by the sovereign. Later the two women chat-ted over tea and cucumber sandwiches. If the denizens of the royal en-closure were staggered at her sudden appearance, they were even more staggered by what she wore—a gray suit in Prince of Wales check. "No one knew whether this was a deliberate statement, or whether it was the only clean thing in her wardrobe"—a reference to Camilla's lighthearted attitude toward her personal turnout.

It was clear to observers by this stage that Diana was not entirely in control of her actions. That week most newspapers carried pictures of the princess making an off-duty visit to the home of her friend Carolyn Bartholemew, in apparent support and approval of Mrs. Bartholemew's assistance of the damaging book. Tipped off by a well-spoken woman who called five newspapers half an hour before Diana arrived at the house in West London, cameramen were waiting for her when she ar-rived.

Mrs. Bartholemew, who, as Carolyn Pride, had been a flatmate of Diana's in the Colherne Court days, said she had "no idea" how the press had learned of the visit. But whoever made the call, behind them was Diana at her Machiavellian best—"Never before had the world's media been manipulated in such a way" said *The Sunday Times*—though it was difficult to see her purpose. Yes, she wanted to show soli-darity with her old friend, but by now she needed to put as much distance between *Diana: Her True Story* and herself as she could.

Reacting, as always, like a supertanker desperately trying to get into reverse, the royal machine took an unconscionable time to decide what to do. As is usual in such cases, courtiers opted for doing nothing in haste—just carry on as normal, was their advice. Five days later a guilt-stricken Diana, faced with the enormity of what she had done in sanctioning the Andrew Morton book—she had not seen the finished text before publication—was on Merseyside visiting a hospice at Southport.

As she arrived, she noticed a group of well-wishers had unfurled a banner that said: "Diana, we love you." The princess shook hands with people in the crowd, then suddenly covered her face with her hands and wept. An eyewitness, Mr. Bob Bird, said: "She was sobbing. She had her hands in her face and was weeping. Her mascara was all over the place. She looked terribly upset." A detective told another onlooker: "It's all been too much for her."

The princess was hastily ushered into an official car and driven to RAF Woodvale, where in the bar of the aero club she asked for a glass of water and to be left alone. The area was cleared and Diana sat with her head in her hands for twenty minutes while her sister, Lady Sarah McCorquodale, doubling as her lady-in-waiting, comforted her. She arrived at her next official destination several minutes late, a police officer explaining that a car in the royal fleet had suffered a "mechanical fault."

The standard "do-nothing" policy, once in place, was not about to be altered. And so it was that, days after delivering this mortal blow, its perpetrator—Diana, Princess of Wales—rode down the course at Royal Ascot along with the rest of the House of Windsor, to the cheers of tens of thousands, just as if nothing had happened.

In preparation for this major, televised event Charles and Diana appeared at the more low-key ceremony of the Order of the Garter at St. George's Chapel, Windsor. Afterward Charles decorously helped Diana by the arm into an open carriage, but the couple did not exchange a glance on the five-minute ride back to the castle. The princess was said to be in emotional turmoil and spending many hours in the company of a personal counselor, Stephen Twigg, who had been treating her for three and a half years.

Charles and Diana appeared together at Royal Ascot simply because no one knew what else to do; they left together, to the confusion of racegoers who the Sunday before had learned even more lurid facts about the royal marriage split. The only open animosity descried by anybody was when Diana walked into the royal box overlooking the course, having just descended from her open carriage, to be brutally snubbed by Prince Philip, the Royal Family plc's chief executive. Underneath the outward harmony, there was tremendous rage at what she had done.

Charles, during this crisis, had spent much time on the telephone at Highgrove discussing with Camilla what was to happen next. Her house was under siege from the press, and she learned then what Diana had discovered over a decade before: that it is permissible, in the mother of all democracies, to be put under house arrest by the Fourth Estate.

Suddenly, she became accustomed to what Diana had been living this past decade. In addition, she was deluged with hate mail. One tabloid newspaper reported:

CAMILLA . . . IS DISTRAUGHT AT THE HUNDREDS OF LETTERS ARRIVING AT HER HOME.

A CLOSE FRIEND SAID: "THE LETTERS ARE ALL BLAMING HER FOR DAMAGING THE ROYAL MARRIAGE. IT SEEMS VERY UNFAIR. SOME OF THE LETTERS HAVE BEEN DISGUSTING AND VERY RUDE.

"THEY BASICALLY SAY THAT PRINCESS DIANA IS A GODDESS AND HOW DARE CAMILLA DO ANYTHING TO UPSET OR HURT HER OR DAMAGE HER HAPPINESS."

In the end the Parker Bowleses were forced to change their telephone numbers and quit their house to seek refuge with friends. Andrew returned to his army work, and Camilla went to stay with her former brother-in-law, Nick Paravicini, in Breconshire. Later she was to travel to Venice in an attempt to shake off the dogged attentions of pressmen.

Meanwhile, Prince Charles drove to Windsor for a crisis meeting with the queen and his wife during which, it was reported, Diana said firmly: "I know my duty." The implication was that she would not walk out on the marriage; she had had her say, and that would be an end to it. This infuriated Charles, but recognizing the crisis for what it was, he agreed that they would turn out as a couple for a state banquet at the end of June when the queen was due to celebrate forty years on the throne. It might just calm the feverish debate now raging outside the castle walls.

Again Charles returned to Gloucestershire while frantic attempts were made by Buckingham Palace to paper over the cracks. So concerned were Charles's friends at the very palpable damage being done to him, on a daily basis, that Lord and Lady Romsey tried to encourage Charles to organize a letter-writing campaign to *The Times*. The idea fizzled out rapidly, and support for the prince continued to hemorrhage at an alarming rate.

Though the couple had already endured a Greek cruise on a luxury ship provided by John Latsis, and promised themselves it was an experiment they would not repeat, it was suddenly decided that a reprise might assuage the ever-thirsty press and convince them that the marriage was still a going concern. The Palace's sudden volte-face on the holiday idea surprised some of the Greek tycoon's staff, who had been told that, however desirous he might be for a prestigious rerun of the previous year's cruise, he could forget it. It was billed, to the delight of Palace officials, as a "second honeymoon"; invited along as extras in the dismal drama were Princess Alexandra and her husband, Sir Angus Ogilvy, and Lord and Lady Romsey.

The cruise had the benefit of being on a sufficiently large yacht that the couple did not have to speak. Diana spent her time waterskiing and topping up her tan; Charles spent his time sketching and telephoning Camilla. They ate and slept apart.

Camilla, meanwhile, had flown to Giudecca in the center of Venice's panoramic lagoon with her sister, Annabel, and their parents. Fellow diners at the Cipriani Hotel noted how tired and pale she looked as she sat beneath a parasol sketching the Venetian scene. At the same time it emerged that Charles had been to visit Camilla at Middlewick House in July, arriving by helicopter.

Back at home, public opinion had swung so far against Charles that the efforts to present a united front alongside Diana—and there were some—came largely from his side. Diana was in pole position, both from the moral standpoint and also from the opinion polls—Charles's popularity rating had sunk to an all-time low. But all that was about to change.

Much has been made of the comical figure of Cyril Reenan, a retired bank manager with a penchant for listening in to late-night telephone calls, who accidentally found himself at the center of an even greater scandal than Diana's confessions to Andrew Morton.

But to Charles and Camilla, closer now than ever they had been, Reenan was a knight in shining armor. Not for him the courtly love, the act of chivalry. No; Mr Reenan listened in to a private telephone conversation, recorded it, listened to it again, then sold it to *The Sun* for a large sum of money. Not everybody's idea of knightly behavior, perhaps, but to Charles and Camilla it was the next best thing.

For Reenan delivered to a public thirsty for new information the Squidgy tapes, a record of conversations between the Princess of Wales and her car-dealer friend, James Gilbey. More than anything, the conversations exposed Diana's frailty of mind at the time of the recording— on New Year's Eve, 1989—and the car dealer's overweening ambition. *The Sun,* with commendable enterprise, broadcast the tapes on an 0898 telephone line, and those with the stomach to eavesdrop on these sad exchanges were able to judge for themselves how far from normal life Diana, their goddess, had strayed.

For Charles and Camilla the publication of the Squidgy tapes was a godsend. In the days that followed there was a merciless pursuit of all those associated with Diana, and in the heat of the moment, the prince and his love were forgotten. Their turn would come, and the damage caused would be infinitely greater, when one of their own private conversations was finally aired; but for the moment they were safe.

In among the scores of lurid headlines about Diana's relationship with James Gilbey, her in-laws, and her husband, there were one or two—but not very many—questions put as to the original source of the tapes. In the end, investigators were drawn to the inescapable conclusion that rogue elements within the British security services had been bugging the royal family; but at the time, the content of the tapes was so explosive that once they had been authenticated, no one paid too much attention to where they had come from.

In the meantime, moves had started at the Palace to draw up the terms of an official separation. The queen's private secretary, Sir Robert Fellowes, and the palace press officer, Charles Anson, were heard in conversation discussing the end of the marriage during the summer of 1992, even though the announcement was some months off and attempts were still being made to fool the outside world that no permanent damage had been done to the royal union. The reasons why this charade was kept up were inexplicable, beyond an innate secretiveness among courtiers who do not like to share even the time of day with the outside world, and possibly—but only possibly—a determination by Charles to breathe life into something that was, in all truth, long dead.

Still they tried to hold it all together. In October the nation gave thanks for victory against the German Army at El Alamein, the most significant land battle of the Second World War, which had been won fifty years before. One of the many combatants to attend was Major Bruce Shand, and with justification. In the days leading up to the historic battle, Shand had been in the Libyan desert when he was suddenly pounced upon by Winston Churchill. The wartime leader was on a surprise visit to the troops, and his eyes had lighted on the ribbons on Shand's chest—which denoted not one Military Cross, but two.

He recalled the encounter thus:

My hand was being vigorously shaken.

"You're a very *young* man. How old are you?"

"Twenty-five, sir."

"Well, well—and a major *and* you've got two of them." He prodded vigorously at my medal ribbon. "How splendid. But you look so thin."

Shand was destined to become thinner. On the night of November 3, as the battle raged and the British troops advanced, he was leading his squadron forward through an unexpected downpour when suddenly he saw vehicles ahead. In his own self-deprecatory way he describes what happened next:

Some of them came nearer, and before I knew what had happened my own [armored] car was being heavily engaged with fire. Something like a whiplash stung my cheek, and Sergeant Francis beside me slumped to the bottom of the car with a large hole in his chest, killed instantly. I could hear all the other cars firing away hard. My mouth was full of blood but I managed to tell Corporal Plant, my imperturbable driver, to turn the car around. I also tried to talk on the wireless but it had become dislocated.

The car started to move but something hit it a tremendous blow, and I saw poor Plant subside over his wheel. A second later the car began to burn. Crawling forward I found that Plant was dead and I prepared to leave the vehicle. I got through the top, jumped down and sheltered under the leeward side. Firing was still going on around me.

I think I must have had a few minutes' blackout as I next remember Edward's car approaching, with him shouting "Jump on." I managed to clamber on and hung rather precariously on to his hand as we began to move. It was then that I was hit in the knee, and in the sudden shock I let go, although he tried to hold me. I do not remember hitting the ground. A buzz of German voices greeted my return to consciousness.

Shand spent the rest of the war in Spangenburg jail, making light of his internment just as he did of his injuries. Fifty years on, he stood in Westminster Abbey with his daughter by his side remembering his brothers-in-arms who died while he lived—"I suffered appalling remorse," he admitted—while statesmen and royalty, who had not endured the hardship of war, occupied the best seats.

Among those wearing medals and finery were the Prince and Princess of Wales. By now their joint public engagements were a rarity, but according to the master plan laid down by the faceless men at the palace, it was incumbent upon them to turn out together from time to time. But this was one occasion when, in retrospect, all wished they hadn't.

For the El Alamein service represented much more than just a single battle victory. It was the land forces' celebration, if that could ever be the word, of their triumphs throughout the Second World War. It was a national moment for reflection, for thanks, and for sorrow at the loss of so many lives in the cause of liberty. But the next morning the headlines in *The Sun* said something else:

MEMORIAL DAY WRECKED BY CAMILLA
PRINCESS SNUBS RIVAL AFTER SHOCK AT MEMORIAL SERVICE

The newspaper reported:

A RARE PUBLIC SHOW OF TOGETHERNESS BY CHARLES AND DIANA WAS WRECKED YESTERDAY—BY THE UNEXPECTED APPEARANCE OF THE PRINCE'S EX-GIRLFRIEND.

THE TROUBLED PAIR HAD TO WALK RIGHT PAST CAMILLA PARKER BOWLES AS SHE SAT IN WESTMINSTER ABBEY FOR A MEMORIAL SERVICE.

CHARLES POLITELY ACKNOWLEDGED HER WITH A KNOWING NOD AND A SMILE AS HE WALKED PAST. BUT HIS UNFORGIVING WIFE LOOKED THE OTHER WAY. THROUGHOUT THE SERVICE OF THANKSGIVING THE TWO WOMEN DID NOT EXCHANGE GLANCES.

THEY ARE KNOWN TO LOATHE EACH OTHER. AND THE PRINCESS EVEN STAYED BEHIND AFTER THE MEMORIAL TO AVOID WALKING PAST CAMILLA AGAIN.

This was, arguably, the lowest point of the whole affair: a national memorial that affected thousands of people besmirched by a petty marital squabble and the distortive media attention on the close proximity, in church, of the three key players. It was a bungle on an amazing scale, demonstrating more than anything how warped the judgment of the participants and their advisers had become in the past few months. Charles was said to know that Camilla would be there; in fact, she took the place of her unwell mother at the last minute, but her presence as her father's escort was entirely justified. Whether, by this late stage, the Princess of Wales should have attended is a matter for debate. Palace officials, pushing the togetherness line, wanted to see Charles and Diana side by side at a national event, no matter the cost to the many other participants. And so she came, adding luster to an occasion whose origins she will have known little of, in a brand-new Catherine Walker outfit with a broad-brimmed hat and gloves. "Camilla," wrote *The Sun,* somewhat missing the point, "wore a dowdy blue suit with long skirt."

But that was not the end of it. Somehow, in the inverted, pro-Diana world, it was deemed that the cuckoo in the nest on this occasion was Camilla. A friend was quoted as saying: "Given the events of the summer, this represents a clear slap in the face for the princess. Everyone knows of Charles's friendship with Camilla and how deeply it has hurt Diana."

The reportage demeaned everyone. The *Daily Mail* proclaimed:

THEY WERE LIKE THE TWIN FACES OF WAR—THE DULLNESS OF DEFEAT AND THE RADIANCE OF VICTORY. AS A PIECE OF THEATRE IT WAS COMPELLING.

THE PRINCESS OF WALES, HER EYES WIDE, BRIGHT, AND OPEN, WEARING A JACKET OF SHIMMERING SILVERY GREY AND TIGHT-FITTING WHITE SKIRT. CAMILLA PARKER BOWLES, A FUNEREAL FIGURE, PALE, THIN, AND HAIR FLECKED WITH GREY, IN SHAPELESS, SOMBRE BLUE.

The burden of this report was that Camilla was a shriveled shell "who looked so much more than her 43 years as she shuffled out of the Abbey"; and that she had no particular reason to be at Westminster Abbey, getting in the way of the more glamorous players. Diana, on the other hand, looked wonderful, and therefore her presence was entirely justified.

Bearing in mind Bruce Shand's own preoccupations that day—of his own life nearly lost, of others who never returned—his response to the grappling paparazzi outside Westminster Abbey who threatened to rob the occasion of its last shreds of dignity was remarkable in its restraint: "It was very good of her to accompany me to the service and she couldn't have been better company," he said. "But I think she found it off-putting to be confronted by 30-odd photographers outside Westminster Abbey." As to her health, he had no doubts. "As far as I am concerned, she is very well and remains in good spirits. The constant Press scrutiny does not seem to have taken its toll on her."

It was bravely spoken, and with decorum. If there had to be a public showdown between the two women in Charles's life, no worse place could be conceived than a memorial for the war dead. But contrary to the reports of the day, it was the Shands who came out with heads held high.

Three weeks later, the ubiquitous Andrew Morton came out with a paperback version of his book. It stated that Diana could not bring herself to speak Camilla's name and instead called her "The Rottweiler." The Mediterranean trip aboard John Latsis's yacht earlier in the summer—the so-called "second honeymoon"—had been a disaster, made worse by Diana's stumbling across her husband making furtive telephone calls via a satellite link to Camilla's Wiltshire home.

Somewhere along the line desperate men thought they could do a patch-and-mend job with The Togetherness Tour. It was a shambles.

Billed as a "business as usual" enterprise by Commander Richard Aylard, it was supposed to be a kiss-and-make-up tour of South Korea.

Aylard madly pulled strings on the eve of departure, in November 1992, to ensure it had a good sendoff. Headlines such as WHY CHARLES AND DIANA ARE BACK TOGETHER in the *Daily Express* and FROM DIANA, THE LOOK—AS HOPES RISE OF A MARRIAGE ON THE MEND in the *Daily Mail* may have raised the expectations of royalists the world over, but did no more than raise a smile from the journalists who had been instructed to write them. It was common knowledge in Fleet Street that the marriage was all over bar the shouting—but the Fourth Estate was allowing Charles and Diana to do whatever they had to do, in their own time.

They did not have to wait long. From the moment the royal jet arrived in Seoul royal-watchers knew the worst. With minutes to go before touchdown, the couple had engaged in a massive row: they emerged angry and red-faced, and stayed that way for the next five days. Observing this unedifying spectacle, one journalist who accompanied the royal tour wrote: "It was a very public, and very humiliating, end to the love story of the century."

So it came as no great surprise to those who had followed the couple closely over the past few months when John Major, the prime minister, rose in the House of Commons on December 9, 1992, and uttered:

It is announced from Buckingham Palace that, with regret, the Prince and Princess of Wales have decided to separate.

Their Royal Highnesses have no plans to divorce and their constitutional positions are unaffected. The decision has been reached amicably, and they will both continue to participate fully in the upbringing of their children. Their Royal Highnesses will continue to carry out full and separate programmes of public engagements and will, from time to time, attend family occasions and national events together.

The Queen and the Duke of Edinburgh, though saddened, understand and sympathise with the difficulties that have led to this decision. Her Majesty and His Royal Highness particularly hope that the intrusions into the privacy of the Prince and Princess may now cease. They believe that a degree of privacy and understanding is essential if Their Royal Highnesses are to provide a happy and secure upbringing for their children while continuing to give a wholehearted commitment to their public duties.

The royal-watchers had known, but the House was shocked. Privy councillors, among them Camilla Parker Bowles's uncle Lord Howe, the former chancellor of the exchequer, had been forewarned. Clearly some of them, including Howe, had been instrumental in guiding the prime minister's hand that day. But when it came, John Major's statement, though brief, made riveting television viewing.

There was not the slightest hint of triumph in Camilla Parker Bowles's public statement, eagerly sought by the newsmen gathered around her Wiltshire home. "Obviously if something has gone wrong I'm very sorry for them," she said.

She added, without even the trace of a smile: "But I know nothing more than the average person in the street. I only know what I see on television."

Then she swept from her home in regal style, driving into the night with her sister in a Mercedes, and followed by a police escort. They headed for Bowood, the home of the Earl of Shelburne, a twenty-minute drive away—and a stately home which was to achieve greater prominence within the space of a few short weeks.

Chapter 8

OOD-BYE, CRUEL WORLD

HILE CHARLES WAS BORN TO EXPECT THE ATTENTIONS OF THE PRESS, AND Diana had come to enjoy and manipulate them, there was one person who found their dogged pursuit disturbing and disorienting: Camilla.

To the woman with a backbone of steel who had endured the Spartan regime of Dumbrells, an institution that would have done credit to Her Majesty's Prison Service, and a fearless horsewoman who would take the most terrifying fences with barely a blink, this new psychological torment—of being perpetually on the run, like so many of the foxes she had chased—was undoubtedly the low point of her life.

But there was yet more agony to endure. With world interest in her affair with Charles showing no signs of abating, suddenly in January came rumblings from half a world away which were to thrust her entirely private life even more before the public consciousness.

In the second week of January 1993 the Australian women's weekly magazine *New Idea* published a full transcript of the so-called Camillagate tapes, less contentious extracts of which had already appeared in two tabloid newspapers in the autumn. Almost simultaneously, the text of the conversation was published in *The Sun* in Britain, and other newspapers worldwide.

By the time the tapes were published, the conversation was three years old, and whatever intimacies had passed between Camilla and her lover might properly be expected to have been lost in the mists of time. But the night before publication in Britain, extracts were read to Camilla over the telephone. Her reaction was one of incredulity and mounting horror. To the reporter designated the ugly task of refreshing her memory of the exchanges, she suddenly blurted: "I can't believe it, I can't believe it. I must speak to my husband. He is on his way home."

That instant reaction gives yet another clue as to the lasting nature of her relationship with Andrew Parker Bowles. Other women, caught in a similar deceit, would instantly turn to their lover for protection; but the mention of "my husband" foxed some editors, who were finding it hard enough to come to terms with the evidence that had been laid before them.

The conversation took place on the night of Sunday, December 17, 1989. Charles was staying at the Cheshire home of his old friend Anne, Duchess of Westminster (referred to on the tape as Nancy), after a heavy week of duties that included a reception at Kensington Palace for his Prince's Trust, acting as a counsellor of state in receiving diplomats, meeting the foreign secretary, hosting a dinner for the Royal Opera House Trust, and hosting receptions for various other organizations with which he was involved. He ended the week with a tour of Wales, which included visits to Greenfield, Mold, and Wrexham; Camilla had hunted with the Beaufort and made her preparations for Christmas.

The fragment of conversation, which lasts eleven minutes, goes as follows:

CHARLES: . . . he thought he might have gone a bit far.

CAMILLA: Ah, well.

CHARLES: Anyway, you know, that's the sort of thing one has to beware of. And sort of feel one's way along with, if you know what I mean.

CAMILLA: Mmmmm. You're awfully good at feeling your way along.

CHARLES: Oh, stop! I want to feel my way along you, all over you and up and down you and in and out.

CAMILLA:	Oh!
CHARLES:	. . . particularly in and out.
CAMILLA:	Oh, that's just what I need at the moment.
CHARLES:	Is it?
CAMILLA:	I know it would revive me. I can't bear a Sunday night without you.
CHARLES:	Oh, God.
CAMILLA:	It's like that programme *Start the Week*. I can't start the week without you.
CHARLES:	I fill up your tank!
CAMILLA:	Yes, you do!
CHARLES:	Then you can cope.
CAMILLA:	Then I'm all right.
CHARLES:	What about me? The trouble is, I need you several times a week.
CAMILLA:	Mmmmm. So do I. I need you all the week, all the time.
CHARLES:	Oh God, I'll just live inside your trousers or something. It would be much easier!
CAMILLA:	*(Laughs)* What are you going to turn into? A pair of knickers? *(Both laugh)* Oh, you're going to come back as a pair of knickers.
CHARLES:	Or, God forbid, a Tampax, just my luck! *(Laughs)*
CAMILLA:	You are a complete idiot! *(Laughs)* Oh, what a wonderful idea!
CHARLES:	My luck to be chucked down the lavatory and go on and on for ever swirling round on the top, never going down!
CAMILLA:	*(Laughing)* Oh, darling!
CHARLES:	Until the next one comes through.
CAMILLA:	Or perhaps you could just come back as a box.
CHARLES:	What sort of box?
CAMILLA:	A box of Tampax, so you could just keep going.
CHARLES:	That's true.
CAMILLA:	Repeating yourself. *(Laughing)* Oh, darling, I just want you now.
CHARLES:	Do you?
CAMILLA:	Mmmmmm.

149

CHARLES: So do I.

CAMILLA: Desperately, desperately, desperately. Oh, I thought of you so much at Garrowby.[1]

CHARLES: Did you?

CAMILLA: Simply mean we couldn't be there together.

CHARLES: Desperate. If you could be here—I long to ask Nancy sometimes.

CAMILLA: Why don't you?

CHARLES: I daren't.

CAMILLA: Because I think she's so in love with you.

CHARLES: Mmmmmm.

CAMILLA: She'd do anything you asked.

CHARLES: She'd tell all sorts of people.

CAMILLA: No, she wouldn't, because she'd be much too frightened of what you might say to her. I think you've got . . . I'm afraid it's a terrible thing to say, but I think, you know, those sort of people feel very strongly about you. You've got such a great hold over her.

CHARLES: Really?

CAMILLA: And you're . . . I think as usual you're underestimating yourself.

CHARLES: But she might be terribly jealous or something.

CAMILLA: Oh! (Laughs) Now that is a point! I wonder, she might be, I suppose.

CHARLES: You never know, do you?

CAMILLA: No, the little green-eyed monster may be lurking inside her. No, but I mean, the thing is you're so good when people are so flattered to be taken into your confidence. But I don't know they'd betray you. You know, real friends.

CHARLES: Really.

CAMILLA: I don't . . . (Pause) Gone to sleep?

CHARLES: No, I'm here.

CAMILLA: Darling, listen. I talked to David[2] tonight again. It might not be any good.

CHARLES: Oh, no!

CAMILLA: I'll tell you why. He's got these children of one of those

150

Crawley girls and their nanny staying.[3] He's going, I'm going, to ring him again tomorrow. He's going to try to put them off till Friday. But I thought as an alternative perhaps I might ring up Charlie.[4]

CHARLES:	Yes.
CAMILLA:	And see if we could do it there. I know he's back on Thursday.
CHARLES:	It's quite a lot further away.
CAMILLA:	Oh, is it?
CHARLES:	Well, I'm just trying to think. Coming from New-market.
CAMILLA:	Coming from Newmarket to me at that time of night, you could probably do it in two and three quarters. It takes me three.
CHARLES:	What, to go to, um, Bowood?[5]
CAMILLA:	Northmore.[6]
CHARLES:	To go to Bowood?
CAMILLA:	To go to Bowood would be the same as me really, wouldn't it?
CHARLES:	I mean to say, you would suggest going to Bowood, uh?
CAMILLA:	No, not at all.
CHARLES:	Which Charlie then?
CAMILLA:	What Charlie did you think I was talking about?
CHARLES:	I didn't know, because I thought you meant . . .
CAMILLA:	I've got lots!
CHARLES:	Somebody else.
CAMILLA:	I've got lots of friends called Charlie.
CHARLES:	The other one. Patty's.[7]
CAMILLA:	Oh! Oh, there! Oh, that is further away. They're not. . . .
CHARLES:	They've gone.
CAMILLA:	I don't know, it's just, you know, just a thought I had if it fell through, the other place.
CHARLES:	Oh, right. What do you do, go on the M25 then down the M4 is it?
CAMILLA:	Yes, you go, um, and sort of Royston or M11, at that time of night.

CHARLES:	Yes, well, that'll be just after, it will be after shooting anyway.
CAMILLA:	So it would be, um, you'd miss the worst of the traffic, because I'll, er, you see the problem is I've got to be in London tomorrow night.
CHARLES:	Yes.
CAMILLA:	And Tuesday night A's[8] coming home.
CHARLES:	No!
CAMILLA:	Would you believe it? Because, I don't know what he is doing, he's shooting down here or something. But darling, you wouldn't be able to ring me anyway, would you?
CHARLES:	I might just. I mean tomorrow night I could have done.
CAMILLA:	Oh, darling, I can't bear it. How could you have done tomorrow night?
CHARLES:	Because I'll be (yawns) working on the next speech.
CAMILLA:	Oh no, what's the next one?
CHARLES:	A Business in the Community one, rebuilding communities.
CAMILLA:	Oh no, when's that for?
CHARLES:	A rather important one for Wednesday.
CAMILLA:	Well, at least I'll be behind you.
CHARLES:	I know.
CAMILLA:	Can I have a copy of the one you've just done?
CHARLES:	Yes.
CAMILLA:	Can I? Um, I would like it.
CHARLES:	OK, I'll try and organise it.
CAMILLA:	Darling . . .
CHARLES:	But I, oh God, when am I going to speak to you?
CAMILLA:	I can't bear it, um . . .
CHARLES:	Wednesday night?
CAMILLA:	Oh, certainly Wednesday night. I'll be alone, um, Wednesday, you know, the evening. Or Tuesday. While you're rushing round doing things I'll be, you know, alone until it reappears. And early Wednesday morning, I mean, he'll be leaving at half-past eight,

quarter past eight. He won't be here Thursday, pray God. Um, that ambulance strike, it's a terrible thing to say this, I suppose it won't have come to an end by Thursday?

CHARLES: It will have done.

CAMILLA: Well, I mean for everybody's sake it will have done, but I hope for our sakes it's still going on.

CHARLES: Why?

CAMILLA: Well, because if it stops he'll come down here on Thursday night.

CHARLES: Oh no.

CAMILLA: Yes, but I don't think it will stop, do you?

CHARLES: No, neither do I. Just our luck.

CAMILLA: It would be our luck, I know.

CHARLES: Then it's bound to.

CAMILLA: No it won't. You mustn't think like that. You must think positive.

CHARLES: I'm not very good at that.

CAMILLA: Well, I'm going to, because if I don't, I'll despair. *(Pause)* Hmmmm . . . gone to sleep?

CHARLES: No. How maddening.

CAMILLA: I know. Anyway, I mean, he's doing his best to change it, David, but I just thought, you know, I might ask Charlie.

CHARLES: Did you say anything?

CAMILLA: No, I haven't talked to him.

CHARLES: You haven't?

CAMILLA: Well, I talked to him briefly, but you know, I just thought I—I just don't know whether he's got any children home, that's the worry.

CHARLES: Right.

CAMILLA: Oh . . . darling, I think I'll . . .

CHARLES: Pray, just pray.

CAMILLA: It would be so wonderful to have just one night to set us on our way, wouldn't it?

CHARLES: Wouldn't it? To wish you Happy Christmas.

CAMILLA: *(Indistinct)* Happy, oh, don't let's think about Christmas. I can't bear it. (*Pause*) . . . Going to sleep? I think you'd better, don't you, darling?

CHARLES: (*Sleepily*) Yes, darling.

CAMILLA: I think you've exhausted yourself by all that hard work. You must go to sleep now, darling.

CHARLES: (*Sleepily*) Yes, darling.

CAMILLA: Will you ring me when you wake up?

CHARLES: Yes, I will.

CAMILLA: Before I have those rampaging children around. It's Tom's birthday tomorrow. (*Pause*) You all right?

CHARLES: Mmmmm, I'm all right.

CAMILLA: Can I talk to you, I hope, before those rampaging children . . .

CHARLES: What time do they come in?

CAMILLA: Well, usually Tom never wakes up at all, but as it's his birthday tomorrow[9] he might just stagger out of bed. It won't be before half-past eight. (*Pause*) 'Night-night, my darling.

CHARLES: Darling . . .

CAMILLA: I do love you.

CHARLES: (*Sleepily*) Before . . .

CAMILLA: Before half-past eight.

CHARLES: Try and ring?

CAMILLA: Yeah, if you can. Love you, darling.

CHARLES: 'Night, darling.

CAMILLA: I love you.

CHARLES: I love you too. I don't want to say goodbye.

CAMILLA: Well done for doing that. You're a clever old thing. An awfully good brain lurking there, isn't there? Oh, darling, I think you ought to give the brain a rest now. 'Night-night.

CHARLES: 'Night, darling. God bless.

CAMILLA: I do love you and I'm so proud of you.

CHARLES: Oh, I'm so proud of you.

CAMILLA: Don't be silly. I've never achieved anything.

CHARLES: Yes, you have.

CAMILLA: No, I haven't.

CHARLES:	Your great achievement is to love me.
CAMILLA:	Oh, darling, easier than falling off a chair.
CHARLES:	You suffer all those indignities and tortures and calumnies.
CAMILLA:	Oh, darling, don't be silly. I'd suffer anything for you. that's love. It's the strength of love. 'Night-night.
CHARLES:	'Night, darling. Sounds as though you're dragging an enormous piece of string behind you with hundreds of tin pots and cans attached to it. Must be your telephone. 'Night-night, before the battery goes. (*Blows kisses*) 'Night.
CAMILLA:	I love you.
CHARLES:	I don't want to say goodbye.
CAMILLA:	Neither do I, but you must get some sleep. 'Bye.
CHARLES:	'Bye, darling.
CAMILLA:	I love you.
CHARLES:	'Bye.
CAMILLA:	Hopefully talk to you in the morning.
CHARLES:	Please.
CAMILLA:	'Bye, I love you.
CHARLES:	'Night.
CAMILLA:	'Night.
CHARLES:	'Night.
CAMILLA:	Love you for ever.
CHARLES:	'Night.
CAMILLA:	G'bye, 'bye my darling.
CHARLES:	'Night.
CAMILLA:	'Night-night.
CHARLES:	'Night.
CAMILLA:	'Bye-bye.
CHARLES:	Going.
CAMILLA:	'Bye.
CHARLES:	Going . . .
CAMILLA:	Gone.
CHARLES:	'Night.
CAMILLA:	Press the button.
CHARLES:	Going to press the tit.

CAMILLA:	All right, darling. I wish you were pressing mine.
CHARLES:	God, I wish I was. Harder and harder.
CAMILLA:	Oh, darling.
CHARLES:	'Night.
CAMILLA:	'Night.
CHARLES:	I love you.
CAMILLA:	(*Yawning*) Love you, press the tit.
CHARLES:	Adore you. 'Night.
CAMILLA:	'Night.
CHARLES:	'Night.
CAMILLA:	(*Blows a kiss*)
CHARLES:	'Night.
CAMILLA:	G'night my darling . . . love you . . .

(*CHARLES HANGS UP*)

The effect on Camilla of the publication of this conversation was shattering. One picture tragically captures her state of mind at the time, as she returned from the newsagents carrying newspapers plastered with banner headlines revealing even more lurid details of her secret life. With a scarf wrapped around her head to shield her from the

---

[1]The home of the Earl of Halifax, friend of Prince Charles and once tipped as a future husband for Princess Anne; married to the ex-wife of Andrew Parker Bowles's younger brother Rick.

[2]Lord Willoughby de Broke, a close friend of both Charles and Camilla, who had a Gloucestershire farm near both Highgrove and the Parker Bowleses' house.

[3]The children of either Marita Crawley or her sister-in-law Sarah, the widows of Randall and Andrew Crawley, who died in the Turin air crash of 1988. Sarah is the daughter of a former chairman of Lloyd's, Murray Lawrence, and has a son; but it is more likely that it was Marita's two children, Aidan and Cosima, who are being referred to. Marita is the present Duchess of Westminster's sister.

[4]Probably the Earl of Shelburne, who was page of honour to the queen in 1956.

[5]The family home of the Earl of Shelburne.

[6]A stud farm near Newmarket in Suffolk. At the time it was owned by Hugh van Cutsem, a longtime friend of the prince and son of the racehorse trainer Bernard van Cutsem.

[7]Patty and Charles Palmer-Tomkinson. Patty was seriously injured in the 1988 Klosters skiing accident that killed royal equerry Major Hugh Lindsay.

[8]Andrew Parker Bowles

[9]It was Tom Parker Bowles's fifteenth birthday

flashes of the photographers' cameras, her face is a picture of uncontrolled anguish and despair.

The hate mail continued. And though it was not revealed until much later, Camilla, who had spent much of her life shielded from the directness of the less privileged classes, suddenly found herself face-to-face with their contempt and derision. She was spotted walking through the car park of Sainsbury's supermarket in Chippenham, four miles from her home, by a group of women who, upon recognizing her, jeered and hurled abuse. Then they dipped into their carrier bags and brought out bread rolls and buns which they threw at her as she attempted to flee. A neighbor, Jessica Webb, said of this extraordinary sight: "Camilla was apparently very upset. The women who did it apparently disapproved of her friendship with Charles."

Buckingham Palace officials, never at their best in an emergency, were caught on the back foot both by the revelations and by public reaction to them. Typically, they said and did nothing while the storm raged on: *The Sun,* the newspaper with the biggest roar, proclaimed: 6 MINUTE LOVE TAPE COULD COST CHARLES THRONE and, in the heat of the moment, probably spoke for nearly every one of its millions of readers.

The Mail on Sunday, in no less forgiving mood, ran a story headlined: CABINET MINISTER'S PLEA TO CHARLES: NEVER SEE HER AGAIN. The newspaper, on harmonious terms with virtually all of John Major's Cabinet, did not specify which minister it had spoken to at length, but the message was clear and stark:

WHILE PRINCE CHARLES IS BELIEVED TO BE RELUCTANT TO END THE LONG FRIENDSHIP, ONE SENIOR CABINET MINISTER SAID LAST NIGHT: "HE WOULD BE WELL ADVISED TO BREAK ALL CONNECTIONS WITH MRS. PARKER BOWLES AND START OFF WITH A CLEAN SLATE."

The Cabinet, said the paper, believed that the British public was "in danger" of becoming deeply disillusioned with the royal family, which could have long-term consequences for the monarchy.

This was a not-particularly-coded message from the Tory government to the Prince of Wales that he was in deep trouble, and that the next step would be a more public breach between Crown and State—

unless something was done to show that Charles was remorseful and intended to mend his ways.

The attack, which sounded nothing like an attack but carried a very heavy threat behind it, came in response to Charles's leaked reaction to the publication of the Camillagate tapes. He let it be known that he thought that the publication of the tape was the "low point in the crisis."

"This was the Sword of Damocles hanging over him," one friend said emotionally. "The worst is over now. Things can only get better."

This impossibly naive view merely served to fan the flames of anger in the Cabinet. Ministers felt that, given the huge deception that had been perpetrated on the British public over the nature of Charles's relationship with Camilla, some small sign of remorse was the very least that could be expected. Instead, the message from Charles's side was foolhardy and upbeat—he would "ride out the storm."

The way he chose to ride it did little credit to someone who could manage to stay in the saddle so ably when playing polo; certainly, it hardly encouraged an increasingly ill-tempered Cabinet. The prince's plan involved repairing to Balmoral with Lord and Lady Romsey and Charles and Patty Palmer-Tomkinson, his skiing friends, for a council of war; officially it was described as a sporting weekend.

Bludgeoned by bad headlines, Charles was unable to tell a drama from a crisis. On hearing what steps he had taken, privy councillors could do no more than look down their noses at the woeful inexperience of the people upon whom the Prince of Wales was calling in his hour of need. They compared most unfavorably with his predecessor's choice of chums, sniffed one, and look what happened to *him*.

But, as the world's media turned its spotlights beyond Charles and Camilla, it was suddenly the turn of the bit-part players in this most extraordinary of dramas. Those suddenly unmasked as co-conspirators in a Machiavellian plot to mislead the nation found their doors being hammered on, and their telephone lines jammed, by those who took it upon themselves to ask on behalf of the nation just exactly what was going on.

Some escaped their notice, like Camilla's former brother-in-law, Nick Paravicini, a polo-playing friend from the days of the couple's fledgling romance in the early 1970s, whose spacious Breconshire home had welcomed Camilla and Charles on more than one occasion; and Camilla's sister, Annabel Elliott, whose house at Stourpaine, near

Blandford Forum in Dorset, had accommodated the lovers on a number of occasions. Also on the list was the Marchioness of Douro, a Prussian princess in her own right, who was married to the Duke of Wellington's heir. A devoted friend of the prince, she lent Charles a country cottage and was rewarded by learning that the Princess of Wales would never speak to her again.

Others were wrongly accused of harboring the lovers, including the Canadian billionaire Galen Weston, whose multinational food-to-retailing conglomerate includes among its smaller outlets the queen's grocer, Fortnum and Mason.

Weston, a close friend of Charles and a man who dines with the queen and named his Vero Beach, Florida, seaside resort community after her Berkshire castle, was someone the press very much wanted to get close to. His British home is Fort Belvedere, an eighteenth-century Gothic Revival folly whose best-known former occupant was Charles's great-uncle and predecessor. The idea that two Princes of Wales should, in succession, make love to their mistresses under the same roof was almost too much to bear. Given Charles's fondness for Weston—and the prince was known to visit the Fort anyway—it *had* to be true, didn't it?

Weston and his Irish-born wife, Hilary, found themselves beleaguered, and turned to Buckingham Palace advisers to ask what should be done. Weston was secure in handling the press when it came to his own multinational empire, but he did not want to say anything that might cause offense or distress to an already hard-hit Prince of Wales. Already he, and Charles, had endured embarrassment the previous summer from an article in an American newspaper saying that Weston had bought Fort Belvedere from the Crown Estates (he has it on a long lease) and was handing it over as a gift to Charles and Camilla.

"They were appalled by the response they got from Buckingham Palace," a friend recalled.

And Hilary Weston revealed: "Galen rang up the press office at Buckingham Palace which gave him the most ridiculous advice, that he write a letter [to newspaper editors] saying 'To the best of my knowledge . . .'—can you imagine anything so stupid? So Galen wrote the only letter you *can* write: 'Mrs. Parker Bowles has never been in Fort Belvedere in her life.'"

It put paid to that particular line of inquiry. Other newspapers, anxious now the relationship was revealed to put a location to these secret and historic assignations, sometimes got it wrong in their haste. A couple of them came across pictures of the Queenwood Golf Lodge on the Earl of Shelburne's Bowood estate, put two and two together . . . and had to offer an apology. Shelburne rightly said that Charles and Camilla had never stayed there; he saw no reason, as he extracted the newspapers' corrective paragraphs, to specify where exactly the couple *had* spent time on his estate.

Once the commentators had had their say on the sexual content of the Camillagate conversation, it was largely forgotten. What remained was a deep sense of unease that the nation had been fooled—even though, as yet, they had only the merest notion of the length of the relationship, and the extent of the knowledge and forbearance of the "injured" parties.

Some of this anger manifested itself in attacks on Commander Richard Aylard, who was accused of manipulating the press, stifling stories, and offering misleading information. The Togetherness Tour was cited—where two mid-market and largely pro-royal newspapers had been fed a completely misleading line; and then *The Sun,* the most forceful voice in Britain, if not the most influential, with a circulation close to four million, weighed in.

They instanced a story they had written the previous summer—at the time of publication of Andrew Morton's book—which Charles, through "a friend," had asked not to be published. In the story the Princess of Wales was described as a "megalomaniac" and a "scheming woman" by a "friend." What he said was: "She has become a megalomaniac. Her behaviour is endangering her marriage, the country and the Monarchy. The book paints the princess as whiter than white, but people must question her motives. Can she really claim to be a loving mother and caring person if she goes to these lengths to damage her husband?"

Another "friend" added: "Diana wants to be the Princess of Wales without the Prince. She is convinced she is the one thing propping up the Monarchy. It is no coincidence that we see lovely family photographs of the Princess with her boys at Alton Towers and Thorpe Park. How do they happen to be taken? It is common knowledge that many of the tip-offs to photographers come from those closest to the Princess."

All woman . . . Camilla flies into the face of the storm, 1992. (*Alpha*)

But the strain begins to tell—Andrew and Camilla at the Guards' Polo Club, June 1992 (*S&G Press Agency*)

The family pulls
together—Andrew, Tom, Camilla
(*Camera Press*)

Two kinds of bravery—Major
Bruce Shand and his daughter,
Westminster Abbey, October
1992 (*Today*)

Anguish as Camillagate finally breaks, 1993

The unrelenting pressure takes its toll: After Camillagate, Mrs. Parker Bowles retreats to Italy. (*Rex Features*)

Even at the supermarket, Camilla could not escape the public attention. She was pelted with bread rolls by angry housewives. (*Joan Wakeham*)

Better than all the rest—a pastoral Camilla at home in Wiltshire (*Alpha*)

Like all good fathers he's never far away—Major Bruce Shand with his daughter
(*Rex Features*)

A picture to stir the blood royal—Camilla at her most irresistible for Charles, as she rides out with the Beaufort Hunt (*Joan Wakeham*)

. . . and with the common touch—Camilla cheers up the workmen on the family estate. (*Rex Features*)

". . . the woman I love" (*Joan Wakeham*)

These quotes had the ring of authenticity about them. Whoever made them, it was Commander Richard Aylard who realized suddenly that they were over the top, and negotiated for their excision from the newspaper.

Much anger was generated by the release of the Camillagate tapes, but in the eye of the storm the eponymous Mrs. Parker Bowles was trying to put her life to rights. Shattered by guilt for the effect all this was having on her husband—he was now forced to run a daily gauntlet with press photographers, and despite taking a large dose of sangfroid before walking out of the door of their London home, his legendary charm was beginning to wear a trifle thin—and worried about the effect of the publicity on her children.

She began to lose weight rapidly. Within two months it is said she had lost nearly thirty pounds, and her face had aged visibly. Bewildered, caught in the headlights, not daring to see her lover, she stayed indoors—under house arrest for the second time in a year. As before—indeed, as always in the time of crisis—she turned to her father. Bruce Shand, by now seventy-six, turned out for the press, ever the gentleman: "I think we'd better keep our traps shut" was his deathless line, though earlier he had opined: "I shouldn't imagine they will ever get divorced. Nothing is one hundred percent certain in this world, but that is the position as of now." The serried ranks of photographers parted in respect as he walked through them.

Indeed, old-fashioned family ties were the thing that kept Camilla going during the early weeks of 1993. Charles, whom she loved as much as when she spoke those fatal words on the night of December 18, was on the rack. Friends say that Camilla felt as much guilt for him as she did for her husband, her children, and her aging parents. But not for her the ministrations of New Age therapists. Diana might go in for holistics and acupuncture and astrological guidance and the whole bag of tricks, but Camilla just lit up a cigarette, poured herself a stiff drink, and got on with the rest of her life as best she could.

"For a time she thought she was the most hated woman in the country," says a friend. "She had the hate mail, she had crank calls, and though Andrew did his best to support her, his patience was wearing thin. She went through agonies about what all this was doing to her children: Tom, particularly, had had a bad time of it at Eton from boys who'd picked up the papers and read extracts from the Camillagate tapes in silly voices.

"On top of all that, what really spooked her was the idea that she was being spied on."

She was not the only person to come to that conclusion. It seemed that there was only one conclusion to be drawn from the fact that the Squidgy and Camillagate tapes had been recorded within the space of sixteen days of each other—*and* that a third tape, eavesdropping on a conversation between the Duke and Duchess of York while Prince Andrew was aboard his ship HMS *Campbeltown*, had been recorded as well.

The royal family had been bugged.

The *Sunday Mirror* reported:

BRITAIN'S SPY BOSSES RECORDED A TOTAL OF 28 INTIMATE TELEPHONE CALLS BETWEEN PRINCE CHARLES AND CAMILLA PARKER BOWLES.

NOW M15 CHIEFS WHO ORDERED THE CAMILLAGATE BUGGING ARE DESPERATE TO STOP MORE OF THE SENSATIONAL TAPES LEAKING OUT.

THE OTHER RECORDINGS ARE SAID TO BE JUST AS INTIMATE [AS THE FIRST].

M15 BOSS STELLA RIMINGTON HAS SET UP A TEAM OF AGENTS TO HUNT THE MOLE WHO LEAKED THE CAMILLAGATE TAPE—AND STOP ANY MORE COMING OUT. SHE BELIEVES THE MOLE IS INSIDE BRITAIN'S MAIN SPY CENTRE, GCHQ IN CHELTENHAM, WHERE THE "PROFESSIONAL RE-CORDINGS" WERE MADE. SOME USED A SPY SATELLITE.

This story did nothing to still the alarm and despondency felt by Camilla since, if true, the mental turmoil she had been through was nothing by comparison with what was to come. Each telephone conversation with Charles—they could not see each other—filled her with fear.

But despite the threat of renewed revelations, nothing more emerged, and though members of Parliament demanded to know what was going on—*were* the security services bugging the royal family, and if so, on whose orders?—no answers were forthcoming. Fleet Street instigated its own inquiry, and came up with nothing.

The most plausible theory put forward was that rogue cells of navy or army intelligence—answerable to neither M15 nor M16—had utilized ultra-sophisticated scanning devices to plot the exact position of the Prince of Wales via his cellular telephone. A further theory was that their operatives analyzed the content of royal conversations "in defense of the realm"—a self-serving, catchall excuse for justifying all levels of espionage.

These were theories, but there were no hard facts. One MP, Geoffrey Dickens, the Conservative member for Littleborough and Saddleworth, introduced a parliamentary question demanding an inquiry into the bugging. His request was disallowed; the Speaker of the House of Commons citing the Birkett Report, which prevented too close a scrutiny of the undercover work of the security services.

The government was in a quandary—to witch hunt or not to witch hunt?—but on the advice of its security advisers it fell back on that time-honored device for getting around a problem—have an inquiry. At the end of March 1993 the prime minister, John Major, published two official reports that cleared M15 and other intelligence agencies of spying on the royal family. The findings were greeted with almost universal derision by members on all sides of the House. Some MPs then insisted on new powers to control the activities of spymasters, their anger fueled by the admission of government officials that there had been no specific inquiries into allegations of involvement in the royal tapes scandal.

The prime minister published one report on phone tapping and another on the security services generally. In the first, the master of the rolls, Sir Thomas Bingham, said a tribunal had found no evidence of breaches. In the second, Lord Justice Stuart-Smith said he could see no reason why the security services would shoot themselves in the foot by bugging the royal family.

These findings simply made MPs even angrier, since it was clear to them that the very inquiries themselves were off target. The Conservative Richard Shepherd summed up the general discontent when he stated: "All we have here is two old buffers saying that in their opinion the security services act with integrity."

One year on, in the summer of 1994, the MP Geoffrey Dickens knew as little as when he asked his original question. "I never got a satisfactory answer—I was told that questions of national security are protected under the terms of the Birkett Report," he told the author. "At the time I was particularly unsettled by the quality of the tapes—I mean, some of them were boat-to-shore, some country-to-city. That quality could not have been achieved by amateurs, it had to have been taped by someone with access to first-class equipment, and that is why I felt it should be investigated.

"The subject matter of the royal tapes was so explosive that I don't believe that it could have just been some amateur tuning in. It must have taken thousands of hours of recording, which made me think that it must have been recorded on a permanent basis. I think in the end it was perhaps a mole in the security services—the whole thing was quite disgraceful.

"The ironic thing is that under the terms of the Birkett Report, even scoundrels in the security services get protected."

In the aftermath of the Camillagate tapes Prince Charles swapped his cellular phone for a portable with a built-in scrambling device. He was by now conscious of the fact that the telephone call between his wife and the car dealer James Gilbey—the Squidgy tape, picked up by the ever-vigilant Cyril Reenan—was a compilation of two telephone calls, tapes of which had been patched together and rebroadcast by persons unknown with the specific intention of being picked by an amateur. There was a danger of its happening again.

This knowledge did nothing to calm the fears of Camilla Parker Bowles; indeed, the cavalier way in which the relevant government agencies misdirected their inquiries could leave her to draw only one conclusion: that she, along with Prince Charles, is bugged by Britain's security services on a round-the-clock basis. And nobody is going to do a thing to change that state of affairs.

But the Camillagate tapes are just as valuable to those with an interest in the future of Britain's royal family as to those, including rogue elements in the spy network, with an interest in its destabilization. They give the clearest possible picture of the nature of Charles and Camilla's relationship, nearly two decades after that fateful night in Annabel's.

That two people should still love each other as passionately after so many years is remarkable in itself: the endearments, when daylight is shed upon them, are of course an embarrassment—but no more so than for any other loving couple who have had their most private moments exposed to the public gaze. Beyond that first hurdle, there emerges a picture of a woman who cares deeply for her man—tenderly concerned for his happiness and spiritual well-being, happily indulgent when he dwells too much upon his own problems.

She is deferential: The conversational confusion over where they will meet next is all Charles's, but she does not hasten to correct him. Charles meanwhile is generous in his praise of her—"Your great achievement is to love me"—and though this seems a backhanded compliment, centering as it does on himself, it comes from a man whose life has been forged on a path toward his own destiny. Unlike most people, Charles is aware that he is part of history in everything he does—and that, in time, history will also mark with greater kindness the role that Camilla has played in his life. Fifty years from now people in supermarket car parks will not feel inclined to throw bread rolls at her.

The conversation highlights the number of friends who are prepared to offer the loving couple sanctuary in their homes, but equally it demonstrates the high level of subterfuge that is required in arranging these trysts. Clearly, as few people as possible must know they are sharing the same roof, and that includes small children as young as six. Additionally, the couple appear to be exercising a very rudimentary form of self-censorship in not directly naming friends or houses.

The speech to which Charles refers was delivered at the Guildhall in the City of London the following Wednesday morning. As president of Business in the Community, he relaunched the Dragon Awards for Community Involvement, then walked to the Brewers' Hall to attend the Community Trust Conference. Not a single one of the hundreds involved in such a high-minded scheme that day could have realized that as he wrote the words intended to spur them on to greater good, his mind had been occupied with Camilla and when he would be able to bed her next.

There was, as one commentator pointed out, a moment of dereliction when the conversation came around to Andrew Parker Bowles. The ambulance strike of 1989 was one of the ugliest industrial confrontations in Britain since the miners' strike. It lasted six months and cost the nation more than £35 million. The police and army hurriedly had to work out a cover system that would provide the same kind of service—and though this was finally achieved, the public inevitably suffered. It was suggested that people had died needlessly because the professionals were out on strike. By the time the strike was resolved in 1990 the police had dedicated an extra 1.1 million hours to ambulance-related duties, which had necessarily taken them away from their core role of crime prevention and detection.

When Charles and Camilla's conversation took place, the dispute was three months old and at its height. Andrew Parker Bowles had a key role to play in providing army ambulance backup, and the job proved demanding and time-consuming. Interestingly, it is Camilla who is apologetic about wishing the strike would carry on so as to keep her husband in London. No such regrets are uttered by the prince—"Just our luck," he says at the thought that he might have to miss his next assignation with Camilla. As a privy councillor and future king he would argue publicly that the restitution of order to the ambulance service was paramount to the health of the nation. But not, it would appear, if it was to interfere with his private life.

Andrew Parker Bowles's response to these ugly intrusions on his life was to maintain a heroically stiff upper lip, not allowing himself even the satisfaction of a sharp word with inquisitive reporters. Part of the reason may have been that, since Princess Anne's separation from Captain Mark Phillips, he had been seeing a great deal of the woman he had once wooed, taking her to the cinema, the theater, and out to dinner at a number of restaurants. She visited his home when Camilla was away, and saw much of him while he was still at Knightsbridge Barracks. In addition, he spent some time in the company of Charlotte Hambro, whom he met and fell in love with a decade before when her father, Lord Soames, was governor of Rhodesia. The gossip was that he wanted to leave Camilla and marry Charlotte, but in the end she married a landowner, Earl Peel. A friend commented: "If Charlotte hadn't married Willie Peel, Andrew would have divorced Camilla and asked her to marry him. But he kept messing Charlotte about and she lost patience in the end."

Interestingly, considering her own extramural involvements, Camilla was less than sanguine about Andrew's romantic life. "Camilla hated the intensity of the relationship with Charlotte. But even if it did go on for quite a long time, she was really in no position to complain," said the friend.

And indeed, whatever accommodation they had reached in their marriage remained unchanged. Andrew Parker Bowles, whose father, Derek, had been, according to some, the queen mother's closest male friend after the death of King George VI, remained a favorite of hers. A tradition had sprung up that he and Camilla would stay at Royal Lodge, Windsor, each spring and travel down to Cheltenham for the National Hunt Festival, that uproarious week of equine excellence. This year was to be no exception, though the queen mother was acutely aware of what the newspapers had written, she saw this as no bar to her friendship with either Andrew or Camilla. The couple, however they were feeling about each other at that particular juncture, were ready to face the world at Cheltenham. For too long now, they told friends, they had been trapped in their own home.

About this time, a very strange story started to circulate about Camilla's father, Bruce Shand. It was said that Major Shand, by now in his mid-seventies, could take no more and had demanded a meeting with the Prince of Wales at Buckingham Palace. When the two men met, he told the prince that his wife was an invalid and that his daughter's life had been ruined; Charles must leave his daughter alone, forever. The prince, it was said, responded by bursting into tears.

When quizzed about this tale, Major Shand did nothing to rebut it: but it was his "trap shut" policy that stilled his tongue, rather than a reticence to tell the truth. The reality was that the meeting never occurred, it was simply the product of fevered imaginations in an overheated atmosphere of intrigue and drama. One persistent rumor that *was* confirmed, however, was the very existence of Charles and Camilla's longstanding relationship at a time when newspapers still fought shy of describing Camilla as anything other than Charles's "confidante." Astonishingly, the confirmation came from Buckingham Palace itself. A member of the press bureau, interviewed by the *Daily Mirror,* admitted as much.

"So what?" he said. "So the prince has had an affair with this woman—it happens in France all the time. Politicians and famous men in all walks of life in France have mistresses and nobody turns a hair."

After all the years of intrigue and subterfuge it was a staggering admission, a princely blunder that showed just how out of control the situation had become.

Indeed, by mid-1993, royal advisers had lost the will to try to control events. Punch-drunk with the seemingly endless barrage of revelations, and with no way of knowing what might yet come spilling out of the woodwork, they simply gave up. No move was made to pacify the renegade Princess of Wales, who was now considered to be an outlaw; this policy in itself was ill-advised since, in her anger and frustration at the way she had been treated—"after all I've done for that family" was her catchphrase—she posed a very grave threat to the House of Windsor in a number of ways.

First, and most dangerous, was the influence she had over her children, and most particularly Prince William. No matter how often the little princes were to be seen at Sandringham Church, treading in their father's footsteps, she saw more of them than did Charles and—if she so chose—was in a position to exercise a malign influence over them, whether in relation to their father, their grandmother, the queen, or the whole royal apparatus. In light of her overexcited state, it would have been reasonable to take precautions to "keep her sweet"—but instead she was treated like an enemy.

Second, she had the capacity to upstage the entire House of Windsor at virtually any event. A carefully staged shopping expedition while Charles made a keynote speech on the environment would drive him off the front pages, a change of hairstyle or the choice of a hat at the annual Service of Remembrance would take all eyes from the queen, a speech on virtually any subject—but especially one that dwelt obliquely on her problems—would absorb the nation's attention, it would seem, for days.

And then there was the ever-present threat that she had not yet finished telling home truths. In the summer of 1994, after her so-called withdrawal from public life, the princess was observed in lengthy discussion with the journalist Richard Kay. It was said that Mr. Kay was planning a book; was this to be a further, and even more damaging, version of *Diana: Her True Story*? The havoc she could wreak on the House of Windsor's national and international standing was incalculable.

Yet nothing, it seemed, was being done by the palace apparatchiks to accommodate her—within the Household, she was simply viewed as someone who had let the side down, someone who had pulled the plug from the bottom of the boat in which they all sailed. There was a great sense of satisfaction when she finally pulled out of Highgrove, getting her sister Lady Jane Fellowes to help her pack personal belongings so she could quit the house she had always felt belonged to Camilla.

In March Charles, spurred on by Camilla, set to work eradicating all traces of Diana from the house. One of the first targets was the princess's sitting room, a first-floor sanctuary close to the pink-and-green master bedroom with its four-poster, which was used mainly by Diana from the early days of their marriage.

In 1981 the room had been decorated in shades of yellow by interior designer Dudley Poplak, who was recommended by Diana's mother, Mrs. Frances Shand Kydd. But now the Wiltshire-based designer Robert Kime, recommended by Camilla, was brought in to strip the walls, pull out built-in bookshelves from the alcoves, and give the room a "more masculine" feel. The changes, unannounced by Charles, gave Diana a considerable shock when she revisited the house in May to spend two nights under its roof in an abortive attempt to give the little princes a taste once again of homelife when both parents were present. It was an experiment that was not to be repeated.

Camilla's stamp would also be placed on Charles's new apartments in St. James's Palace, where he had moved from Kensington Palace in the wake of the separation. And Diana, too, was ready to quit the London marital home for somewhere nonroyal: she saw Kensington Palace as "secure, but a gilded cage." She encountered more difficulty in relocating.

Meanwhile, Andrew and Camilla Parker Bowles put a brave face on the deluge of damaging revelations. The queen mother, for one, was not about to dump them simply on the basis of what she would perceive as pernicious gossip; they were her guests in March at Royal Lodge, Windsor, before the Cheltenham Festival race meeting. Indeed, it was the queen mother's influence—she had, after all, signed the register as principal witness to the couple's wedding twenty years before—which governed the queen's own reaction to the scandal of the tapes. Unsure now what her relationship should be with the man who had been her Silver Stick in Waiting, the woman who was the daughter of a trusted member of the Queen's Body Guard, and her own son, she adopted the attitude of her mother, who blithely saw the whole issue as a blip on the dynastic horizon.

But while at the heart of the royal family there seemed a determination to overcome any slight embarrassment Charles's love for Camilla may have caused, there was no letup outside in the real world. In April 1993 Andrew and Camilla allowed themselves to be photographed ostensibly giving a luncheon party at Middlewick House for a dozen friends: but this display of marital solidarity was rudely shattered by the too-close attentions of the press, who not unreasonably demanded some clarification of this historic ménage-à-trois. Andrew slammed the door shut on them.

His own relations with the press had recently taken a dip. Unsure what they could justifiably say about a man whose wife was having an affair with the Prince of Wales, they had skirted decorously around the soldier. He, in turn, had treated even the more rapacious representatives of the Fourth Estate with an uncommon courtesy, with the result that, while Camilla came in for wholesale criticism, from her looks to her clothes to her morals, he remained exempt.

However, the brigadier's highly successful army career had recently hit a rocky patch. Having headed the Household Cavalry, he was now given a new command, as director of the Royal Army Veterinary Corps. For the two-hundred-year-old corps, this came as a heavy and demoralizing blow—for never before in its history had anyone who was not a qualified vet led them.

It prompted the instant resignation of the corps's colonel commandant, Brigadier Robert Clifford, who had served for more than thirty years with the RAVC. He wrote to the Ministry of Defence: "I have just been notified by the director that his successor is to be Colonel A. H. Parker Bowles, OBE, late Blues and Royals.

"As Officer Commanding Household Cavalry, Silver Stick in Waiting to HM the Queen and Steward of the Jockey Club, he is no doubt eminently qualified for the promotion, but he is not a veterinary surgeon." This rather sour tally of Parker Bowles's achievements constituted an unprecedented attack on a brother officer, and led to accusations that the protest had less to do with the brigadier's want of professional qualifications and more to do with his extramural activities and friendships. Moreover, he was accused—though not by Clifford— of having ducked foreign postings that would have carried brigadier rank in preference to remaining in London: "The army had to look round for a suitable position and that was the only brigadier's job available, so they gave it to Andrew," said a friend. "It caused a lot of resentment."

Indeed, Brigadier Clifford was not alone—he was joined by other retired brigadiers from the corps who launched an attack via the Royal College of Veterinary Surgeons, claiming the appointment of a non-vet was unethical. "They were very upset and demanded some immediate action," said a member of the college.

The Ministry of Defence climbed down. It decreed that when Brigadier Parker Bowles took up his controversial appointment he would limit his orders to management, and keep out of the clinical field. This meant, inevitably, that the veterinary workload of other senior officers would increase. But it also meant that his last command before retiring from the army in December 1994 would be a bed of nails; he would be surrounded by brother officers who would continue to mutter, with little justification, that he got the job because of his contacts, not on merit. For a man who, in Rhodesia, persuaded a group of guerrillas to lay down their weapons while he himself was unarmed, this was a bitter pill to swallow. Veterinary surgeons were hardly frontline troops.

The tensions at work and at home took their toll on Andrew and Camilla, and for the first time friends started to discuss quite seriously the possibility that the couple might part after twenty years of marriage. The *Daily Express* columnist Ross Benson observed: "Despite an almost superhuman effort to come to terms with the revelations of the past few months, the tension generated has pushed them to breaking point." Camilla was now rarely to be seen at home; she had made a visit to Italy in the wake of the Camillagate scandal, and was now spending considerable amounts of time in London. What the article did not say, although the inference was clear, was that she was seeing Charles. It was easier to be anonymous in London than risk his visiting her house, or her going to Highgrove. Their carefully constructed network of "safe houses" had been blown, at least for the time being—and Camilla and Charles desperately needed to see each other.

Soon the talk of divorce became a roar, but such defeatism from friends drew a sharp rebuttal from Andrew's cousin Lord Beaverbrook, a former lord-in-waiting to the queen, who protested: "This is totally preposterous. Anyone who knows Andrew will understand that he will stand by his wife in these difficult times."

Andrew's younger brother Simon—who introduced the couple all those years ago while working for Major Bruce Shand's Mayfair wine merchants—said: "Both Andrew and Camilla have said they will never divorce and, while the relationship is rather eccentric, it appears to work. They get on well."

Maybe the pill was sugared somewhat by the publication of a racy novel on one of Andrew's favorite sports, *Polo* by Jilly Cooper. The narrative was enlivened by a character called Drew Benedict, a dashing captain whose name, and possibly exploits, were inspired by the brigadier. The fictional captain's Christian name is a diminutive of Andrew, and Benedict a neat reference to his Roman Catholicism. Parker Bowles was said to be highly amused by this canonization in print.

It was a brief moment of levity in an otherwise grim drama. Fearful of being bugged, desperate that their continuing relationship should not be further uncovered, Charles and Camilla were at pains to put distance between them. Camilla's by-now-traditional spring sojourn at Birkhall on the Balmoral estate was canceled, and she and Andrew made an effort to be seen together publicly—as much for the sake of their children as anything else.

In May the couple turned out for the wedding of twenty-five-year-old Sarah Ward at the village church of Chilton Foliat in Wiltshire. But as the bride was given away by her father, Gerald Ward, Camilla's thoughts must have strayed back to the night in 1972 when he and she and Prince Charles and Princess Anne danced the night away at Annabel's, and to what might have been if things had worked out differently.

During this period, in the summer of 1993, Charles and Camilla's relationship intensified under the immense pressure both were facing. Charles, attacked on all sides, had lost the confidence of the nation. Opinion poll after opinion poll offered alternative solutions to his acceding to the throne, mostly involving his passing the kingship straight on to Prince William; his popularity sank to an all-time low, way beneath the errant Duchess of York's.

"Despite all the talk about him having no real job, Charles has always had a clear-cut picture of his own destiny," one royal source observed. "Though he could be frustrated by the wait for kingship, he had created what he considered a worthwhile role for himself, championing the common man against the bureaucrats and taking a swipe at political correctness where it prevailed over traditional values." All fine and dandy, except that it was now rendered worthless by the publication of a telephone call.

The royal disinformation machine kicked in. In June the *Daily Express* ran the headline: CHARLES GAVE UP CAMILLA 2 YEARS AGO, and underneath its royal correspondent wrote:

> FRIENDS CLOSE TO THE PRINCE, WHO IS BEGINNING TO GROW IN CONFIDENCE AS HE PUTS THE CONTROVERSY OF HIS MARRIAGE BEHIND HIM, ARE ANXIOUS TO PLAY DOWN THIS LATEST OUTBURST. ONE SAID: "THERE IS NOTHING MORE THAT CAN COME OUT ABOUT THE PRINCE'S RELATIONSHIP WITH CAMILLA. AS FAR AS WE ARE CONCERNED, IT IS ALL OLD HAT."
>
> IT WAS ALSO CLAIMED THAT THE PRINCE'S RELATIONSHIP WITH CAMILLA HAS BEEN OVER FOR MORE THAN TWO YEARS, A FULL 12 MONTHS BEFORE ANDREW MORTON'S BOOK *DIANA: HER TRUE STORY* WAS PUBLISHED.
>
> "IT WAS ALL SO UNNECESSARY," SAID THE FRIEND. "ALL THE HUMILIATION, PAIN AND HEARTACHE THAT FOLLOWED COULD HAVE BEEN AVOIDED. THE PRINCE ENDED HIS RELATIONSHIP WITH CAMILLA TWO YEARS AGO IN THE SPRING OF 1991. HE KNEW HE HAD TO GIVE HER UP AND HE DID."

This was one of the most mendacious pieces yet planted in a journalist's ear. The source was sufficiently highly placed for the reporter to believe what he was hearing—it was, after all, a carbon copy of Commander Richard Aylard's briefing to selected newspapers, months before, about the Togetherness Tour. But now, as then, the information was misleading. The source went on to vouchsafe that Charles had made a concerted effort to save his marriage but Diana had rejected all his approaches, and that it was on the ill-fated tour of Korea—the last Charles and Diana would ever undertake—that the princess had flatly refused to consider a reconciliation.

This last adumbration neatly got over any embarrassment Commander Aylard may have felt about misleading the press into believing there was life in a long-dead marriage, but it lacked conviction. Nevertheless, the source went on: "After that trip he knew his marriage was finished, but suggestions that he again turned to Camilla are just not true. The prince feared that if he was ever seen with Camilla again it would finally wreck his chances of becoming King. The people would not accept him."

So, went the source, in an "emotional meeting," Charles said he wanted to end the friendship so he could make a final effort to save his troubled marriage, and that since then, Charles had "stuck to his word" and not pursued Camilla.

The report concluded:

In fact, it was 45-year-old Camilla, now beginning to lose her looks, who could not cope with being dumped by the man she cherished. She pursued him. In January, after the Camillagate scandal hit the monarchy even further, the prince made a gentleman's agreement with Brigadier Parker Bowles never to see his wife again.

The report was arrant nonsense, but the Machiavellian men who provided its synthesis were by now desperate. The twenty-fifth anniversary of Charles's investiture as Prince of Wales was now just a year away, and the task of Tippexing the Tampax was proving considerably more difficult than at first envisaged.

Meanwhile, the strain on Camilla was becoming ever more visible. By June friends were expressing alarm at the state of her health and talked about the "intolerable pressure" she was under: "I am genuinely worried about her. The spark has gone out of her life and she looks haunted and hunted," said one. As her forty-sixth birthday approached she was said to be looking older than her years: friends conceded that she was "in touch" with Charles, though maintained the fiction that she had not seen him for six months. This not wholly credible version nonetheless put paid to the claims of Charles's "friend" who averred they had not met for two years.

But the stakes were high in the game to win back the affections of the British public in time for Charles's first great anniversary, and the end justified the means.

In the early autumn Camilla's spirits had revived sufficiently to embark on a tour of India with Gerald Ward's wife, Amanda, and with Emilie van Cutsem, whose house, Northmore, had featured in the Camillagate tapes. But fears which remained that she had undergone a nervous breakdown during the summer were quashed by Andrew Parker Bowles, who declared: "She is perfectly all right. She has gone away on holiday with another couple of girls, that's all." He added with uncharacteristic frankness that the couple were working hard to make their marriage work: "Everything is all right between us."

Days later, on her return, Camilla neatly avoided Diana at a memorial service for the Earl of Westmorland, the former Master of the Queen's Horse. Unlike the El Alamein service a year before, there was no confrontation between the two women, but observers were able to assess the comparative damage that events had inflicted on each of them: Diana, the nervous, self-obsessed bulimic who had made theatrical attempts at suicide, sparkled radiantly in black. Camilla, the steely horsewoman whose resolve had stiffened Charles's backbone, looked shattered and almost old enough to be Diana's mother. Though she had regained some of the curves which her prince found so appealing, it was an ironic twist to see such a difference between the two women.

At this point, disbelievers who still clung to the hope that the events of the past few months had been simply a weird and distressing nightmare were finally disabused when Andrew's sister-in-law Carolyn gave an interview to an Australian women's magazine. The Parker Bowles marriage, she said, was a "convenient and unusual" one.

"Everyone knows Camilla and Andrew have an arranged marriage," she said. "Ever since they married they have had a fairly free life together." However, she dismissed the suggestion that the couple might divorce: "Why would they? They get on very well and what they do suits them both quite well."

The effect of the Camillagate tapes' publication had changed their subject's life: "She just doesn't go out, except to private parties. Can you blame her? Imagine going to the supermarket after you have had those tapes quoted at you in all the newspapers and magazines."

The public, by now almost as battle-fatigued as the players in this drama, took this first admission from a member of the Parker Bowles family—that Charles and Camilla had had an affair—with remarkable calm. Christmas was coming, and after nearly a year of scandal and intrigue, they felt they'd heard the worst.

Two or three days later she made a brief appearance in front of the cameras to demonstrate how unmoved she was by her sister-in-law's comments. Indeed, she looked remarkably healthy and confident as her brother-in-law Simon confirmed that she was feeling much better. Close friends had helped her through a bad patch, he said, and added: "Things have really picked up for her. She's been out much more than before. I don't know what her relationship is with Prince Charles at the moment, but she seems happy."

He added that royal circles were still what he described as a "no go area" for Camilla: "The one thing she would never do is embarrass the royal family," he said. As if to underline this, she authorized friends to let it be known that there would be no divorce between her and Andrew. Discussions had taken place over their respective positions which had managed to resolve whatever problems existed in their highly unusual marriage. A two-sentence statement, issued jointly but unofficially, proclaimed: "We will never divorce. It is not something that has been considered."

Into this flurry of feelgood communication with the outside world suddenly stepped the surprising figure of Bruce Shand. Now seventy-six, he declared he had never given an interview before—but suddenly he was ready to do so, and one must surmise that since he had nothing in particular to sell, this was to be his own small contribution to his daughter's rehabilitation.

In the event, the interview was remarkable for what it did not say, rather than what it did. His feelings on sexual permissiveness: "It's a pity that the ties of marriage have been so destroyed by it." Has the country gone to the dogs? "There's been a tremendous deterioration of conduct and respect." He revealed a potentially embarrassing encounter with the queen—not over his daughter and her son, but in his role as a member of the Queen's Body Guard ("always dressed for the Battle of Water-loo").

His most arduous duty, he said, was to carry the queen's standard on state occasions. Once, cramped for room when he was required to lower the standard to the queen as she passed through the royal gallery, he managed to hook the handbag of a French visitor on its butt end. "That was dramatic, what? The Queen was very amused by the whole thing."

It was a deft and charming display, without giving a thing away.

* * *

When the Princess of Wales wrested away the initiative from her husband with the publication of *Diana: Her True Story,* she must have known it was only a matter of time before she lost the advantage she had gained. From the moment in June 1992 when it hit the bookshops, courtiers and royals alike were searching for a solution. And, it must be said, their judgments were tinged with more than a hint of revenge.

It took eighteen months. But by December 1993 the die had been cast—and the princess was forced into a humbling withdrawal from public life which left politicians, churchmen, and the public gasping in amazement.

The statement was so effectively stage-managed that no one grasped that her withdrawal was involuntary. In the unlikely surroundings of the London Hilton Hotel, the princess announced: "I will be reducing the extent of the public life I have led so far. Over the next few months I will be seeking a more suitable way of combining a meaningful public role with, hopefully, a more private life."

Should anyone, in the heat of the moment, suddenly remember to ask why the princess was making this astonishing announcement, a barely veiled reason was contained in the section which read: "When I started my public life twelve years ago, I understood that the media might be interested in what I did. I realized then that their attention would inevitably focus on both our public and private lives. But I was not aware of how overwhelming that attention would become; nor the extent to which it would affect both my public duties and my personal life, in a manner that has been hard to bear."

This part of her statement touched the hearts of her audience, drawn from supporters of the Headway National Head Injuries Association, for within the previous month sneak photographs of the princess working out in a West London gymnasium had been published by the Mirror group, to universal disgust. But still, her declaration stopped just about short of humbug, for the present crisis, which had kept the House of Windsor's name in the headlines on a daily basis for the past eighteen months, was entirely of Diana's making.

Blaming the message bearers is an old trick, much beloved by politicians, and here Diana used it to great effect; but one academic, Dr. David Starkey of the London School of Economics, was unimpressed: "She wanted not only to protect her privacy, but have all the indulgence and pleasure of the private life of a rich young woman," he said. "But you can't do it, especially when you've paraded your private life before the public when it suits you. She is now complaining of media intrusion, but who was it who spilled the beans on every detail of her married life to the press via Andrew Morton's book?"

Initially, at least. But upon closer scrutiny the message she gave out was riddled with inconsistencies. In June 1992, at the time of the Morton book, the message she delivered via intermediaries to *The Sunday Times* was interpreted thus:

SHE HAD A GREATER UNDERSTANDING OF HERSELF AND A SURER SENSE OF PURPOSE. IN HER WORK WITH THE SICK, THE DYING AND THE DISTRESSED, SHE HAD FOUND A CALLING.

In December that year, at the time of the separation announcement, she delivered a public message which went, in part: "I want you to be certain of this—our work together will continue unchanged."

But even as she spoke, the machinery was in motion to put Diana on the back burner—and off the hob altogether in due course. For in the aftermath of the separation she perceived a globetrotting role for herself where she would become a figure on the world stage. Friends of the princess revealed that she would return to a scaled-down public life in the spring. "She will no longer be the Princess of Wales but a princess for the world," said one, somewhat grandiosely. "She will concentrate on the international side of her charity work, while the royal side of her life will diminish."

Another version, authorized to be leaked by the princess, continued the "dynamic new role on the international stage" theme. Plans were under way for her to head a charitable foundation, working as an executive and decision maker rather than simply a photogenic figurehead, it was hinted. This independent organization would be dedicated to offering help and encouragement to the disadvantaged around the world, with Diana concentrating her efforts on overseas issues, leaving her husband to work on projects in Britain without the inevitable clashes. In any event, reports of her going into exile were "grossly exaggerated," she said.

But Charles was having none of it—his advisers warned him that his own role would continue to be diminished all the time Diana continued on the public stage. A squabble arose over separate trips to Russia—both wanted to go, neither was prepared to back down.

In a meeting with the prime minister, Charles made it clear that he had to stand alone on the royal stage, and that if he was to become an effective king, there must be no distractions from his center-stage position. While the premier remained transfixed by indifference over this royal push-me-pull-you, his foreign secretary, Douglas Hurd, wasted no time in coming to Charles's aid.

Hurd, the Old Etonian son of an obscure life peer, had distinguished himself in the diplomatic service before carving an equally successful career in politics. He was, most people thought, sufficiently "Establishment" not to be dazzled by royalty, yet the encomium he delivered on Charles's behalf was positively embarrassing in a politician holding the second-highest political office. Charles, he claimed joyfully, was "a star."

"I have seen him in action in many different circumstances and he is a star," he said. "He would be a star even if he were not the Prince of Wales.

"We must use his particular gifts, which go beyond the ordinary matters of royalty into the interests which he has developed, sometimes business, sometimes social, sometimes environmental.

"Thank heavens," he proclaimed, that Charles would one day be king. It was difficult to imagine that the rest of the Cabinet felt quite as Douglas Hurd did; maybe, felt some observers, he was overcompensating for the indifference or downright hostility some ministers felt toward someone who had let the side down.

In October Diana, too, had a meeting with John Major in which she outlined her plans for the future to include more trips like her recent successful tour in Tibet. Even at that late stage, she harbored the belief that she would have a future as a roving ambassador—she and the overseas development minister, Baroness Chalker, had reached an understanding and mutual respect, and saw much fruitful work ahead together in the underdeveloped countries of the world. At that stage it seemed possible that she might attract the support of John Major, who was not slow to recognize her international appeal: "He has always taken an interest in the royal marriage, and took the unusual step of announcing the separation himself when it was widely regarded that the Palace should have done it," said a government source. "He believes she is a very important figure as she is the mother of the future king, so he feels it is his business to make sure she is given a suitable role."

Diana even drafted in Sir Gordon Reece, a deft and dapper image burnisher, to help in her attempts to set up her own secretariat and her own agenda. But it all came to nothing, for in the end Charles, as future king, pulled rank. Sir Gordon told Diana she was fighting a losing battle, and with few other big hitters behind her to support her case—she had, after all, no constitutional position even though she was wife and mother of future kings—the bid for her own platform collapsed.

It would not be entirely misleading to suggest that palace sources, briefing the press and thereby the world, did not contradict anyone who suggested that Diana's decision to quit was hers, and hers alone. Was it hasty? Possibly. Emotional? No comment.

One seasoned observer, looking at Diana's plight, commented: "It was a classic mistake, and a classic ploy used by the royal family. Whenever they want a problem to disappear they manipulate that person into a corner so that they inevitably go abroad or disappear from sight. You have only to look at the way they dealt with the Duke of Windsor or the Duchess of York. They believe 'out of sight, out of mind,' and by the look of it, Diana has fallen for their plan—hook, line, and sinker."

Even so, one other figure—as bizarre in his way as Sir Jimmy Savile, who all those months ago had tried to broker a reconciliation after Charles's self-imposed exile at Balmoral—emerged as a supporter at this time: Lord Archer.

The former deputy chairman of the Conservative party and bestselling novelist was summoned to Kensington Palace the day before Diana's speech and invited to read it and offer suggestions. Archer later commented: "I was very sad when I read it. We discussed how and when she would speak, and the best way to do it with dignity."

A measure of decorum was achieved that day, but Diana's next outing was anything but dignified. On the following Monday she turned out at Heathrow Airport to name a new Virgin Atlantic jet. She was subjected to a humiliating ordeal at the hands of the effervescent head of Virgin, Richard Branson, who popped champagne corks, put his arm round her, and treated her like an actress from a television soap opera.

It was a demoralizing rout, and she headed for anonymity with her head down and the tears once again welling in her eyes. Her husband, meanwhile, spent two hours in the company of Camilla Parker Bowles that night.

This was something that would not have found favor with the Reverend Tony Higton, a vociferous member of the Church of England Synod and the long-standing vicar of Hawkwell in Essex. "It is with great sadness," he began, "that I have reached the conclusion that Prince Charles is not fit to be the next king of England.

"I believe that Charles can only become king if he totally denies he committed adultery with Camilla Parker Bowles. Alternatively he should make a public expression of remorse and penitence. And if he really said that he was sorry, and confirmed that any romance was over, then I think that he could still be king.

"But in the absence of either of these options, I have to say I think he is unfit to be king, and I think it would be better if the crown passed straight to Prince William—provided he maintained the highest standards in his private life."

Mr. Higton was, perhaps, one of the most clamorous of the clergy, but he nonetheless spoke for a still significant Establishment body—the Church of England. Charles's road to respectability was barred by their surpliced figures; he needed their sanction before he could be fully rehabilitated in the eyes of the populace.

"We require even higher standards from people in public places today than we did in the past," continued Mr. Higton. "We must take a firm stand on adultery—I think it is very unfortunate if people in such high places as Prince Charles cannot behave morally.

"This country has one of the highest divorce rates of any country in the world and I believe that we have all got to start pulling together to put right this moral decay. We should have strong leadership from our royals."

And Arthur Leggatt, secretary of the five-thousand-strong Church Union, said: "It would compromise the teachings of the scripture which says clearly that a person taken in divorce has committed adultery. An adulterer should not be head of the Church of England."

The Church, silent all these years, had suddenly found its voice.

Chapter 9

$\mathcal{T}$HESE TURBULENT PRIESTS

HE WORDS "CONSTITUTIONAL CRISIS" STRIKE TERROR INTO THE HEARTS OF the royal family and their supporters. There has already been one this century, and the healing process after the Abdication was a long and slow one, jerkily started by King George VI but more smoothly developed by his daughter.

Ever-conscious of the waxing and waning appeal of monarchy worldwide—the rise of King Juan Carlos of Spain is matched by the final deroyalization in 1994 of King Constantine of Greece—the House of Windsor remains sensitive to its critics. Though during the royal marriage crisis no active republican movement emerged, it became perfectly clear that the royal family's greatest enemy was the nation's contempt. Britain stood back and watched with indifference as its first family dug their own grave.

Certainly in the early stages, it seemed that others were more alive to the growing crisis than were the royals themselves. Following the announcement in the House of Commons by the prime minister that Charles and Diana were to separate, a jittery Church of England moved swiftly to dispel any idea that the prince's future position as Supreme

Governor could be jeopardized. Prevented by his absence in Sri Lanka from making any personal statement, the Archbishop of Canterbury, Dr. George Carey, instructed the Archbishop of York to go to the House of Lords to deliver the Church's own deliberations on the crisis.

On December 9, 1992, the same day as the prime minister's historic statement, Dr. John Habgood told a thunderstruck upper chamber: "We urge the public to react with compassion and understanding, and not to add unnecessarily to the pain already suffered by those involved. The interests and feelings of Prince Henry and Prince William should be borne constantly in mind."

The archbishop went on: "Questions will inevitably be raised about the implications of the separation for His Royal Highness's position as future Supreme Governor of the Church of England.

"From a legal viewpoint, marital status does not affect the succession to the throne and hence to the title of Supreme Governor. The monarch is Supreme Governor of the Church by virtue of being the Sovereign: there is no other legal requirement. Under the Act of Settlement of 1701 the Sovereign must be a communicant member of the Church of England.

"In the case of unsuccessful marriages, the Church of England accepts that there are sometimes circumstances, however sad, where separation is the lesser evil and hence the best way forward. To undergo such an experience and take such a decision does not in itself in any sense disqualify a person from holding the title of Supreme Governor."*

Thus, the Church's position was set out in clear and unequivocal terms—Charles would be Supreme Governor when he became king. But things were far from being that simple. And within a year discussions would have taken place, the purpose of which was to prevent Charles from ever becoming the Church's figurehead.

Cynics in a nonreligious age might ask what difference it makes in Great Britain if the established church and the royal family should part company. Though Anglicanism is the nation's official religion, only a small

---

*Six weeks later, the archbishop's position appeared to have hardened somewhat. Appearing on the BBC television show *The Heart of the Matter,* he said that while he did not agree that recent exposure in the media of the Prince of Wales's relationship with Camilla Parker Bowles had made it difficult for him to become Supreme Governor of the Church of England, "all tolerance has its limits."

percentage of the population now attends church regularly; since the Coronation of 1952 an increasingly multiracial society has evolved, with more and more Britons belonging to other religions. If Charles is to reign as king, he will be these people's sovereign too, and—his supporters argue—the backing of the established church is far less crucial to successful kingship than at any time since the reign of King Henry VIII.

Having pledged to investigate these minorities—Sikhs, Muslims, Hindus—in his travels up and down the country, and having familiarized himself with their lives and culture, however superficially, Charles had adopted a somewhat diluted view of the importance of the Church of England. Certainly that was the prevailing opinion from within the Church's ranks; but while many grumbled few, initially, wished to upset the status quo.

But the seismic rumblings among a powerful minority within the Church of England finally erupted on December 5, 1993, when the Archdeacon of York, the Venerable George Austin, spoke up for many disaffected fellow clerics when he launched an outright attack on the Prince of Wales.

"Does he have the right to be trusted with the role of king, if his attitude to matrimony is so cavalier?" he asked.

"Prince Charles made solemn vows before God in church about his marriage, and it seems he began to break them almost immediately. He has broken the trust on one thing, and broken vows on another. How can he then go into church, into Westminster Abbey, and take the Coronation vows?"

He concluded, to devastating effect: "Are we to believe him that he will keep those? It brings into question the whole attitude of Charles to vows, trust, and so on. The Church forgives of course; if I as Archdeacon of York fiddled the books or cheated on my wife or broke my ordination vows, God would forgive me if I repented. But I might be totally unsuitable at the end of it to be Archdeacon of York."

The response was instantaneous, and dramatic. Though Austin's position in the Church was acknowledged as that of a dedicated antiliberal and was thus discounted by many of his senior colleagues, his statements echoed the notorious speech made by the Bishop of Bradford, the Right Reverend Walter Blunt, on December 1, 1936, to an annual diocesan conference.

Spoken in the dying days of Edward VIII's brief reign, it had the effect of opening the floodwaters of criticism, which for too long had been held back. Ingenuously, Blunt later claimed he had meant something else when he commended the king to God's grace "which he will so abundantly need—for the King is a man like any other—if he is to do his duty properly. We hope that he was aware of this need. Some of us wish that he gave more positive signs of such awareness." Many took this to be a reference to the king's all-consuming and destructive love for Mrs. Simpson.

Whatever their original purpose, Blunt's words had the effect of finally releasing a nation's newspapers from the yoke of degrading self-censorship. At last—when the Abdication crisis was almost over—Fleet Street felt free to reveal to its readers the appalling truth of what had been going on for many months in Buckingham Palace and in the corridors of power.

Almost fifty-seven years to the day, in December 1993, the more superstitious courtiers in Buckingham Palace sensed a similar disaster in the offing. Though the "bush telegraph" had given them warning of earlier shocks in the press, they could not be certain that other embarrassments, which had been held back—just as the Squidgy tapes had been, for many months—were not about to be released.

This new assault, from within the heart of the Establishment, would give Fleet Street the justification it had long been seeking to reveal even more damaging material. Or so the official thinking went. Certainly, no one from the queen down could have contemplated the existence, let alone the publication, of the Camillagate tapes—was this the moment when Charles would be hit with a final coup de grace?

Nothing happened immediately. But three days later the archdeacon of York returned to the attack, in *The Times*.

Half a century before, the country's most respected newspaper held the line, along with the rest of Fleet Street, in its silence over Edward and Mrs. Simpson, though, in its bookish way, it managed to convey to the cognoscenti a whiff of the hushed-up scandal by publishing a letter that included the lines from Racine's *Berenice*:

. . . so vile a thing,
Tied to thy train—a hopeless, throneless King,

Loathesome to men below, to gods above,
A sad example of the sleights of Love.

But half a century later it was *The Times* which, this time more forth-
rightly, was to spur a nationwide debate. In his article of December 8,
Dr. Austin wrote of his conviction that Prince Charles began to break
his marriage vows soon after promising lifelong faithfulness to the Princess of Wales.

Referring to the vows Charles would make at his coronation as king,
he observed: "If his attitude to his vows of matrimony was so cavalier,
has he the right to be trusted in this second solemnity?" He repeated
what he had said on BBC radio—that he would feel duty bound to re-
sign if he cheated on his wife, because he would have betrayed the trust
placed in him. "It may be that Prince Charles has gone too far for that
same trust to be restored," he concluded.

To the dismay of the prince and his advisers, it was learned that
several senior bishops were also privately expressing their reservations
about Charles's fitness to succeed to the throne.

The Bishop of Sodor and Man, the Right Reverend Noel Debroy
Jones, went one step further by going public on the issue. He declared
that the breaking of the marriage vows was "an indication of a moral
flaw which would be worrying. It is scriptural to think that of those to
whom much is given, much should be expected." He added: "I think
marriage vows are vows and I do not happily accept the remarriage of
divorcées in Church."

He concluded: "It would be right for us to say that anyone who
aspires to a position of real high office must also have really high morals. If you cannot take that on, you should not actually do it.

"If I had a future monarch who was divorced I would find it very
difficult to say I was giving allegiance to that person."

Next it was the turn of the Bishop of Kensington, the Right Reverend John Hughes, who delivered an equally devastating analysis: "The
Church might well remind him that the royal family is fighting for its
credibility. Some attempt to repair his family life would be the best example he could give to the nation. He ought to be looking in a positive
way at the restoration of the family.

"To marry a divorcée would render his position untenable. If he were to marry a divorcée he would have to renounce the Crown."

The many pro-Establishment figures within the Church wishing to preserve unaltered the relationship between sovereign and Church kept their own counsel. Others, however, felt strongly that the ties were loosening. The Right Reverend Peter Coleman, suffragan bishop to the Diocese of Exeter, stated ominously: "If Charles were divorced, depending on the reason, this would be a matter of serious anxiety vis-à-vis his Coronation. Most of us will be realising that there are real difficulties ahead."

The implication was quite clear: Could an utterly discredited king summon sufficient bishops to crown him? These anxieties were echoed by the Archdeacon of Canterbury, the Venerable Michael Till. "There may come a point where the credibility has disappeared," he said. "People are holding their breath about it. There is a question-mark. Whether that fades into silence or is consolidated depends upon the next weeks, years and months." He added that the prince's position would be undermined by divorce and would worsen still further if he remarried a divorcée. "I think the Church would find it difficult, as would the congregations. All those people who have kept their marriages going would find it very hard to handle."

These comments rained like hammer blows upon the prince and his advisers. It is not unusual for members of the royal family to suffer criticism by politicians, the press, and pressure groups. But such a concerted display of displeasure from within the ranks of the religious establishment could do nothing but cause acute alarm.

The prince's friend Nicholas Soames, long ago his equerry but now a government minister and bound into the affair by his sister Charlotte's relationship with Andrew Parker Bowles, could remain silent no longer. As The Times printed the Archdeacon of York's attack on the prince, Soames insisted that the archdeacon spoke for no one but himself. He declaimed: "What he has said is a disgrace. The suggestion that being heir to the throne is a lottery is completely inappropriate. To be heir to the throne is not an ambition, but it is a duty and an obligation which will befall the Prince of Wales at a sad moment later in his life.

"The Archbishop [of Canterbury] has made it plain that the Archdeacon speaks entirely for himself and not for the Church of England.

What was said today was utterly outrageous. I am very surprised by what this man has said—it is disgraceful, wounding, ignorant, and hurtful."

Some interpreted this vigorous and unscripted defense of his best friend as an indication of the panic that had set in at St. James's Palace. But Mr. Soames had not finished. "The Archdeacon shows a remarkable ignorance of the true feelings of most people in Britain who want to see the happiness of the Prince of Wales and the stability of the throne with everything that implies for British life. I do not think the vapourings of a completely unrepresentative archdeacon will make any difference. But it was still quite, quite disgraceful."

If Soames felt this quixotic attack was sufficient to turn the tide, others did not. Clerics rarely drawn into public controversy were suddenly determined to be heard. That so many voices, despite Soames's belief, sang in unison against the prince impressed itself upon the nation—and in the absence of any real indicators, official or otherwise, of what was to happen next, most came to the conclusion that the publication of the Camillagate tapes must result in divorce for the Parker Bowleses. That in turn led many to believe that Charles would marry Camilla. His expressions of devotion on the tapes made it plain that he had been distracted from the course of duty by her. Who was to say what would happen next?

Into this crisis charged more men with a message. The Archdeacon of West Ham, the Venerable Timothy Stevens, warned: "There would be many in the Church of England who would argue that to marry a divorcée would make it untenable for him to be head of the Church." And the Archdeacon of Chesterfield, the Venerable Charles Phizackerly, added: "There will be those who will be very disappointed that the full ideals and standards of Christian family life are not being embodied. I think those people would not want him to be Head of the Church. I think it is sad from that point of view that an icon of family perfection is tarnished."

Within the space of days, a survey was taken of 100 members of the 574-strong Synod, which is divided into three houses of bishops, clergy, and laity. Of this sample, 47 percent thought the Prince of Wales should not become Supreme Governor upon accession, while 27 percent thought he should not become king if it were shown to be true that he had had an affair with Camilla Parker Bowles. A significant but by no means overwhelming proportion—38 percent—supported a general disestablishment of the Church, while the same proportion thought it would be necessary to disestablish if Charles became king.

A day after these findings were published, *Today* newspaper reported that a worried prime minister had ordered his ministers to come out in Charles's defense. This was an unprecedented step in twentieth-century politics and cannot have been done without full consultation with the queen's private secretary, Sir Robert Fellowes, and the prince himself, since for one political party to deviate from a neutral line on the royal family invites the Opposition to take the contrary view; and bringing the royal family down into the cockpit of domestic politics is something successive monarchs and their advisers have tried hard to avoid.

Nevertheless, John Major's instructions resulted in Foreign Secretary Douglas Hurd glibly describing Charles as a "star." Other ministers, including John Gummer, William Waldegrave, and Lord Wakeham also offered their opinions—consistently favorable—on the heir to the throne. Wakeham, the head of the Privy Council, added there were grave dangers "if churchmen vandalise our monarchy," deftly omitting from his attack that the churchmen's voiced opinions had only been triggered by Charles's own dual standards of morality.

In addition, an irritating, but inescapable, point was raised by the former Bishop of Birmingham, the Right Reverend Hugh Montefiore. What, he asked, would happen if the queen dropped dead tomorrow? There was no way you could have Diana—officially separated from Charles as she was—crowned as queen. His comments exposed a massive flaw in the leisurely distancing process going on between the princely husband and wife; and more important, they dealt a death knell to the optimistic claims by Buckingham Palace and Downing Street that Charles and Diana's separation had "no constitutional implications."

Dr. Montefiore said: "The separated Princess of Wales cannot be crowned Queen. It would be abhorrent to a large proportion of the English people. The question is bound to arise whether the Archbishop [of Canterbury] would in good conscience be able to crown her."

Just at that moment, this debate on the succession seemed an arbitrary one—yet within weeks the queen, now sixty-seven, had fallen heavily from her horse while wearing no protective headgear. If the accident had taken place on a paved road, or the horse had rolled on her, the argument would not seem quite so abstruse after all. There would be the coronation of a new king. By then it would be too late to ask the question, What to do with Diana, still married to the king, still mother of the next king?

None of this was lost on courtiers at St. James's Palace, who felt on the one hand a very real anger that their attempts to reestablish Prince Charles's credibility were seen to be built on shifting sands, yet on the other had no means of venting their frustration on those they felt were truly to blame for the present impasse—the press, the Church, and, inevitably, Diana herself. Theirs was truly a no-win situation.

At that point, in late 1993, there was a very real danger that the issue could turn from an ugly row into something permanently damaging. Privy Council sources leaked their grave concern that Charles's relationship with Camilla showed no signs of abating and, more important, that Mrs. Parker Bowles now appeared to be wielding considerable influence over him—to the extent that she was said to have put her foot down on an attempt during the summer to create a new working relationship between Charles and Diana.

This, if true, put Camilla Parker Bowles in a new and far more sinister position. It was one thing for her to be the prince's mistress, tending to his every need and soothing his fevered brow—that, to some, was bad enough. Far worse was the idea that she should now step between the Prince and Princess of Wales and ordain what Charles should, and should not, do. This, if true, really was the exercise of power without responsibility.

But it was not true. Any views Camilla expressed on Palace attempts to kick-start the failed marriage were merely mirror images of what the prince himself had said—that it was too late, that Diana had gone too far, and that his wife now posed a very grave danger to the stability of the monarchy in Britain.

But by now even privy councillors, let alone senior clergymen and other leading public figures, were feeling jumpy. No one had anything to gain by a major constitutional crisis breaking just now, but the difficulty was that no one knew what Charles's next move was going to be. Would he divorce? Would he marry Camilla after she had obtained a divorce? Would he do what he had secretly threatened to do—quit the country of his birth and set up a home with Camilla in Florence, where Alice Keppel ended her days? There were many questions, but no answers. Charles, striving to maintain his equilibrium, had decided on the policy of "least said, soonest mended." It was hard to put over to him the highly anxious state of others, who had rather more vestigial roles in this drama.

One political source, referring to the alarming lack of information over Charles's intentions, revealed: "Some of the most senior Palace and Anglican figures believe that Charles will face enough difficulties if he insists on going ahead with a divorce from Diana, without any further complications.

"They feel that if Mrs. Parker Bowles comes back into the picture, Charles would be publicly signaling his intention to renounce the throne at a future date and step aside in favor of Prince William. That would be contrasted unfavorably with the position of his aunt Princess Margaret, who put duty before love when she agreed to break with Group Captain Peter Townsend." The not particularly coded message— tell us what you plan to do, Charles, before the entire Establishment turns against you.

What was not generally known was the part that the Archbishop of Canterbury was playing in the whole drama. Unlike his remote predecessor in the Margaret/Townsend imbroglio, George Carey took it upon himself to become an honest broker in the Waleses' decaying marriage. During the summer months of 1993 he emerged as a firm friend and supporter of the Prince of Wales in the high-profile war with Diana for public support, yet attempted at all turns to use his mediating skills.

Carey had the added advantage, to Charles, of believing that the prince was his own sternest critic. He told fellow clerics that while divorce might not be a bar to his becoming king, Charles would be "acutely sensitive" to any risk of damaging his status within the Church. But Carey's message contained an ominous note: Any chance of Prince Charles's being crowned would evaporate completely if his liaison with Camilla took on a more public profile.

But all this sub-rosa activity went on without the knowledge of the rest of Carey's Church. They were less happy with the way things were turning out—*Today* newspaper interviewed a cross-section of clergy and reported: "While several supported Charles, the majority showed mounting support for the disestablishment of the Church."

In fact, according to some highly placed sources, the debate had already been in progress for some time within the higher echelons of the Church. Suddenly, and to some shockingly, it was hinted in *The Times* that senior bishops had been discussing a range of options with the queen at Buckingham Palace over a change to the 460-year relationship between the sovereign and the Church. This crucial reexamination resulted in a general conclusion that future legislation should be introduced shortly before or after the next coronation (though not within the queen's lifetime) to amend the sovereign's position. Such a move would fall short of disestablishment, but would go some way toward placating those who were dissatisfied with the present relationship between Church and State.

It would take a fly on the wall at Buckingham Palace to tell whether this was a plot by a mother against her erring son, but the proposed amendment would weaken the traditional links by abolishing the sovereign's position as Supreme Governor, while maintaining the title of Defender of the Faith. The model to be used was that of the Church of Scotland, which was established by law as the national church in that country, while acknowledging Jesus Christ as the sole king and head of the church.

Not everyone in the Church of England believed that the debate had advanced as far as this; indeed, some seasoned observers hinted at the hand of the troublesome priest George Austin in the rumors that were billowing like smoke over a guttering fire.

But of one thing most senior clerics were certain: Prince Charles was now an unwelcome figure in the Church of England. One observer commented: "In the eyes of many within the Church, the prince's image is in need of drastic improvement if he is to win back confidence and take on the role as figurehead.

"At present, in the Queen as Supreme Governor, they have an exemplary role model. To have someone with a quite frankly sleazy reputation such as Prince Charles in this position is a completely different matter. He has a difficult task ahead of him, and it is unlikely that he realizes just how far he will have to go to win back general favour within the Church.

"His image must be improved immeasurably, and that improvement can only be done by diligent work. There has to be an indication that he is attempting to do deeds for the good of society, and there is a need for years of celibacy."

To a society whose mores have changed incalculably within the space of a generation, this last may seem an excessive penalty. Outside the Roman Catholic Church, few people in Britain are prepared to listen to lectures on their sex lives, and the Prince of Wales was likely to be no exception. He was faced with the frustrating example of his ancestors—some near, some far—few of whom were beset by such moral strictures, and many of whom enjoyed their sexual *droit du seigneur* unhindered by nagging clerics.

Indeed, it might seem to the rationalist in an age where the Church has an increasingly weak grip over morality, that in seeking to impose their rules not upon the whole nation but upon one man, the bishops had completely lost the plot.

Nonetheless, the hard-liners were backed up against Charles. One insider explained: "The major problem is Charles's inability to realise the importance of his role, and the consequences of his behaviour. He felt he could carry on in the adulterous manner he had seen his father and great-uncle behave in; but he had reckoned without the combined forces of his wife, the Church, and the tabloid press. He is under scrutiny in a way no other future monarch has been, and he doesn't seem to be able to understand that the rules have changed."

Of course, the argument ran two ways—while Charles would be diminished without the Church, so the Church would be diminished if its traditional ties to the monarchy were severed. There was a genuine fear among some senior members of the Anglican hierarchy that of the two, the Church would come off worse, and the Archbishop of Canterbury set about gagging his bishops on the subject of Charles's suitability as a future Church governor.

A secret memo reflecting Dr. Carey's views was circulated in the wake of the outspoken criticism of some junior clergy. One newspaper, seeking to canvass the views of forty-five bishops on Charles's fitness to be king, discovered that two thirds of them refused to respond at all and rapidly discovered the existence of a memo from Lambeth Place which stated: "We expect Her Majesty the Queen to reign for many years yet and therefore are not prepared to respond to hypothetical questions." A spokesman later claimed that the memo was simply advice to the bishops, which they could accept or reject according to their own consciences; but its effect was to still further talk among senior clergy on this contentious issue.

Indeed, such was the determination within the Establishment to play down any hint of a constitutional crisis at this time, there appeared to be a general agreement that the standoff between Charles and the Church of England would come only when the queen died. But then, at his coronation, the new king might well find that the wording of the monarch's ceremonial vows had changed.

In the traditional coronation oath, the Archbishop of Canterbury asks the new sovereign to solemnly swear to govern the peoples of Great Britain according to the law, then asks:

"Will you to the utmost of your power maintain the laws of God and the true profession of the Gospel? Will you to the utmost of your power maintain in the United Kingdom the Protestant Reformed Religion established by law? And will you maintain and preserve inviolably the settlement of the Church of England, and the doctrine, worship, discipline and government thereof? And will you preserve unto the bishops and clergy . . . all such rights and privileges as by law shall apertain to them?"

The sovereign answers: "All this I promise to do"—*but can only do so if the question is put.* At the time of writing there was a growing belief that this section of the coronation ceremony would be rewritten, with or without Charles's consent, and that he might no longer find himself with the title Supreme Governor.

Does all this make for a constitutional crisis? Inevitably the answer must be in the affirmative; and the reasons why need to be delineated in some detail.

On the one hand, it would appear that the Church is a waning influence. In a population of roughly 60 million, membership in the Church of England now stands at 1.4 million, of which 1.1 million regularly attend church services and 2 million attend at Christmas and Easter. And although membership in the Anglican Church is 70 million worldwide, only the Church of England itself is directly linked to the monarch.

When compared to statistics from other churches, the Church of England's clout seems weak indeed. The Roman Catholic Church in Britain has around 5.6 million members, the Methodist churches nearly half a million, and the combined figure of all other Christian churches—Baptist, Orthodox, Presbyterian, and others—adds up to over 37 million Christians in the United Kingdom. When coupled with the non-Christian community, of which Muslims number 1.5 million, Sikhs 400,000, Hindus 350,000, and Jews 300,000, it becomes clear that the Church of England is, these days, very far from representative of the whole population. Thus, despite its name, it cannot be considered to be the church of the whole United Kingdom.

Yet the Church of England is part of the British Establishment, the principal denomination of the nation, its history originating in the conflict between Church and State during the Middle Ages, which culminated in the Act of Supremacy issued by King Henry VIII in 1534.

The Church's unique link with the State is secured by the fact that all sovereigns, from Mary Tudor in 1553 to the present queen, have been crowned by the Archbishop of Canterbury. This bond among church, legislature, and throne is an act of mutual support which allows the Church's bishops to sit in the House of Lords, the prime minister to advise on the appointment of bishops, and the requirement of parliamentary assent for new Church legislation.

Any sovereign may take himself out of this historic linkage, or be taken out, and survive. But if Prince Charles were to lose the support of the supposed bedrock of the Establishment, if he were to find that the Church was disputing his fitness for kingship, there would indeed be a crisis of epic proportions—one that would make his great-uncle's abdication seem piffling by comparison. Disentangling State from Church, crown from miter, would fundamentally weaken them both and dissolve the glue that binds together the nation's fabric.

As Sir Douglas Lovelock, the first Church Estates Commissioner, argued, one or all of the main pillars of the Establishment may be changed, "but history shows that once one aspect of a structure is altered, people quickly start asking if the whole thing is worth retaining."

Charles had courted the support of a wider spectrum than merely the Church of England, but only the established church could assist him in his attempts to surmount the constitutional hurdles he faced.

Catholic loyalties will always lie first with Rome, Muslim with Mecca, and the support he needed most—from a purely pragmatic standpoint—was from the religion that felt the greatest unease about his personal behavior.

Given the content of the Camillagate tapes, and the real sense of shock felt throughout the Church of England after their publication, it surprised many churchmen that the prince made no special effort to recapture their support. Successive public statements from Palace aides hinted at irritation, anger, and depression at the furor that had been created in the wake of Camillagate. Never once was there a hint of contrition.

To the Church, once the monarchy's greatest supporter, it seemed almost as if Prince Charles believed that when his time came, like Henry VII half a millennium ago, he could pick up a crown from some wayside bush and, settling it on his own head, pronounce himself king.

Chapter 10

OUT OF THE DARKNESS

THE PRINCE OF WALES'S 1994 TOUR OF AUSTRALIA BEGAN AMID A WELTER OF new opinion polls, both in Britain and the host country, which showed his popularity had sunk to an all-time low.

In Britain, one poll showed that only the Duchess of York, still stumbling in the dark after the public humiliation of her toe-sucking activities in the South of France with John Bryan two summers before, had a lower popularity rating.

In another he found that, infuriatingly, only 3 percent of people polled blamed Diana for the breakdown of their marriage, though there was some small consolation to be found in the fact that 57 percent in a nationwide poll did not think that his relationship with Camilla Parker Bowles made him unfit to rule.

Nevertheless, he was swimming against the tide in this, his twenty-fifth year as Prince of Wales. He learned with anger that the highly respected Labour MP Frank Field had called for a committee of privy councillors, chaired by the prime minister, to oversee the upbringing of Princes William and Harry, and although—unsurprisingly—nothing came of this suggestion, it was yet another shot across Charles's bow.

The previous month Charles had been on an official visit to South-wark, South London, to meet workers involved in the Gateway Project, an enterprise designed to provide accommodation and job training for the homeless and unemployed. When he arrived on December 8, the street was empty. Newspapers next day carried a tally of people who'd come to see him: photographers—13; reporters—10; members of the public—2. "He's obviously as unpopular as everyone makes out," said the crowd-control policeman whose skills, perforce, went unused that day. When finally he found himself indoors, Charles, with his usual panache, tackled twenty-one-year-old Barry Holden, who told him one of the reasons he ended up homeless was that his parents separated when he was six years old.

"Really?" said his royal inquisitor. "Why did they divorce?"

"It was due to my dad going out with another woman behind my mum's back" came the reply. Charles smiled wanly. It was time to move on.

Diana, meanwhile, was in Belfast on one of her last public engage-ments. Although, for security reasons, her visit went publicly unan-nounced the newspapers made another tally: photographers—30; reporters—10; members of the public—160. No wonder Charles could not wait for his wife's enforced retirement, for it was clear he was now being threatened with the worst fate that any future king could face—he was in grave danger of being ignored by his future subjects.

In Australia, a nation whose political leader, Paul Keating, had al-ready signaled that becoming a republic was not a matter of if but when, Charles arrived to barely veiled indifference and sparse crowds. Reports suggested that advisers had to work hard to get Charles to go to Aus-tralia at all, but a major public relations victory was needed, and could more easily be won abroad.

As he arrived in the last week in January, Charles had with him a portfolio of justificatory speeches designed to catch whatever mood he and his advisers could sense and turn to their advantage. But despite this extensive groundwork, no plans had been laid to cope with what came next.

His first major engagement was at Tumbalong Park in Sydney. A police band played "Waltzing Matilda" and "I Still Call Australia Home." Onstage the prince prepared to present prizes to a group of schoolchildren. Before him in the arena was spread a genial crowd of fifty thousand or so, but as Charles stepped forward for the prizegiving, one member of the crowd, a twenty-three-year-old anthropology student, David Kang, stood up and pulled out a gun. He sprinted toward Charles, firing in the air. For a moment no one took in what was happening and Charles failed to react, merely fiddling with his cuff links. Then with a leap up the steps Kang was on the stage, firing again. Then he tripped on a microphone cable and crashed to the floor. He was overpowered, aptly enough, by a man who had just been named Australian of the Year, yachtsman Ian Kiernan.

The gun had contained only blanks; Kang had been making an ill-considered protest about the Cambodian boat people. He made his point, but more effectively, it instantly brought a sharper focus to Charles's visit. Those who had viewed it with contempt or indifference found themselves impressed with the way Charles brushed it aside, and his comments that such alarms were all part of the job. He added wryly to the still-stunned audience: "It's all right for you, at least you've all had a drink."

Two days later an opinion poll was published as the royal roadshow hit Perth. Charles was given a rapturous reception by a newly respectful public as the poll revealed that now 63 percent of Australians believed him fit to be king. Only one in five thought he was doing a bad job, and 53 percent thought he set a good example. Compared with the findings of the poll back in Britain, this was a remarkable turnaround.

Suddenly there was a new impetus to the royal tour, given extra thrust by the new enthusiasm of ever-increasing crowds.

So what happened next would seem to many to be a logical step. Royal reporters accompanying the tour had been given unofficial briefings by courtiers who labeled it the "Tippex the Tampax" tour: Australia was the chance of a new beginning for the prince, a chance to put the past behind.

Until the gun attack, that had seemed a pretty forlorn hope, but in the wake of it, and assisted by some eulogistic analysis pieces by British journalists, maybe this was the moment to move things up a notch.

Whatever the reasoning behind it, and whatever the source, on January 30 the London *Mail on Sunday* newspaper ran as its front-page lead a story headlined: PRINCE CHARLES SEVERS ALL LINKS WITH CAMILLA PARKER

BOWLES: MY DUTY BEFORE LOVE. Under this dramatic headline ran a story by Nigel Dempster that stated that Charles had "renounced" his friendship with Camilla.

"He has decided to sacrifice his close friendship with the mother-of-two for the sake of his duty to the country," wrote the journalist.

"The Prince has resolved, after months of heart-searching, to remove any obstacle to his succession by finally severing their 24-year relationship. According to a royal confidant the Prince has come to an 'irrevocable decision' on the matter."

The article went on to quote the unnamed source as saying: "The Prince says he has every intention of becoming King in the fullness of time and, as long as that is his intention, there is no room in his life for Mrs. Parker Bowles.'

Dempster continued: "Now Prince Charles has decided they must lead separate lives, which cannot cross at any point.

"Camilla is said to be 'frantic' over her rejection.

"The source said: 'Camilla has found that the Prince is no longer taking her calls and is very unhappy about it.' "

If she was, she had a remarkable way of showing it. Confined to the shadows for many a long month by a self-imposed purdah to beat the press's unquenchable thirst for more information about her, she emerged from her house—confident that the world's press was waiting for her—and took coffee to workmen chopping logs in the grounds. She spent long enough in their company for photographers to get the pictures they needed—of a Camilla utterly at ease with herself and wreathed in smiles. One of the coffee mugs she bore out to the workmen carried the word LOVE in large print on its side: a not particularly coded message which would wing its way to the other side of the globe.

Nonetheless, the British press believed they had a story—and a historic one at that. Some papers talked of the "months of heart-searching" by Charles "to remove any obstacle to his succession." While this was palpable nonsense, since nothing short of premature death could stop Charles from coming to the throne, there was a belief—buoyed up by who knows what—that there was substance to the story. As is often the case among headstrong editors, the desire to see a story in print sometimes has the blinkering effect of pushing away all contrary arguments.

Some sections of Fleet Street saw the parallels between Edward and Mrs. Simpson and Charles and Camilla slipping away. Instead, they portrayed a prince determinedly walking away from his nemesis. An unnamed Cabinet minister was quoted thus: "This decision is a clear indication that he takes his future responsibilities very seriously. It is entirely right that he should put his duty first, and he should be respected for this decision."

It did not take long for the dream to evaporate. By the following morning a very strong counterargument was running—that Charles and Camilla's love was as strong as ever, that the prince resented this new interpretation on his attitude to her, and that everything was as it had been.

To this end, a stray piece of information surfaced—that Charles and Camilla had enjoyed a lengthy telephone conversation while he was actually undertaking his Australian tour—which demonstrated more implacably, and more than any other single piece of information in the months since the publication of the Camillagate tapes, that the couple were still deeply involved.

The call came to Charles at his official residence overlooking the Sydney Opera House. Camilla made it from the home of a family friend somewhere in the south of England—and a place unlikely to be bugged. Other calls followed, and the ongoing relationship continued without a hitch. Those who enjoy such parallels would later recall that after King Edward VII was shot at (a recurrent problem, apparently, to successive Princes of Wales) as he passed through Brussels in 1900, he immediately telegraphed to Alice Keppel in Weymouth that he was unharmed. It is fair to suppose his successor instantly made a similar, though technologically more advanced, communication with Mrs. Keppel's great-granddaughter.

The scoop of the year evaporated as quickly as morning mist. One source told the *Daily Mirror*'s James Whitaker: "These two are in love. And even if the affair had cooled down, which it hasn't, the prince is not the sort of person to dump friends. He is immensely loyal and it is insulting to his integrity to suggest he now won't take Camilla's calls."

This theme was taken up by another well-sourced journalist, who wrote: "One friend who regularly has the Prince's ear complained during a New Year house party in the Caribbean that, for all his endeavours, Charles and Mrs. Parker Bowles seemed determined to carry on."

He quoted a singular exchange that demonstrated the depth of

Charles's loyalty. The prince told a companion: "I would never treat anyone like my great-uncle did Mrs. Dudley Ward." This was a reference to David, Prince of Wales's treatment of his mistress Freda Dudley Ward once he took up with Mrs. Simpson: He cast her aside by the simple expedient of ordering the Buckingham Palace switchboard that she was not to be put through to him anymore.

Apocryphal maybe, but this anecdote does demonstrate Charles's lasting qualities. Though in truth there was another, glaringly obvious reason why he could not give up Camilla—he could not do without her. So why the sudden rush of blood to the head that had the world's press believing Charles had just thrown away a twenty-two-year-old love affair?

The prevailing theory as to the placing of the leaks was that well-meaning friends felt his already high profile in Australia would be given an upward nudge and increase his slowly thawing popularity back home. Instead, it turned out to be a disaster. After initial incredulity that the prince would let it be known he had dumped Camilla, there was the predictable backlash: one newspaper headline read, HE BEDS THEM THEN HE BETRAYS THEM, a reference to both Diana and Camilla.

Charles's most prominent biographer, Anthony Holden, tartly alluded to "the different ambitions of his so-called 'friends,' anxious to be associated with a future King rather than another Duke of Windsor." And he accused Charles's friends of telephoning the press with the information in an attempt to force the prince's hand on the Camilla issue.

There was general agreement that the prince himself was unaware the leaks were taking place. He was outraged at their effect. In making his painstaking preparations for the Australasia tour, Tippexing the Tampax meant eradicating *all* references to his relationship with Camilla—he did not want his name in any way connected with hers at a crucial time in his repairing fortunes. He was furious.

Disinformation spread alarmingly in the ensuing witch-hunt. In a quick backtracking movement it was suggested that the friends planted the information, not because Charles had dumped Camilla, but because the physical side of their relationship was over and the world would feel more comfortable knowing that. This was yet another version, as risible as those that preceded it. According to these sources, the couple had not been lovers since November 1992, a month before Charles and Diana separated. It was all over, and the "obstacle" of adultery could therefore no longer be part of the debate about Charles's fitness to be king.

This logic had the distinction of being both ingenuous and disingenuous. It was intensely stupid of Charles's friends to suppose that, simply because he and Camilla were no longer in an adulterous relationship, the Church of England could ignore the two decades of adultery that had already taken place. When it came to their deliberations on Charles's fitness to head the Church, whether the relationship was active or passive would make very little difference.

And there was something deeply suspicious in the scenario that was created by those friends: "They mutually agreed to cool it but remained in close touch," said one. Then, shortly before Christmas, 1993, elaborated the friend, the couple took the final step to stop their regular telephone calls.

The fact that Camilla called Charles in Australia twenty-four hours before the gun incident, and that this should be leaked to the press accompanying the royal tour, effectively destroyed that testimony. Charles and Camilla *were* talking, *were* seeing each other, and if the physical side of their relationship had become nonexistent, it owed more to the passage of time than to any conscious decision by the parties involved. But as the days wore on, even that one seemed increasingly unlikely.

In the midst of this confusion came a moment of light relief as a popular novelist, Una-Mary Parker, dipped her toe into the already muddied pool.

Her qualifications for speaking about the royal marriage were, to say the least of it, scant. It is true that she had been married for some long while to the society photographer Archie Parker. It is true that Parker, along with Andrew Parker Bowles, was descended from the sixth Earl of Macclesfield, whose long-suffering wife produced for him a record eleven sons and four daughters.

But Una-Mary's marriage to Parker had foundered some years before, and in any event, he was dead and thereby disbarred from quizzing his distant cousin on the latest turn of events. Nevertheless, Mrs. Parker saw this as no bar to her deliberations and proclaimed that Charles was considering a reconciliation with Diana for the sake of their children. Referring to the press reports, she declared: "It is part of a master plan in which Diana and Charles are working for a reconciliation."

This was greeted with hoots of laughter back in Australia by the royal camp.

As spring approached there were, of course, no sightings of Charles and Diana together. Despite her emotional announcement that she wanted to quit public life, Diana was not very often out of the newspapers. Photographers captured her on an almost daily basis taking out her sons, shopping, emerging from a restaurant after lunch, diving into a Chinese foot-massage parlor. After over a decade of public work, it could be argued, it was only right that she should take time out to reorder her life and reconsider her priorities. But it soon became plain that she had walked into a vacuum and that, stripped of her duties and with no great hobbies or pursuits to indulge, she had nothing to do. There were an awful lot of pictures of a woman with nothing to do that spring.

Soon after Charles arrived back from Australia, his campaign managers pleased with the overall success of the feelgood tour, it was revealed that he had been in touch with Camilla to discuss the success of his trip. His call to her was confirmed by the same source that revealed how Camilla had telephoned Charles in Australia. At the same time it emerged that Diana had told friends that she had never accepted that her husband's relationship with Camilla had ended—she was convinced it was still on. In that, she was entirely correct, even if the frequency of the lovers' meetings had been scaled down.

Life went on. Charles and Camilla both continued to hunt with the Beaufort, though now chose alternate days so they should never be seen together. As the summer approached, Charles took up polo again and Camilla tended her garden. His anxiety over coping with Prince William and Prince Harry when he had them to stay was overcome by the appointment of a "surrogate mother," Alexandra Legge-Bourke, who had previously run a London nursery school called Mrs. Tiggywinkle's. The boys took to her instantly. After a tumultuous two years, life was beginning to return to normal, though it would never be the same again. Such events as Camilla would once have attended without a second thought—the wedding of a friend, the annual National Hunt Festival at Cheltenham—she now chose to avoid. The public was naturally fascinated to see the woman whom the Prince of Wales truly loved, and for many years yet she would be an object of fascination to millions.

In February Charles's private apartments in St. James's Palace were burgled, and a quantity of jewelry, including a number of sets of cuff links, was taken. Immediately Palace officials were asked, Did the thief steal Camilla's famous cuff links, the ones with the entwined Cs, which the prince so foolishly wore on his honeymoon?

They never existed, came back the stony answer. The officials had got out their Tippex again, trying desperately to put over their message to the outside world—*this woman does not exist, she has never existed, please forget about her.* But theirs was a hopeless task, for it would take years for the nation to forget Camilla Parker Bowles, and indeed, having overcome the initial shock of her existence, it felt, rather encouragingly, very much less antagonistic toward the idea of her.

Meanwhile, the rehabilitation went on apace. Charles turned out for a Status Quo concert at the Royal Albert Hall. This, in a previous life, was the sort of event he would leave to his wife—on the odd occasion when he did turn out, he would make no secret of his discomfort, as with the Live Aid concert in 1985 when he wore a suit while everyone else did not. His interest in rock music, never strong, was over by 1967 when The Troggs, already chart toppers with "Wild Thing" and "I Can't Control Myself," invited the prince to accompany them on their next hit with his cello. He declined, and from then on immersed himself in music from the classical and baroque periods. Now he was back, tapping his feet to the Quo as they explored the limits of their three-chord repertoire, and smiling a great deal. It required a great deal of effort.

But there was a greater challenge ahead. A year before, in April 1993, Charles had found himself floundering in a welter of criticism and abuse for the way he had handled himself after the shocking death of two young boys, Johnathan Ball and Tim Parry, who died in an IRA attack on the northern town of Warrington.

The boys' death touched a nerve in the nation. A televised memorial service was arranged, to which the prime minister, the leader of the Opposition, and the president of the Irish Republic all readily gave their agreement to attend. The question was then asked: Which member of the royal family will be there?

Charles was the obvious candidate, since he had paid a fleeting visit to the town immediately after the bomb and Warringtonians had been pleased by his apparent concern. But on the day of the memorial, Charles was in Spain attending the funeral mass of Don Juan de Borbón y Battenburg, the father of the king of Spain.

There was little purpose in his presence, though his critics claimed that he did not like missing the opportunity of rubbing shoulders with Europe's crowned heads—it made him feel superior. If anyone should have represented the British royals, it should have been Prince Philip, whose mother was a cousin of Don Juan. Charles, as a cousin twice removed, may have looked resplendent in his naval uniform in this Ruritanian procession in the Spanish sun, but in the chill and rain of Warrington they waited for him in vain.

The MP Ian McCartney declared: "As the King-to-be, he should have known that his place was with his future subjects at such a traumatic time." Nobody disagreed with that. Where the dissension began was when the townspeople of Warrington discovered that while Charles would not be attending the memorial, he had banned his wife from being there. The Princess of Wales had expressed an urgent desire to go to Warrington, and had spoken at length on the telephone to the mother of one of the boys. But Diana fell victim to Charles's determination to marginalize her, and a nation chafed at the ineptitude of the House of Windsor at such a time. If politicians could bury their differences to mourn the dead—and make the considerable journey from London—why couldn't Charles?

The best that can be said is that overenthusiastic courtiers offered faulty advice, and Charles took it. But it was a mistake he could never make again; and in his stride forward to public acceptance this was a major setback.

When in March 1994 there was a chance to redress the balance, an older and wiser Prince Charles did not fail. At the Hall Garth School at Acklam, near Middlesbrough, a masked gunman who also carried a knife burst into a mathematics classroom on the second floor and ordered the pupils to kneel down, shouting: "They have killed me, now they have killed all of you." He stabbed to death twelve-year-old Nikki Conroy, and injured two other pupils, Emma Winter and Michelle Reeve, before being tackled and disarmed by two members of the staff.

The nation was in a universal state of shock, not only for the loss of a bright and pretty child, but also from the realization that no school was immune from the dangers of sudden attack. Into this scenario came the Prince of Wales, who was on a tour of the Cleveland area, which incorporated Middlesbrough.

He arrived at Hall Garth School bearing a wreath of yellow and white carnations, lilies, and roses, to which he had attached a handwritten card saying: "In deepest sympathy, Charles." He gathered around him the children and staff who had witnessed the attack and addressed them gently. In a ten-minute conversation he spoke of his own pain, anger, and grief at the loss of Earl Mountbatten, murdered by the IRA in 1979, and he urged the children to talk to each other about their feelings and about Nikki.

The school's headmaster, Peter Smith, said: "They were friends together and the prince made it very easy. We were very touched by the whole visit and the trouble he has obviously gone to to try to make it right." And a sixteen-year-old pupil, Claire Barry, added: "I think it's good that he came here. It's not just Prince Charles coming to see us—it's more important than that. He represents the whole country."

The country took his decorous behavior, so very different from that of the previous year, to its heart. It was even ready for another earful of Prince Charles on the dreaded subject of architecture.

In March Charles launched his own architectural magazine, *Perspectives*, with a celebrity-laden (and shrewdly rehabilitative) launch party at St. James's Palace. *Perspectives* was never likely to be a publication to send the nation rushing to the bookstall, but everyone was polite about it. The only complaints were that, as one of the richest men in the land, he served inferior drink at the launch—and that he appeared to have appropriated the magazine's name from another equally worthy architectural tome.

There was no mention in *Perspectives* about Poundbury, Charles's well-intentioned plan to raise a perfectly balanced mini-town on the edge of Dorchester in Dorset. Yet when in 1994 the project, years after its much-publicized conception, finally gave birth, it could contribute very little to Charles's comeback. Though admirable enough in principle, its scope had been so whittled down by market forces and the world recession that all that was left was a few homes for a group of startled first timers who found their designer-made properties stuck between a barren agricultural spread and a council estate. With money too tight to provide much infrastructure, it looked as if they might have to wait a decade to get a corner shop.

But that did not stop Charles from inveighing against other planners and developers. In May he sounded off against the Russians for attempting to build a vulgar high-rise block to kickstart the dormant economy in St. Petersburg. What was charming about Charles was that some things in his life were immutable. Architecture and polo were two. Mrs. Parker Bowles was another.

And suddenly there was Mrs. Parker Bowles playing—without any great seriousness, it has to be said—the power game which the Princess of Wales had enjoyed so much in her heyday.

San Lorenzo, the renowned Knightsbridge restaurant which plays host to the likes of Eric Clapton, Dustin Hoffman, Joan Collins, and a host of the rich and famous who like to pay a lot to eat not very much, was the headquarters for Diana during her ill-starred love game with James Gilbey. Its Italian proprietor, Mara Berni, became one of Diana's closest friends and, during the height of her clandestine liaison with Gilbey, would lend the key to her family house around the corner so that Diana and Gilbey could retreat there to be alone. Moreover, the restaurant was used as a dead-letter drop during the period when Diana—with or without justification—believed that her mail at Kensington Palace was being intercepted.

But now, in May, all that had changed. Camilla Parker Bowles, not renowned for her lunching activities and, unlike Diana, never photographed by the clamorous, unwashed paparazzi as she strolled out into Beauchamp Place to a double-parked car festooned in parking tickets and *billets doux* from compliant traffic wardens, suddenly made an entrance. And just as suddenly she was clasped to the ample bosom of Mara Berni. To the jet set, this simple gesture would be a sign that they had arrived. But to Camilla, it meant no more than another of many genial encounters with people one barely knew who adopted a strange familiarity after thirty seconds' conversation. She was not the kind of woman who ever needed the approval of restaurateurs.

But in any event, she would never be far away from any story concerning the Prince of Wales. In May Charles launched a sustained attack on the fashion of political correctness, which he said was destroying much of the fabric of British society. It was a sweeping condemnation of fashionable theories, from child care to education and literature, in which he urged ordinary people to resist "intellectual fanaticism" and stand up for well-tried principles. But the ordinary people he spoke for were just as interested in the fact that Charles had lost his Jack Russell terrier, Pooh, somewhere on the Balmoral estate. And even more fascinated when they discovered that Pooh's sister was owned by Camilla, and that she had commiserated with the prince over the loss of the dog. Human-interest stories, especially with an animal thrown in, were as likely to touch their hearts and bring Charles the support he so desperately sought, as the high-minded lectures he delivered for the greater good.

From this, at last, Charles should have been able to see something that had so far evaded him: that royalty, for the masses, does not exist at street level but hovers somewhere high above and out of reach. That makes the loss of a prince's dog a matter for concerned discussion, where the loss of a hundred other dogs would pass without remark; equally it means that any debate instituted by him would be treated, by the majority, in the same otherworldly way. Not being taken entirely seriously is a burden he has to bear, even though he has devoted his career to being accepted as a credible figure.

The long haul back to respectability following the publication of the Camillagate tapes is, for Charles, far from over. Both he, and those who serve him, desperately wanted to show the world, on the occasion of the twenty-fifth anniversary of his investiture as Prince of Wales, what his contribution has been. Fate denied him the opportunity to clap himself on the back, and some future anniversary will have to suffice for a proper assessment of the role he has played.

Part of that assessment will include the way he handled his recovery from the Camillagate scandal. To perpetrate the deception of a happy marriage upon a nation when you are in love with another woman is, in an all-seeing age, unacceptable behavior. To then deny the existence of the woman you love in an attempt to find favor with your people is no less unacceptable.

Somewhere in between, there is a life for Charles and Camilla, one in which the outside world will accept the blow of fate that brought them together, and kept them together. It is a solution that has to be worked out and gently tested on the world, for one thing is certain: A nation will no more love a man who abandons the woman he loves in order to secure the throne, than they did a man who abandoned the throne for the woman he loved.

$\mathcal{I}$ N D E X